Ties That Bind

Ties That Bind

Maternal Imagery and Discourse in Indian Buddhism

REIKO OHNUMA

OXFORD
UNIVERSITY PRESS

OXFORD
UNIVERSITY PRESS

Oxford University Press, Inc., publishes works that further
Oxford University's objective of excellence
in research, scholarship, and education.

Oxford New York
Auckland Cape Town Dar es Salaam Hong Kong Karachi
Kuala Lumpur Madrid Melbourne Mexico City Nairobi
New Delhi Shanghai Taipei Toronto

With offices in
Argentina Austria Brazil Chile Czech Republic France Greece
Guatemala Hungary Italy Japan Poland Portugal Singapore
South Korea Switzerland Thailand Turkey Ukraine Vietnam

Published by Oxford University Press, Inc.
198 Madison Avenue, New York, New York 10016

www.oup.com

Library of Congress Cataloging-in-Publication Data
Ohnuma, Reiko.
Ties that bind : maternal imagery and discourse in Indian Buddhism / Reiko Ohnuma.
p. cm.
Includes bibliographical references and index.
ISBN 978-0-19-991565-1 (hardcover : alk. paper)—ISBN 978-0-19-991567-5
(pbk. : alk. paper)—ISBN 978-0-19-991566-8 (ebook)
1. Buddhist literature—India—Themes, motives. 2. Motherhood in literature.
I. Title. II. Title: Maternal imagery and discourse in Indian Buddhism.
BQ1029.I42O57 2012
294.3'8—dc23 2011043000

1 3 5 7 9 8 6 4 2

Printed in the United States of America
on acid-free paper

For Attie, Astro, and Rich

Contents

List of Illustrations

Conventions

(1) All Pali canonical and commentarial sources are cited from the Tipiṭaka (and commentaries) established at the Chaṭṭha Saṅgāyana or Sixth Buddhist Council held in Yangon, Myanmar, 1954–56, and available online at www.tipitaka.org. However, as is customary, the bibliographic references given are to the standard Pali Text Society editions, as noted in the Abbreviations.

(2) All translations from Pali and Sanskrit are my own, unless otherwise stated. The original Pali or Sanskrit text is provided in the notes only when an especially significant word or brief phrase is involved; otherwise, the original text is not provided.

(3) For names and words that have different forms in Pali and Sanskrit, the Sanskrit form is always used, unless the name or word is appearing within a direct quotation from a Pali text, or the name or word appears within a discussion that is wholly limited to a Pali passage; in these cases, the Pali form is used.

(4) All Chinese names, terms, and titles are cited in Pinyin.

Acknowledgments

Bits and pieces of this book have been presented over the years in many different venues, including the Center for Buddhist Studies at the University of California at Berkeley, the Five Colleges Buddhist Studies Faculty Seminar at Smith College, the Fifteenth Congress of the International Association of Buddhist Studies at Emory University, the University of Toronto, McMaster University, the Buddhist Studies Forum at Harvard University, the Religious Studies Colloquium of the College of Charleston, the American Academy of Religion Annual Meeting, and, at Dartmouth College, the Department of Religion Faculty Colloquium and the Feminist Inquiry Seminar. I owe thanks to all of the people who invited me to speak and to everyone who showed up to question, praise, and criticize. Sharing my ideas in public does not come naturally to me, so I am grateful for all such situations in which I am committed to doing so. Plus, my very best ideas have often begun with thoughtful comments from the audience.

Thank you to Dartmouth College for awarding me a Senior Faculty Grant that allowed me to spend all of 2009 in splendid isolation, and thus gave me the time to write this book. John Strong, Liz Wilson, and Julie Puttgen were especially conscientious and careful readers of the original manuscript and offered many valuable suggestions, almost all of which I have tried to follow. Cynthia Read and Charlotte Steinhardt have made my first experience publishing with Oxford University Press a very pleasant one. A special thanks, also, to the Department of Religion at Dartmouth College, whose faculty has been endlessly patient with my antics and given me a happy home since 1999.

This book is dedicated with boundless love to those who made me a mother myself and thus sparked my passion for the subject—my children, Attie and Astro, and my co-conspirator, Rich.

Ties That Bind

Introduction

THE VENERATION OF mothers, both human and divine, has been a pervasive and persistent feature of South Asian religious culture. On the level of the divine, the vast Purāṇic compendia composed in Sanskrit throughout the latter half of the first millennium CE are full of mother goddesses who have been feared, loved, and respected—in benevolent, nurturing forms, such as those of Lakṣmī or Pārvatī, and in terrifying, horrific forms, such as those of Kālī or Cāmuṇḍā. The life-giving rivers of the Indian subcontinent are divinized as nurturing mother figures (the voluptuous goddess Gaṅgā is perhaps foremost among them); vermilion-smeared stones are still worshipped as aniconic forms of local mother goddesses in many villages today; and cows are held to be sacred as divine symbols of maternal love. On the human plane, as well, Indian social ideology, while often oppressive to women, idealizes their roles as wives and mothers. In the literature of the *Dharma Śāstras,* a woman is largely defined in terms of her status as wife and mother, and mothers are frequently celebrated for the nurture and love they give to their children. According to Manu in the *Manusmṛti*: "The teacher is ten times greater than the tutor; the father is a hundred times greater than the teacher; but the mother is a thousand times greater than the father."[1] The role of the mother is also sacralized, since it is she who makes her husband immortal by giving him a son.

These expressions of veneration for the mother come primarily from the Hindu tradition, however. In many ways, the Buddhist tradition of India could be seen as a minority strand of Indian culture that consciously resisted and rejected this veneration of the mother. Early Buddhism in India was largely unconcerned with mother goddesses or the veneration of human mothers. Buddhism promoted as its highest goal the complete rejection of an ordinary, worldly life and all of the social and familial relationships that such a life entails. Following the model of the Buddha himself, the Buddhist renunciant was defined as one who severs his or her ties with parents, spouse, and children and takes a vow of celibacy that prevents him or her from ever procreating again. This rejection of family and society was seen as a necessary prerequisite to following the long and arduous path to nirvana—complete liberation from the round of birth and death, and the ultimate goal of the Buddhist religious path. Nirvana was obtained by overcoming all worldly desires and attachments, thus putting a stop to the processes of karma and rebirth. Desire for and attachment to the things of this world were thus the primary enemies the Buddhist renunciant had to overcome.

Within this context, it is easy to see why Buddhism rejected the "cult of the mother." Veneration of mother goddesses was useless, for the task of attaining nirvana was a human task alone. In undertaking this task, motherhood itself was an integral part of the familial life one had to reject, and the ideal Buddhist renunciant was sometimes described as one who no longer acknowledged any relationship with his or her own mother. Women, too, tread the path to nirvana, and this required them to reject the idealized role of the mother for themselves. Women who became Buddhist nuns took a vow of celibacy that would prevent them from ever becoming mothers, while those who already had children were supposed to leave their children behind once they had entered the monastic community. Even when mothers acted as pious laywomen who were praised for giving alms (and, sometimes, their children) to the Saṃgha, motherhood itself remained wholly profane in nature and had no part in salvation or immortality. Motherhood was an essential component of samsara, and samsara was to be vanquished and overcome. In short, one would not be off the mark in describing early Buddhism as a decidedly "mother-rejecting" tradition.

As the anthropologist Mary Douglas has noted in another context, however, "that which is negated is not thereby removed," and thus "the most complete philosophies . . . must find some ultimate way of affirming that which has been rejected."[2] This book begins with the assumption that Buddhism in India was not merely and simply a mother-rejecting tradition. In fact, Buddhism had a complex and ambivalent relationship with mothers and motherhood—symbolically, affectively, and institutionally. Symbolically, motherhood was a double-edged sword, sometimes extolled as the most appropriate symbol for buddhahood itself, and sometimes denigrated as the most paradigmatic manifestation possible of the attachment to the world that keeps all benighted beings trapped within the realm of rebirth. Motherhood was a lightning rod, a privileged symbol used in an iconic fashion to stand for both the best and the worst. On an affective level, as well, motherhood was viewed with the same ambivalence: In Buddhist literature, warm feelings of love and gratitude for the mother's nurturance and care frequently mingle with submerged feelings of hostility and resentment for the unbreakable obligations thus created, and positive images of self-sacrificing mothers are counterbalanced by horrific depictions of mothers who kill and devour. Institutionally, the formal definition of the Buddhist renunciant as one who has severed all familial ties seems to coexist uneasily with an abundance of inscriptional evidence demonstrating monks' and nuns' continuing concern for their mothers, as well as story after story addressing a variety of unexpected familial entanglements. On every level, it seems, motherhood, though it may have been profane in nature, was hardly treated with indifference. The title of the book, *Ties That Bind,* is meant to indicate that motherhood was a lingering tie that simply *could not be broken,* despite one's renunciation of worldly life.

This book seeks to make sense of this tie by engaging in a wide-ranging—though also partial and highly selective—exploration of maternal imagery and discourse in South Asian Buddhist texts. What are some of the common ways in which mothers, motherhood, maternal love, and maternal grief are depicted in South Asian Buddhist literature? How is motherhood used as a trope to give expression to Buddhist values, and sometimes to undercut them? How does the trope of motherhood differ from and relate to the trope of sonhood or the trope of fatherhood? What special significance attaches to the figures of the Buddha's own mothers, Māyā and Mahāprajāpatī? Why are Buddhist images of motherhood so often ambivalent, contradictory, or oppositional in nature? And how might such images of motherhood reflect the emotional world of the renunciant Buddhist monks who composed and passed down these traditions?

In exploring the maternal imagery and discourse characteristic of South Asian Buddhism, I have limited myself to the Mainstream and Mahāyāna Buddhist traditions.[3] The development of Vajrayāna and Tantric forms of Buddhism in the latter centuries of Indian Buddhist history was an exceedingly complex phenomenon that witnessed an explosion of female symbolism—much of which departed, in significant ways, from what came before. Because Vajrayāna and Tantric maternal imagery are worthy of separate and sustained treatment—and because I lack the expertise that would be necessary to do the subject justice—I felt it better to limit myself to non-Vajrayāna forms of Indian Buddhism.

Even given these limitations, my treatment is by no means exhaustive or complete. I have followed my own interests and inclinations, allowing my exploration of maternal imagery and discourse to meander in whatever direction it happened to take. My focus is limited, however, to textual depictions; apart from a few cursory comments, I have left aside the rich evidence offered by South Asian Buddhist art. The major sources I draw on come primarily from premodern South Asian Buddhist literature preserved in Sanskrit and Pali—including, for example, the texts of the Pali Canon of the Theravāda school (along with their later commentaries), Mainstream Buddhist literature preserved in Sanskrit, and Mahāyāna sūtras and *śāstras* preserved in Sanskrit. In addition, I also draw occasionally on Chinese and Tibetan translations of Indian Buddhist texts no longer extant in Sanskrit or Pali (relying wholly, in these instances, on other people's translations), as well as making very limited use of art-historical and inscriptional evidence from India. My choice of sources has been determined by the specific interests of the project, and I make no attempt to limit myself to a particular school, type of Buddhism, or genre of literature. Historically speaking, these sources date anywhere from perhaps a few centuries BCE well into the medieval period and cover a very wide geographical region. What holds them together is nothing more than the broad and constructed category—rather loosely conceived—of "premodern South Asian Buddhism."

The historical diversity of my sources is a direct reflection of the methodological concerns that have motivated my scholarly work in general. Throughout my scholarship, I have been most interested in uncovering and trying to understand a general "Indian Buddhist discursive world" that displays remarkable consistency over time in terms of narrative themes, character-types, plotlines, conventional tropes, similes, metaphors, and images. This is a consistency that stretches across the linguistic borders between Sanskrit, Pali, Tibetan, and Chinese, as well as extending over many centuries and throughout a large geographical region. It is also referential and intertextual in nature, with texts from widely varying historical contexts referring to one another, playing off one another, and often seeming to "speak to" one another in ways that might be historically impossible. Thus, just as my previous book[4] argued that texts from widely varying historical contexts belong to the same "Indian Buddhist discursive world" and offer a remarkably consistent discourse on the bodhisattva's gift of his body, so the present book makes a similar argument for a consistent discourse on motherhood. This discourse reveals itself, however, only when one places the theme of motherhood in the foreground and allows *it* to determine which sources are used, rather than—for example—looking at the local production of meaning in one particular time and place. I am aware that my methodology, which is historicist only in a very broad sense, goes against the current cult of historicity that has increasingly come to characterize both Buddhist Studies and the humanities as a whole. Nevertheless, I remain convinced of the usefulness and validity of such an approach.

In much the same spirit, on several occasions throughout the book I venture well beyond the category of "premodern South Asian Buddhism" to examine texts or evidence taken from other Buddhist contexts that may or may not have any direct connection to India itself—including, for example, my discussions of several Chinese apocryphal sūtras in chapter 3, Tibetan exegetical literature in chapters 1 and 6, medieval Theravāda literature from later Southeast Asia in chapter 7, modern ethnographic accounts of Buddhism in chapter 8, and the relationship between Buddhism and recent feminist theory on motherhood in the conclusion. In these instances (all of which are clearly marked as such), my intention is *not* to imply that the ideas expressed must have ultimately derived from an Indian context and can therefore be taken as representative of South Asian Buddhism. Instead, I use these discussions merely to suggest that Buddhists in other times and places, while developing the Buddhist discourse on motherhood in their own unique ways, were also seeing and making use of certain suggestions and possibilities that were inherent in the Indian discourse itself. Again, these discussions are meant to be suggestive and illuminating, not to offer concrete, historical arguments.

A few words are perhaps in order concerning the nature of the "mother" I focus on here. First, this book is *not* concerned with any notion of a Universal Mother, Archetypal Mother, or Eternal Feminine Principle—*Mother* with a capital *M*, as it were—because Indian Buddhism itself was not overtly concerned with such. Although mothers and motherhood are often used in a symbolic manner, these depictions never rise to the level of an all-encompassing divine principle. Motherhood is sometimes idealized, but it is not sacralized or divinized. The figure of the mother remains worldly, mundane, and very human. My focus, then, is on the *human mother* and how human motherhood and maternal emotions are deployed in Buddhist texts. While Buddhism did, of course, exist within a larger South Asian religious context that often involved the sacralization of motherhood and the worship of mother goddesses—indeed, we will see some of the ways in which Buddhism interacted with this larger context—nevertheless, human motherhood remains my primary concern.

Second, with the exception of chapter 8, which does attempt to broach this subject, I am concerned not so much with *actual* human mothers as with how such human mothers are imagined, invoked, and utilized in Buddhist texts. Actual human mothers lie beyond the scope of what can reasonably be uncovered, not least because Buddhist texts were written not by mothers but by their sons—that is, the male Buddhist monks who were responsible for creating, preserving, and passing down the surviving body of Buddhist texts. These sons, I believe, had little interest in the depiction of actual human mothers. In their hands, motherhood more often functions as a symbol, an image, a metaphor, or a simile. Motherhood is a trope that is used to express Buddhist values, ideas, and beliefs and that is often deployed in combination with other tropes, such as the trope of sonhood or the trope of fatherhood. It is for these reasons that the subtitle of the book describes its focus not as "mothers and motherhood in Indian Buddhism" but, rather, as "maternal imagery and discourse in Indian Buddhism." I am interested in the *theme* of motherhood and the *figure* of the mother as important components of South Asian Buddhist discourse and of the South Asian Buddhist imaginary.

One primary argument I will advance throughout this book, in fact, is that these texts often treat motherhood not just symbolically or metaphorically, but also *iconically*. In other words, motherhood is not just one of many images used to represent whatever quality it is meant to stand for; rather, it is often treated as an iconic embodiment or paradigmatic manifestation of that very quality. Similarly, certain maternal emotions—foremost among them maternal love and maternal grief—seem to be foregrounded above all other possible emotions that might be experienced by actual mothers, and to achieve an iconic status as being particularly characteristic or emblematic of motherhood. More often than not, the mother is depicted as the very embodiment of such emotions, rather than as a fully rounded individual who experiences a full range of human feelings. The Buddha's own mothers, Māyā and Mahāprajāpatī, also share in this "iconic" quality even though they are individualized figures. They are not so much unique individuals as they are "types" or interpretations of motherhood. Much of the book will focus on these various "iconic" uses of motherhood.

At the same time, however, I have also tried, throughout this book, to hang on to the notion that I might be able to catch at least an imaginative glimpse of *actual human mothers*—more specifically, the mothers of those men who produced this discourse on motherhood. I occasionally speculate, for example, about how such Buddhist authors may have felt about their own mothers, and how they may have expressed their feelings through their depictions of motherhood. At bottom, my inquiry is driven by the assumption that the male monastic authors who composed Indian Buddhist texts and dominated the tradition as a whole were not only learned Buddhist monks who had renounced all familial ties. They were also the sons of their mothers. The vast majority of them most likely grew up within a patriarchal, patrilineal, and patrilocal family structure that perpetuates a strong emotional bond between mother and son[5]—yet they also adhered to an elite religious tradition that often denigrates women and encourages the repudiation of all familial ties. In short, they were conflicted human beings—complicated and interesting human beings. Just as psychoanalytical theory gives us the picture of a young infant who is so overwhelmed by the omnipotence of his mother that he ends up "splitting" the mother in two, so I imagine male monastic authors writing stories about mothers and using maternal imagery in a manner that reflects such feelings of conflict and ambivalence. These are feelings that we ourselves, as the children of our mothers, can identify with and try to understand, despite the enormous historical and cultural differences that characterize the practice of motherhood in different times and places. While this book is not interested in hazarding guesses about the early childhood experiences or subconscious psychological motivations of authors so distant from us in time and space, it does ultimately rest on a desire to understand Buddhist texts as the products of people much like ourselves—the sons (and daughters?) of their mothers.

The book is organized as follows. Chapter 1 focuses, in a general way, on Buddhist depictions of mother-love and introduces some of the standard maternal tropes that reappear throughout the remainder of the book. Chapter 2 focuses on the *grieving mother* as an iconic figure of attachment and suffering and looks at several different ways in which Buddhist texts depict the spiritual transformation of the mother in grief. Chapters 3, 4, and 5 focus on traditions surrounding the two mothers of the Buddha himself—Queen Māyā or Mahāmāyā, and her sister, Mahāprajāpatī Gautamī. These chapters argue that the Buddhist tradition has consciously shaped Māyā and Mahāprajāpatī into a contrasting pair, using this pair to explore two alternative visions of motherhood in a highly nuanced, imaginative, and complex fashion.

Chapters 6 and 7 turn their attention to some of the biological processes surrounding motherhood. Chapter 6 focuses on the many ways in which *pregnancy* and *gestation* are used as metaphors for the process of attaining buddhahood, examining five different contexts in which "metaphorical pregnancies" define the Buddhist path. In a similar manner, chapter 7 focuses on several different ways in which *breastfeeding* is used as a metaphor for the compassionate deeds of buddhas and bodhisattvas.

Finally, chapter 8 turns away from the discourse on motherhood illuminated in the first seven chapters, and attempts to look briefly at the relationship between motherhood and Indian Buddhism as it actually existed "on the ground." The limited nature of the evidence in this chapter also leads me to draw on a wider context of contemporary Buddhist ethnography to make sense of the data at hand. Final thoughts are offered in the conclusion and are framed in relationship to some recent feminist theorizing on motherhood.

I

"A Mother's Heart Is Tender"

BUDDHIST DEPICTIONS OF MOTHER-LOVE

MOTHERHOOD IN SOUTH Asian Buddhist literature seems to be characterized, first and foremost, by a single, defining emotion: mother-love, or the love a mother has for her child. Mother-love constitutes a powerful trope in this literature and is used not randomly, but in a number of consistent ways.[1] In many contexts, the mother is treated in company with the father, and little distinction is made between them. In multiple passages from the Pali Canon, for example, both parents are praised and celebrated for the innumerable services they perform on behalf of their children and their constant willingness to place their children's needs before their own. "Mothers and fathers do much for their children," the Buddha says; "they take care of them and nourish them and show them this world."[2] Because of these many services, "parents have attained a high position" and are "worthy of praise," "worthy of reverence," and "equivalent to [the deity] Brahmā and to the ancient teachers." Emphasis is often placed on the debt children owe to their parents and how this debt should be repaid. Children who are wise will "honor and esteem" their parents with "food, drink, clothing, bedding, bathing, anointing, and washing the feet."[3] Such children should be known as "superior people" (P. *sappurisa*)[4] who are "praised by the wise right here in this world and rejoice in heaven after death"[5]—while those who fail to serve their parents should be known as "outcastes" (P. *vasala*)[6] who will see their wealth perish, go to ruin, or be reborn in hell.[7] Parents, in fact, do so much for their children that it is almost impossible to repay them adequately:

> If a man were to carry his mother on one shoulder and his father on the other shoulder for as long as he lived, for a full one hundred years, and if he were to anoint and massage their bodies, bathe them and knead them, while they were to piss and shit all over him . . .

> [and even] if he were to establish his mother and father in kingship and lordly sovereignty over this [entire] great earth abounding with the seven treasures, even so, Monks, he would not repay or requite his mother and father![8]

On the other hand, causing harm to one's parents is the greatest of all possible sins. Thus, patricide and matricide are classified throughout Buddhist literature as two of the five "sins of immediate retribution" (Skt. *ānantarya-karma*)—"crimes so heinous," as Jonathan Silk describes them, "that their inevitable karmic result of descent into hell takes place immediately and necessarily in the next life, rather than at some unspecified vague point in the future." These are, in fact, "the most serious crimes catalogued and studied within Indian Buddhist literature."[9]

Despite the presence of many such passages that pay equal attention to both parents, however, there are also subtle ways in which the mother is sometimes highlighted: Speeches promoting the benefits of serving both parents, for example, are often addressed to monks who are specifically designated as "supporters of their mothers" (P. *mātiposakabhikkhu*)—and even monks who are explicitly described as serving both parents are likewise referred to as "supporters of their mothers."[10] The commentary to the *Aṅguttara Nikāya* passage cited above, in which a man is imagined to carry both parents around on his shoulders, carefully specifies that the mother should occupy the right (or auspicious) shoulder, whereas the father should occupy the left.[11] Subtle clues such as these suggest that the mother has a distinctive role to play that distinguishes her from the father. Likewise, though both patricide and matricide result in immediate rebirth in hell, when the five "sins of immediate retribution" are hierarchized, Buddhist sources "almost uniformly rank the murder of a mother more severely than that of a father."[12] According to the *Aṅguttara Nikāya Commentary*, this is because "the mother is responsible for difficult tasks, and is very attentive to her sons."[13] As Silk has further noted, this favoritism shown toward the mother is common to Hindu sources as well; in the *Mahābhārata*, for example, we are told: "Neither mother nor father is to be blamed, since they are both one's former benefactors. But, since she has endured suffering in carrying [one during pregnancy], of the two the mother is more venerable."[14]

Perhaps one of the best examples of this tendency to favor the mother within a context that presumably deals with both parents can be found in the *Sonananda Jātaka* (*Jātaka* No. 532), in which the bodhisattva is a wise man named Sona who instructs his younger brother Nanda on the virtues of looking after one's parents.[15] While clearly advocating the support of both parents, Sona in fact pays an inordinate amount of attention to the mother. Here, we begin to see not only the favoritism sometimes shown toward the mother, but also her particular association with the affective emotions of love, compassion, and tenderness. In a long series of verses (along with their accompanying commentary), Sona depicts maternal love in a highly idealized and emotional manner as the purest, most compassionate, and most self-sacrificing type of love possible—while saying nothing about the love of the father.

Even before the child's conception, Sona notes, the mother anxiously "worships the gods and questions the stars and the seasons"[16]—wondering, for example, "under which constellation will a long-lived son be born?"[17] Once she succeeds in becoming pregnant, she immediately "gives rise to love (P. *sneha*) for the offspring in her womb" and should therefore be known as his "goodhearted friend" (P. *suhadā*).[18] Upon the baby's birth, she "soothes her crying child with breastmilk and lullabies,"[19] "nestles him in between her breasts, suffuses him with the touch of her body, and wraps him up in the cloak of her arms."[20] She "pleases and appeases him,"[21] "protects her innocent child from frightful wind and heat,"[22] "treats him with tenderness" (P. *mamaṃkārana*), and "looks at him with a loving heart" (P. *siniddhena hadayena*).[23] As her son gets older, she guards and protects the family wealth, thinking, "Someday, let it go to our son."[24] Hoping that her son will be virtuous, she "suffers hardship and wears herself out" (P. *vihaññati kilamati*), constantly admonishing him, "Please, my son! No, my son!" But in all too many cases, despite her tireless efforts, "when her son has attained maturity, he is careless and visits the wives of others." She "knows that he is not coming home, and with eyes full of tears, she watches the path, and she suffers and wears herself out."[25] This emotional portrait of the mother who longs to be reunited with her son finds its reflection in the actual mother of Sona and Nanda, for when Nanda returns home after an extended period away, his mother "goes to him and embraces him, smells and kisses his head, and extinguishes the grief in her heart."[26] "Seeing Nanda at long last," she exclaims, "my heart trembles, like the tender shoot of a fig tree, fanned by the breeze."[27]

It is only after this extended mother-son love story, highly charged with the emotions of love, separation, and suffering, that the text suddenly reverts to a series of rather bland verses advocating the support and service of both parents. Thus, while both mothers and fathers do much for their children, and children owe a corresponding debt to both parents, it is the mother alone who seems to be surrounded by such intense emotions and made the object of such intimate descriptions. Much as Alan Cole has described in the case of medieval Chinese Buddhist literature, maternal love often seems to serve as the emotional "hook" that guarantees the son's devotion to the patriarchal family.[28] It is in this sense that the mother can be distinguished from the father: The obligation to the father is a call of duty, whereas the obligation to the mother is a pull of love.

The special nature accorded to maternal love is also evidenced by the number of contexts in which its qualities are alluded to in a proverbial manner, as if understood and assumed by everyone. In a story from the *Dhammapada Commentary*, for example, when a mother and father are struggling to cross a wilderness during a famine, and the father wishes to abandon their baby son, the mother's steadfast refusal to do so is explained by the narrator with the statement: "They say that the heart of a mother is tender" (P. *mātuhadayaṃ nāma mudukaṃ ti*).[29] Elsewhere in the same text, another mother also refuses to abandon her baby, even though he is deformed and repulsive, "for powerful is the love [of a mother] for the son who has dwelt in her womb."[30] In the *Uraga Jātaka* (*Jātaka* No. 354),[31] when a young man suddenly dies, the deity Sakka is unfazed by his father's failure to cry, yet surprised that the same is also true of his mother: "My good woman," he asks her, "a father, since he is a man, must not cry, but a mother's heart is tender (P. *mātu hadayaṃ pana mudukaṃ hoti*), so why do you not cry?"[32] For Sakka—and, presumably, for this text's audience—so proverbial is the mother's "tender heart" (P. *muduka-hadaya*) that this mother's lack of it seems to violate the very definition of "mother." Thus, while both parents are celebrated for the love and service they show to their children, it is primarily mother-love that is described in such intimate, affectionate, and emotional terms.

More significantly, for our purposes, it is also primarily mother-love that comes to serve, in many contexts, as the most appropriate metaphor for the love and compassion that a buddha or bodhisattva radiates outward toward all beings. Here, we move from the depiction of maternal love itself to the use of maternal love as a religious metaphor. Buddhas and bodhisattvas, though frequently imagined or described as fathers, have an intense and compassionate love for all beings that is strongly associated with the love of the mother. Only mother-love, it seems, can convey the ardor, fervor, and intensity with which buddhas and bodhisattvas love sentient beings, and in countless Buddhist texts we are told that buddhas and bodhisattvas love all beings "just as a mother loves her only son." The constant repetition of this cliché, and the corresponding lack of any such comparison involving fathers loving their daughters, husbands loving their wives, and so forth, suggests that the *mother's love for the son*, in particular, was idealized as an example of pure, compassionate love.[33] Ordinary monks engaging in the cultivation of "loving-kindness" (P. *mettā;* Skt. *maitrī*) toward all beings—one of the standard varieties of Buddhist meditation—are likewise instructed to imitate the love a mother has for her only son. One classic, early instance of this metaphorical use of mother-love can be found in the chapter devoted to "loving-kindness" in the *Sutta Nipāta*: "Just as a mother would guard with her life her own son, her only son," the text tells us, "so one should cultivate an unbounded mind toward all living beings, and loving-kindness toward the whole world."[34] Mother-love here is the very best model for the monk who wishes to cultivate loving-kindness.

Despite this positive valuation of mother-love, however, a closer consideration of the above passage (and others like it) will reveal that mother-love, when used in this way, is really a double-edged symbol that simultaneously succeeds and fails. Both its success and its ultimate failure hinge on its *particularity* or *exclusivity*—that is, the fact that it is love for one particular person. On the one hand, it is precisely because of this particularity that mother-love is able to reach the intensity that makes it such an appropriate metaphor for the Buddhist virtue of loving-kindness. This is why the Buddha's loving-kindness for all beings is so often compared specifically to the mother's love for "her own son, her only son" (P. *niyaṃ puttaṃ, ekaputta*). Because one's own children are more highly valued than other people's children, because sons (in premodern South Asia) are more highly valued than daughters, and because an only child is more highly valued than one of many children, it is only the mother's love for "her own son, her only son" that reaches the intensity that allows it to serve as an appropriate metaphor for the love of the Buddha.

On the other hand, of course, it is precisely this same particularity that ultimately distinguishes mother-love from the Buddha's love and turns them into polar opposites. For while mother-love is particular to one's own child alone and does not extend to anyone else, the Buddha's love is universal and extends, with equal intensity, to all living beings. There is thus a stark contrast between *one person* and *all beings*, or between *particular* and *universal* love. Mother-love may serve positively as a metaphor for the Buddha's love, but mother-love, as an actual entity, is ultimately undercut and devalued. Particularistic love for one's own child is, in fact, wholly incompatible with the Buddhist ideal of universal love, since it obviously leads the mother to favor her own child over everyone else. The particular, from this perspective, is *not* highly valued; in fact, the particular must be overcome and abolished in order for the universal to occur. (Within the Buddha's own life story, this is emphasized as much as possible by the fact that he renounces the world to seek enlightenment for all beings on the very day that his first son is born.)

In fact, mother-love, when considered from this perspective, is often negatively portrayed in Buddhist texts as being a potent manifestation of desire, attachment, and clinging—all highly negative emotions that keep one bound within the realm of samsara. This, again, sharply distinguishes it from the Buddha's love, which, despite its intensity, is said to be practiced with perfect detachment, dispassion, and equanimity toward all—those qualities that lead one to nirvana. Once again, we can see this as a necessary consequence of the contrast between the particular and the universal: Because mother-love is directed toward someone particular to the mother alone, it is, by definition, the result of selfish attachment. The mother's love for her own child alone is just a reflection of her constant grasping after "I," "me," and "mine"—the same delusional belief in a permanent self that keeps us bound within the realm of birth and death. In contrast, because the Buddha's love is directed equally toward all living beings, it is, by definition, selfless, detached, and dispassionate in nature, a reflection of the Buddha's superior insight into reality and his understanding of the truth of no-self. As an especially pernicious form of attachment, then, mother-love, perhaps more than any other type of human emotion, is inconsistent with the detachment necessary for spiritual progress to occur. Despite its positive uses as a metaphor, mother-love, as an actual entity, is ultimately incompatible not only with the universal compassion of the Buddha, but also with the perfect detachment of the arhat. This is not to deny that mother-love is often praised, celebrated, admired, or encouraged within a worldly scale of values, as we have already seen, but only to observe that ultimately it is judged to be incompatible with Buddhism's highest soteriological goals. Though clearly other forms of attachment (such as romantic love) are also incompatible with these goals, mother-love, I contend, is made to seem *especially so.*

A brief consideration of the complex depiction of mother-love in several different Buddhist contexts will perhaps help to illustrate some of these ideas. I will begin with a narrative motif that exists in both Hindu and Buddhist versions, the differences between which illuminate the

Buddhist ambivalence toward mother-love. In an ancient Hindu ritual text known as the *Baudhāyana Śrauta Sūtra*, we are told a very brief story in which a man named Ṛtuparṇa, who is the father of several sons, angers the deity Indra.[35] He is punished by being transformed into a woman, and as a woman, she becomes the mother of several more sons. The deity Indra then kills all of the sons, but later decides to bring some of them back to life and gives Ṛtuparṇa the choice of which sons should be restored—those of whom she is the father or those of whom she is the mother. She immediately chooses those of whom she is the mother, and the text itself concludes: "This is why they say that sons are dearer to a woman."[36] The story is simple and straightforward, and its point is crystal clear: Mother-love is always greater than father-love—even when the same person is both mother and father.

Now let us consider the same narrative motif, as found in a story from the *Dhammapada Commentary*.[37] In this case, a man named Sorreya, who is the father of two sons, is suddenly transformed into a woman through the negative karmic consequences of a lustful thought. As a woman, she gives birth to two more sons, but later on, after repenting for the lustful thought, she is once again transformed back into a man. Whenever people hear this remarkable story, they ask Sorreya which sons he loves the most—those of whom he is the mother or those of whom he is the father. And he always gives the same reply: "Friends, I have a stronger love (P. *sineha*) for those [sons] who were born from my womb."[38] Thus, just as we saw in the Hindu story, mother-love is celebrated as being greater in intensity than father-love. But the Buddhist story does not end there. For Sorreya, being "ashamed" (P. *harāyamāna*) of giving this reply, subsequently becomes a Buddhist monk, withdraws into meditative solitude, and quickly attains nirvana and becomes an arhat. And from then on, whenever people ask him which sons he loves the most, he answers: "I have no love at all for anyone."[39] At the end of the story, the Buddha, commenting on Sorreya's attainment of arhatship, pronounces verse 43 of the *Dhammapada:* "Neither mother nor father nor any other relative can do that which a well-directed mind can do far better."[40]

The Buddhist adaptation of this narrative motif may be subtle, but it is striking in its implications about mother-love. Gone is the simple celebration of mother-love, and in its place, we get a more ambivalent message: Yes, mother-love *is* greater and more intense than father-love—yet this intensity itself suggests that mother-love is that much farther away than father-love from the perfect detachment of the arhat, who has "no love at all for anyone." This subtle condemnation of mother-love is further underscored by the fact that Sorreya's initial transformation into a mother is depicted as the negative karmic consequence of a sinful thought of lust, while his retransformation into a father is depicted as the positive karmic consequence of repenting for that thought[41]—as well as by the fact that Sorreya is "ashamed" of the greater attachment he experiences as a mother. Clearly, the father is closer to being an arhat than the mother is—and this is manifested, the story suggests, by his lesser attachment to his children. Finally, the Buddha himself enunciates the larger point of the story: When it comes to attaining nirvana, personal, familial bonds such as that between mother and child are useless; only a well-directed mind really matters. When *all* parental love is spiritually impotent, in other words, the mother's greater attachment to her children takes on a different cast and becomes a sign of weakness rather than strength.

Just as mother-love may be particularly incompatible with the detachment necessary to attain nirvana, we can also find passages suggesting that the reverse is equally true—that is, one who *does* attain nirvana can be imagined as a mother who has eradicated all mother-love from her heart. This is precisely what we find, in fact, in an intriguing discussion from Buddhaghosa's *Visuddhimagga*.[42] At a fairly advanced stage on the path leading to nirvana, Buddhaghosa informs us, the Buddhist practitioner observes the way in which all phenomena of the past, present, and future are constantly arising and then disappearing—an ephemeral flow of existence that is terrifying to ordinary human beings. Buddhaghosa then compares the meditator's reflection on past, present, and future phenomena to a mother accompanying her three sons to the execution ground: "Seeing that her oldest son's head had been cut off, and that her middle son's head was being cut off, she let go of [any] attachment (P. *ālaya*) for her youngest son, [thinking:] 'This one, too, will be just like them.'"[43] Buddhaghosa explains the metaphor as follows:

> Here, the meditator's discernment of the cessation of past phenomena is like that woman seeing her oldest son's head [already] cut off; his discernment of the cessation of present phenomena is like her seeing her middle son's head being cut off; and his discernment of the cessation of future phenomena—[thinking:] "Phenomena that arise in the future, too, will also break up"—is like her letting go of [any] attachment to her youngest son, [thinking:] "This one, too, will be just like them."[44]

In this intriguing metaphor, the Buddhist meditator comes to realize that both his past and his present have been characterized by the enormous suffering caused by the impermanence of all phenomena—a suffering that is likened to a mother watching her two oldest sons die. He thus makes a conscious decision to remain detached from all phenomena in the future in order to avoid any further suffering—a decision that is likened to a mother who forsakes any attachment to her youngest son after watching the first two die. Thus, the ordinary mother who loves her children is used as an image of delusion, while the mother who turns her back on motherhood and forsakes all mother-love is used as an image of enlightenment. The potency of mother-love as an image here is further underscored by the second metaphor Buddhaghosa offers for the same scenario—that of a woman who gives birth to eleven sons, the first nine of them stillborn, the tenth one dying in her arms, and the eleventh one still in her womb: "Seeing that nine of her babies had died, and the tenth was dying, she let go of [any] attachment for the one in her womb, [thinking:] 'This one, too, will be just like them.'"[45] Here, the vivid imagery of pregnancy, repeated stillbirths, and a baby dying in his mother's arms is put to effective use to capture the dramatic turn from bondage to enlightenment. (Somehow, one imagines that a metaphor involving fathers would not pack quite the same punch.)

Lest we forget the double-edged nature of mother-love, however, it is also pertinent to point out that in another section of the *Visuddhimagga*, we find Buddhaghosa equally willing to draw on its more positive connotations. For in his section on the four "immeasurables" (P. *appamaññā*)—that is, four highly valued emotional states that the disciple is supposed to cultivate in meditation and then gradually extend outward until they pertain to all living beings—Buddhaghosa draws upon mother-love as the most appropriate metaphor for such states.[46] He first tells us that "loving-kindness" (P. *mettā*) is the emotion of wanting to do good for others, "compassion" (P. *karuṇā*) is the emotion of wanting to remove misfortune from others, "sympathetic joy" (P. *muditā*) is the emotion of wanting to rejoice in others' happiness, and "equanimity" (P. *upekkhā*) is the emotion of treating all beings equally and not being overly preoccupied with any one. He then tells the meditator to cultivate each of these four states by imitating the mother's attitude toward a baby son, a sick son, an adolescent son, and an adult son who manages his own affairs, respectively. Thus, loving-kindness is the attitude of a mother who wants to nourish and properly care for her baby son, compassion is the attitude of a mother who wants to remove illness and suffering from her sick son, sympathetic joy is the attitude of a mother who wants to rejoice in the successes of her adolescent son, and equanimity is the attitude of a mother who is not overly anxious about her adult son. When it comes to positive and nurturing emotions toward others, Buddhaghosa can think of no better comparison than a mother's love for her children. He consciously chooses, in this context, to invoke a mother rather than a father.

What is intriguing about Buddhaghosa's metaphor, however, is that despite its obviously positive depiction of mother-love, the metaphor itself contains the same tension I alluded to above between the particularistic love of the mother and the universal love so highly valued in Buddhism. For within the schema of the four "immeasurables," it is equanimity—or the calm, dispassionate, and even-minded attitude toward all beings alike—that is considered the highest state. In fact, each of the other three states is supposed to be cultivated until they themselves reach the state of equanimity—in other words, until they extend evenly to all beings without exception. Thus, equanimity is the highest of these four states—and yet, as we saw above, it is precisely the universality implicit in equanimity that stands in conflict with the mother's exclusive love for her own children alone. We can see this tension clearly within Buddhaghosa's comparison: On the one hand, mother-love is a natural and easy metaphor for positive emotions such as loving-kindness and compassion, but on the other hand, the only way to extend this metaphor to the most highly valued state of detached equanimity is to cite the example of a mother who has no anxiety about an adult son managing his own affairs. In other words, only the *weakest* and most attenuated version of mother-love can stand for equanimity—and not very effectively, I might add. We can easily see, in fact, that equanimity would be much easier to imagine through consideration of the feelings of a *father*. This again betrays the fact that mother-love is inherently bound up with particularity, exclusivity, and selfish attachment.

One final feature of mother-love that is suggested in several contexts, as a concomitant to its partiality, intensity, and selfishness, involves its general *lack of effectiveness*. Though mother-love is undoubtedly more intense than father-love, this intensity itself seems to make the mother less effective than the father in those situations that really matter. As an excessive form of attachment, maternal love renders the mother somewhat mindless, easily carried away by her emotions, and thus impotent in situations in which her child is really in danger—whereas the detached and dispassionate love of the father makes him a more effective agent who can successfully help a child in need. This is a common theme in Buddhist literature. In the *Śyāmaka Jātaka* of the *Mahāvastu*,[47] for example, an old mother and father live as ascetics in a hut in the forest, where they are cared for by their loyal son Śyāmaka. When Śyāmaka is mistakenly killed by a king who is out hunting, his mother immediately gives way to grief and lamentation, clasping Śyāmaka's head to her bosom, bemoaning her "dear child" (Skt. *vatsa*) and "beloved, only son" (Skt. *dayita ekaputra*), and cursing the gods who have failed to protect him.[48] It is only Śyāmaka's *father* who keeps his wits about him and effectively responds. "Do not grieve, Pāragā," he scolds his wife, "for there is no point in weeping and grieving! All who are born in the world of beings must inevitably die. Besides, we are celibate and have abstained from sexual intercourse for a long time. We will speak a statement of truth, and by it, we will destroy the poison in him."[49] Thanks to the level-headed detachment of his father, Śyāmaka is thereby restored to life.[50]

In a Mahāyāna context, as Alex Wayman has pointed out,[51] this same contrast between the *effective father* and the *ineffective mother* is sometimes used to exalt the superiority of the Mahāyāna bodhisattva (father) over the inferior, Hīnayāna disciple (mother)—despite the many other contexts (as discussed above) in which the bodhisattva's love is likened to that of a mother. In a Sanskrit Mahāyāna sūtra known as the *Sāgaramatiparipṛcchā*, for example, an only, beloved son falls into a terrible cesspit, and his mother is so overcome with grief and sorrow that she never thinks of entering the cesspit in order to bring the boy out. It is only the *father*, with his superior detachment, who refrains from grieving, calmly assesses the situation, and succeeds in rescuing the boy.[52] From the perspective of this Mahāyāna polemic, the father stands for the Mahāyāna bodhisattva, who loves all beings in a detached and therefore effective manner, whereas the mother stands for the inferior, Hīnayāna disciple, who lacks the necessary detachment to effectively rescue beings—no matter how much love and compassion for them he may have. This is not a contrast, then, between a loving mother and an indifferent father, but, rather, a contrast between the mindless and impotent attachment of the mother and the effective and dispassionate altruism of the father. Within such passages, as Wayman notes, "mother love—wonderful as it is—is not a rescue mentality. The latter role is credited to the father."[53] Mahāyāna polemic aside, however, the metaphor only works because of its basic assumptions about mother-love: The mother's love is ineffective precisely because it is so caught up in desire, attachment, and grief.

I hope that this random scattering of textual passages—chosen from many that might have been cited—will suffice to demonstrate the consistently ambivalent manner in which mother-love is treated in South Asian Buddhist texts: On the one hand, mother-love is idealized as intense, compassionate, and self-sacrificing in nature, made akin to the Buddha's love for all beings or the Buddhist meditator's cultivation of loving-kindness, and consistently elevated above father-love in this regard; on the other hand, mother-love is negatively portrayed as being overly exclusive and ultimately selfish in nature, perceived as a pernicious form of attachment keeping one bound within the realm of samsara, and sometimes condemned as impotent in comparison to the dispassionate love of the father. As I have tried to demonstrate, much of the ambivalence shown toward mother-love hinges on its *particularity*—which accounts for its intensity and thus its usefulness as a religious metaphor, but also puts it into outright conflict with the universal ideals espoused by Buddhism. As metaphor, maternal love is idealized; as reality, it is ultimately condemned. This ambivalence is sometimes displayed even within the confines of a single text: For example, in the *Mahāyānasūtrālaṃkāra*, Asaṅga states that the bodhisattva has a love for beings "as great as [that which a mother has] toward an only son"[54]—yet the bodhisattva's love, in truth, is "nothing like that which other beings have, even toward those such as an excellent only son."[55] The comparison is—finally—just a foil for the contrast.

Good and Bad Mothers

In addition to considering the mother as opposed to the father, another way of approaching the ambiguities surrounding mother-love is by taking a closer look at the *good mothers* and *bad mothers* who populate Buddhist texts. Mothers in Buddhist literature are rarely neutral figures; instead, they tend to appear in diametrically opposing forms.[56] Thus, on the one hand, we find depictions of good, nurturing, and self-sacrificing mothers whose boundless love for their children is admired and celebrated; on the other hand, we find depictions of cruel and horrific mothers who may lack any love for their own offspring and often kill and devour the offspring of others. These two figures are antitheses of one another, and in many contexts, as we would expect, the "good" mother is celebrated while the "bad" mother is condemned. Yet good and bad mothers, although polar opposites, also have a strange tendency to morph into one another: The good mother whose motherhood is somehow frustrated can easily transform into a hideous mother-ogress, while the bad mother who eats babies for pleasure can be tamed and converted by Buddhism into a benevolent and nurturing force. The good mother and the bad mother, on some level, appear to be the same figure. As Bernard Faure has noted, "There is a fine line in Buddhist legend between blind love and ghoulish desire: even ogresses feel motherly love, but conversely, even loving mothers have something of an ogress in them."[57] In some instances, moreover, rather than praising one and condemning the other, the Buddhist tradition subtly condemns *both* good and bad mothers in favor of the link between fathers and sons.

This mercurial nature of motherhood makes sense, I believe, in light of the ambiguities surrounding mother-love that I discussed above. For as we have seen, on the one hand, mother-love can be *likened* to the Buddhist values of love and compassion—and from this perspective, the "good" mother, who embodies Buddhist values, may be exalted over the "bad" mother, who doesn't. But on the other hand, mother-love is also fundamentally *opposed* to such values—and from this perspective, the distinction between "good" and "bad" mothers becomes blurry, perhaps suggesting that both are ultimately subject to the same fate and that mother-love in any form must finally be transcended—often in favor of a spiritual connection between fathers and sons. In lieu of a more complete discussion, it is this latter possibility alone—that is, the ultimate equivalence of "good" and "bad" mothers from a perspective that finally condemns *all* mother-love—that I would like to explore further here by considering the pairing of "good" and "bad" mothers in three closely related Buddhist tales.

One common image found in many narrative sources is that of the would-be "good" mother whose motherhood is somehow frustrated, and who then becomes a "bad" mother who is vindictive toward the children of others. In some cases, this tendency to morph from one extreme to the other results in a vicious cycle, running over multiple lifetimes and involving two different mothers. In the *Dhammapada Commentary*,[58] for example, we find the story of a man who has both a barren wife and a fertile wife. On three different occasions, the fertile wife becomes pregnant, but the barren wife, out of jealousy, gives her a drug that makes her miscarry, whereupon the fertile wife vows to get revenge on her in a future rebirth. She gets her revenge when she is reborn as a cat and the barren wife is reborn as a hen. The cat devours the hen's eggs on three different occasions, whereupon the hen vows to get revenge in a future rebirth. The hen is reborn as a leopardess, the cat is reborn as a doe, and the vicious cycle continues. Finally, the same two beings are reborn as a demoness (P. *yakkhinī*) and a woman. The demoness succeeds in devouring the woman's first two sons, but on the third occasion, the woman successfully gives birth to a baby boy. When the demoness tries to devour him, the woman runs into a nearby monastery, lays her son at the Buddha's feet, and asks him to keep her son safe. The Buddha puts an end to this cycle of frustrated motherhood and its attendant violence. He admonishes both the demoness and the woman for their mutual hatred over multiple lifetimes, and he concludes by pronouncing verse 5 of the *Dhammapada:* "For not by hatred can hatreds ever be appeased here in this world. By the absence of hatred are hatreds appeased. This is an eternal law."[59]

Here, it seems that "good" mothers and "bad" mothers are almost completely interchangeable. The "good" mother who loves and protects her children very soon becomes the "bad" mother who kills and devours the children of others, and vice versa. These are not two distinct species of women—they are the *same woman,* and they turn on a dime. This equivalence is emphasized even further by depicting an even number of lives, so that the "bad" mother and "good" mother from the beginning of the story end up as the "good" mother and "bad" mother at the end. What makes these two mothers interchangeable, moreover, is the quality of mother-love they share. It is because the "good" mother loves her children so much that she immediately transforms into the "bad" mother once those children are taken away. Good and bad mothers may seem different on the surface, the story suggests, but ultimately both of them are subject to the same fatal weakness of mother-love: Mother-love is attachment, attachment leads to suffering, and suffering is implicated in violence and revenge. Only the Buddha can break this cycle of maternal attachment and its attendant suffering. Under his influence, the good and bad mothers are finally reconciled. The woman, in fact, hands her baby to the demoness, whereupon the demoness kisses the baby and returns him to his mother.

The same theme of frustrated motherhood and the same equivalence ultimately drawn between good and bad mothers can also be found in the *Ayoghara Jātaka* (*Jātaka* No. 510).[60] In this story, once again, the rivalry between a barren woman and a fertile woman leads to their being reborn as a demoness and a queen, with the demoness determined to devour the queen's offspring. The demoness succeeds in devouring the queen's first two sons, but the third son—the bodhisatta—is spared when his mother and father lock him up in an iron house so that the demoness can't get to him. The story thus establishes an initial contrast between a "good" mother—the queen—who loves her son and tries to protect him, and a "bad" mother—the demoness—who becomes "bad" when her own motherhood is frustrated, and who then sets out to destroy the children of others. The "good" mother protects her son, while the "bad" mother wants only to kill him.

Despite this contrast, however, it is striking to note what the son himself—the bodhisatta—has to say when, at the age of sixteen, he is finally released from the iron house and learns the entire story surrounding his birth. The son, rather than contrasting the "good" and "bad" mothers, draws a direct comparison between his imprisonment for sixteen years within the iron house and his original imprisonment within his mother's disgusting womb, which he refers to metaphorically as an "Iron Cauldron Hell" (P. *lohakumbhiniraya*) and a "Hell of Shit" (P. *gūthaniraya*).[61] Thus, just as the "bad" mother was responsible for his imprisonment within the iron house, so too the "good" mother was responsible for his imprisonment within the womb, which is itself likened to a hell of iron. Though this comparison perhaps has more to do with Buddhist perceptions of the female body than with its perceptions of motherhood, there is still a subtle message being conveyed here about mothers. From the son/bodhisatta's perspective, we might say, both forms of imprisonment, as well as the mothers who bring them about, are ultimately the same: Both are equally unsatisfactory, both equally partake of the futility of samsara, and therefore the son does the only thing that makes sense for him: He renounces the world—and he brings his *father* along with him. Taking the story as a whole, then, we find a superficial contrast between good and bad mothers, their ultimate equivalence from the perspective of Buddhism, and the Buddhist son's rejection of both mothers in favor of a spiritual link between father and son.

Occurring just three stories later in the Pali *Jātaka* collection, the *Jayyadisa Jātaka* (*Jātaka* No. 513) has a very similar setup but provides us with a new twist.[62] Once again, this story involves a demoness who vows to devour the offspring of a queen because of frustrated motherhood and jealous rivalry in a previous lifetime. Once again, the demoness succeeds in devouring the queen's first two sons, whereas the third son—the bodhisatta—survives. In this case, however, just as the demoness is about to devour the third son, the baby mistakes the demoness for *his own mother*, puts his lips to her breast, and thus awakens within her a powerful feeling of mother-love that stops her from killing him and instead causes her to hide him in a cave and lovingly raise him as her own child. Here we get a slightly different perspective on the equivalence between good and bad mothers: Just as the "good" mother can become a "bad" mother if her mother-love is somehow interrupted or frustrated, so too the "bad" mother can become a "good" mother once her mother-love again finds its proper outlet. In a sense, what this story suggests is that the difference between good and bad mothers is not a true moral difference. It is only a difference between the satisfaction of one's selfish desires and their frustration. This suggestion underscores the idea that mother-love is ultimately a form of craving or desire rather than a positive moral quality.

The remainder of this story, I believe, is also significant. Though the plotline is too complicated to narrate fully here, what happens, in brief, is that the son/bodhisatta, after growing up in the cave under the care of his demoness foster-mother, is rescued from the cave by his own nephew, reunited with his older brother (who is now a king), and renounces the world to become an ascetic living under his brother's protection. Various *male* relatives, in other words, come to the fore to help the young man escape from his imprisonment and renounce the world, while the two mothers recede wholly into the background. The difference between good and bad mothers is thus shown to be irrelevant in comparison to the Buddhist values of renunciation and detachment, which are supported here by relatives who are male. Spiritual connections between sons and their metaphorical fathers thus take precedence over the clinging grasp of the mother—whether "good" or "bad."

In these latter two stories, we see a common family dynamic that involves the son's rejection of his mother in favor of his father. Many feminist scholars of Buddhism have written of the way in which samsara in Buddhist literature is implicitly coded as feminine, while entrapment within samsara is perceived primarily as a male dilemma—an idea expressed narratively through such episodes as that in which Prince Siddhārtha sees the disgusting bodies of the sleeping women in his harem and decides at that very moment to renounce the world, or the many stories in which shipwrecked sailors are held captive on an island by cannibalistic female ghouls.[63] As Liz Wilson puts it, samsara is a "man-trap" in which "women are the agents of incarceration."[64] The latter two stories discussed above also fall into this general pattern, both presenting a scenario in which the essential task of the male hero is to escape from the clutches of the feminine. What is particular to these two stories, however, is that "feminine" and "masculine" take on the specific forms of "mother" and "son." The son's renunciation of worldly life is also an escape from his mother(s) and is often aided through an association with his father. "To 'leave the house,'" as Bernard Faure puts it, "was to leave the mother"—in favor of a Saṃgha composed of "symbolic fathers."[65] Psychologically, of course, this is reminiscent of the way in which the male child's successful psychological development is said by some to involve a necessary break in his identification with his mother in favor of a more mature identification with his father. We might speculate that in stories such as these, the developmental journey of the male child, from the domestic realm associated with the mother to the public realm associated with the father, has been mapped onto the soteriological journey demanded by Buddhism, such that the move from samsara to nirvana becomes symbolized as a rejection of the mother and an identification with the father.[66] The essential point to emphasize here, however, is that this "mapping" is further reinforced by the Buddhist depiction of mother-love itself as an excessive form of attachment, perceived as suffocating by the son, whether or not the mother is "good" or "bad." The reduction of both "good" and "bad" mothers to that which must be rejected further underscores the Buddhist tradition's ambivalence toward the love of the mother.

Finally, it is also interesting to note the manner in which these three stories might relate to a larger South Asian religious context. All three stories share the motif of a woman whose own motherhood is somehow frustrated and who then, after death, becomes a vengeful devourer of the children of others. Historically, it seems clear that all three of them can be related to a long-standing and continuing South Asian folk religious belief that the spirits of women who suffer either an untimely death themselves or some other unnatural interruption of their domestic roles—for example, the untimely deaths of their husbands or children—have the potential to come back and haunt the living, whether through demonic possession, the infliction of epidemic diseases, or a variety of other malign visitations. The usual solution to this problem is to appease the spirit of the unfulfilled woman by divinizing her, turning her into a minor mother-goddess, and making her the object of a continuing cult of worship, in hopes that she might be persuaded to nurture and protect the local community rather than harming it. These potentially vengeful mother-goddess spirits make many appearances in classical Hindu literature—for example, in the shadowy group known as the *mātṛkās* ("Mothers") found throughout the Purāṇas—and they are still widely worshipped on the village level throughout the Indian subcontinent today.[67]

But although our stories seem to draw on this wider complex of beliefs, they finally use it for wholly different purposes. The Buddhist stories discussed above are not concerned with demonstrating how to appease the spirits of frustrated mothers by instituting regular cults of worship on their behalf. Instead, they use the theme of frustrated motherhood in the service of the overall discourse on mother-love I have tried to elucidate above: Alternating pairs of frustrated mothers who pursue each other endlessly in life after life finally serve to demonstrate that good motherhood and bad motherhood are merely two sides of the same coin, that the loving care and protection bestowed by the "good" mother has its source in the very same selfish attachment as the vengefulness and cruelty of the "bad" mother, and that Buddhism offers people a path that lies beyond the faults of motherhood altogether.

Mother-Love versus Son-Love

Just as mother-love may be elucidated by comparing mothers to fathers, or by comparing good mothers to bad mothers, so it may be further elucidated by comparing mothers to sons. In other words, the particularity, exclusivity, and selfish attachment that characterize mother-love in Buddhist literature can be brought into greater relief by contrasting the mother's attitude toward the son with the son's proper attitude toward the mother. How do Buddhist texts advise the good son to view his mother? As we might expect, the good son is encouraged repeatedly in Buddhist literature to honor his mother, be grateful for the many services she has performed on his behalf, take care of her in her old age, and do everything he can to repay the enormous debt he owes to her. The son's love of the mother, in other words, should be just as particular, exclusive, and intense as the mother's love for the son. Buddhist literature is full of stories, in fact, featuring loyal sons who are wholly devoted to the welfare and benefit of their mothers. (Perhaps most famous of all was the story of the Buddha's disciple Maudgalyāyana, who searched the entire cosmos to discover the postmortem fate of his mother—a story that would blossom in East Asia into an entire "Mulian saving his mother" tradition.)[68] There is nothing unusual in this, of course, and it is fully what we would expect. Buddhist ethics pay significant attention to harmonious, cooperative, and respectful family relationships and strongly inculcate a child's sense of love and duty toward his parents.

But what if we were to reframe the question not in terms of the ordinary "good son" but, rather, in terms of the idealized male figures of Buddhism—the ideal monk, the perfect arhat, or the male bodhisattva? Though these figures, as well, are frequently described as loving and taking care of their mothers, it is striking to note the number of contexts in which such idealized "sons" are encouraged to cultivate emotions and attitudes that in some way militate *against* the particularity of the mother-son bond—either by encouraging the son to recognize *no mother* or by encouraging the son to recognize *many mothers*. Both strategies, whether by elimination of the mother or extension of the mother, have the effect of undercutting the bond between one particular mother and her son. Both strategies thus work to draw a distinction between the overly attached mother and the liberated Buddhist son.

Buddhist texts that promote the virtues of detachment, evenmindedness, and equanimity, for example, often posit the *nonrecognition of one's mother* or the *nonrecognition of any special relationship to one's mother* as an ideal manifestation of such qualities. Because one's mother is generally one's earliest object of attachment, as well as the focus of a lifelong and intimate personal relationship, it stands to reason that one's refusal to acknowledge or recognize this relationship in any way would constitute a superior display of detachment. Thus, in the *Visuddhimagga*'s chapter on the subjects of meditation, Buddhaghosa discusses ten "obstacles" (P. *paḷibodha*) to effective meditation, the second of which is one's family (P. *kula*):[69] The monk who is preoccupied with his family will be distracted, and his success in meditation will suffer. The ideal monk, on the other hand, is one for whom "even mother and father are no obstacle" (P. *mātāpitaro pi paḷibodhā na honti*).[70] To illustrate this ideal, Buddhaghosa cites the case of a monk who has not seen his parents in many years, but then ends up spending the rainy season retreat in a dwelling donated to the Saṃgha by his parents. He knowingly dines with his parents in their home every single night, yet he never identifies himself to them as their son (Buddhaghosa doesn't explain, however, why his parents fail to recognize him). After speaking of both parents, Buddhaghosa then turns his attention to the mother alone. The mother has been waiting anxiously for news of her long-lost son, "crying and lamenting" when she thinks he might be dead.[71] But when someone finally tells her that the monk who was their nightly guest for three months was, in fact, the son in question, she marvels at his superior detachment: "Though he ate for three months in the home of the very mother who gave birth to him, still he never said: 'I'm your son, you're my mother.' Oh! What a wonderful man!"[72] Not only is the mother (rather than the father) singled out for special attention, but in addition, the lingering attachment of the mother, as she waits anxiously for news of her son, is contrasted with the calm detachment of the son, who refuses even to recognize his own mother.[73] The opposition between these two attitudes is further heightened by having the mother herself marvel at the "wonder" of her son's detachment. Clearly, mother and son inhabit opposite ends of the spectrum. The father, on the other hand, is largely ignored.

Elsewhere in the *Visuddhimagga*,[74] Buddhaghosa invokes a second, though somewhat different, type of scenario in which the failure to distinguish one's own mother again testifies to one's superior nature. One way to combat any feeling of "hatred" (P. *paṭigha*) that might arise in the course of one's meditation, Buddhaghosa tells us, is to recall the many previous lives during which the bodhisatta displayed complete forbearance and equanimity even toward those who were evil to him. He then refers to the *Culladhammapāla Jātaka* (*Jātaka* No. 358),[75] in which a queen, "filled with love for her son,"[76] is playing with her seven-month-old baby Dhammapāla—the bodhisatta—and thus fails to stand up when her husband enters the room. Her husband, the king, being enraged at this slight, calls for the executioner and, in quick succession, has the infant Dhammapāla's hands, feet, head, and flesh cut off. Though the *jātaka* itself, as it appears in the *Jātaka* collection, tells us nothing about what the baby is thinking during all of this, Buddhaghosa informs us that he is cultivating perfect evenmindedness by making no distinction whatsoever between the father who kills him and the mother who weeps for him: "Now, right now," the baby admonishes himself, "is the time for you to restrain your mind, you fool! You must be evenminded (P. *samacitta*) toward these four beings—the father who gives the order to cut off Dhammapāla's head, the man who cuts it off, the mother who laments [over it], and yourself." And with this thought, Buddhaghosa concludes, "he did not experience even a single wicked thought."[77]

Although Buddhaghosa obviously cites this scenario in order to highlight the bodhisatta's forbearance toward his evil father, it is equally remarkable to consider the baby's attitude toward his mother. To be "evenminded" toward everyone within this scenario necessitates not only an absence of anger toward the father who orders his execution, but also a corresponding lack of any particular attachment to the mother who "adorns him, plays with him, and bathes him with fragrant water."[78] This, of course, is exactly what "evenmindedness" means—it means having the *same mind* (P. *samacitta*) toward everyone—and even the ordinary Buddhist meditator is advised by Buddhaghosa to engage in various mental exercises that are similar to that posited for Dhammapāla. In the cultivation of "loving-kindness" (P. *mettā*),[79] for example, Buddhaghosa advises the meditator to develop a feeling of "loving-kindness" first toward himself, then toward a friend, then toward a neutral person, and finally toward an enemy—thus moving from the easiest state of mind to achieve to the most difficult. Once all four states of mind are well established, however, the meditator should then strive to "break down the barriers"[80] between them—that is, to develop a feeling of "loving-kindness" toward all four categories so equally that no distinctions between them are possible. As an illustration of the "breaking down of barriers," Buddhaghosa says that if oneself, a friend, a neutral person, and an enemy were all being attacked by a robber who wished to kill one of them, the one who has "broken down the barriers" would be completely *unable* to choose which of the four people should be killed. In other words, he would look upon these people with much the same attitude as that of the baby Dhammapāla.

The fact that evenmindedness, by definition, necessitates the equal consideration of all beings alike is, therefore, nothing surprising or unusual. The point I wish to emphasize here is only that this idea seems to take on particular force when it is imagined—as it so often is—in the specific terms of *mother* and *son*. To describe a seven-month-old baby who makes no distinction whatsoever between a loving mother and a murderous father not only illustrates the meaning of "equanimity" in a particularly stark manner; it also draws on certain cultural connotations surrounding "mother" and "son"—in essence, using "equanimity" as yet another opportunity to contrast the overly attached mother and the idealized Buddhist son (a contrast further heightened by the maturity of the mother and the infancy of the son). This particular *way* of illustrating equanimity, in other words, fits into a larger pattern in the Buddhist discourse on mother-love.

A second manner in which idealized Buddhist "sons" are encouraged to cultivate attitudes that cut against the particularity of the mother-son bond is by advising them to recognize *many mothers* rather than none. Here again, we can find several such examples. In an episode from the *Mahāvastu*, when the Buddha's son Rāhula decides to renounce the world and become a monk, his mother Yaśodharā gives him some advice on how to be a good monk. "My son," she says, "in order to attain the nirvana you have not yet attained, you must guard yourself well. And why is that? Because, my son, venerable, pleasant, and beautiful women will come to venerate the feet of the Blessed One—and toward them, my son, you must establish the idea that they are your mothers" (Skt. *teṣāṃ . . . mātṛsaṃjñā upasthāpayitavyā*).[81] A precedent for Yaśodharā's advice may be found in a passage from the *Saṃyutta Nikāya,* in which a king asks the Buddhist elder Piṇḍola Bhāradvāja how the Buddha's monks manage to maintain a state of celibacy even when in the prime of life, and the elder replies by quoting the Buddha's own advice: "Come, Monks, toward those women old enough to be your mother, generate the thought of 'mother' (P. *mātumattīsu mātucittaṃ upaṭṭhapetha*); toward those women of a proper age to be your sister, generate the thought of 'sister'; and toward those women young enough to be your daughter, generate the thought of 'daughter.'"[82] Yaśodharā, however, rather than promoting the view of women as mothers, sisters, or daughters, recommends the mother alone—and this focus on the mother is further heightened by the fact that Yaśodharā *is,* in fact, Rāhula's actual mother. The mother herself thus advises her own son to view *all women* as his mothers.

Clearly, the admonition to view all women as one's own mother is intended to minimize any sexual attraction to such women that a monk might otherwise feel. In this sense, the admonition is not concerned with motherhood per se, which is why the *Saṃyutta Nikāya* passage considers the viewing of women as sisters and daughters to be equally effective. Nevertheless, the final effect of Yaśodharā's admonition for any monk who takes it seriously is that the identity of "mother" will be extended from a single woman to the category of women at large. In the service of maintaining his celibacy, the good monk will train himself to see *all women* as his mothers. This diffusion of motherhood from the perspective of the ideal son thus stands in stark contrast to the particularity of sonhood from the perspective of the mother. We might even speculate that the celibacy associated with the former stands in subtle contrast with the eroticized attachment associated with the latter.

A similar but even greater diffusion of motherhood can be found in one of the standard Mahāyāna meditative techniques for generating universal compassion—a technique that was ultimately based on Indian sources but was to be particularly well developed in Tibet. Here, the Mahāyāna bodhisattva is encouraged to begin his cultivation of compassion by first remembering his own mother and all of the many services and sacrifices she performed on his behalf. Having generated a feeling of compassion for his mother's suffering and a strong urge to ease her burdens, he should then use his knowledge of the ceaseless round of samsara to reflect on the fact that *all* sentient beings, at one time or another, have served as his mother and have similarly suffered for his welfare. In this way, his compassion for his mother will gradually be extended into a universal compassion for all "mother sentient beings."

The clearest Indian source for this form of meditation may be found in two verses from Candragomin's *Śiṣyalekha*:

> Who on earth, even the lowest of the low,
> could force himself to abandon
> those beings who were once his mother,
> whose milk, joined with their affectionate love,
> he drank as a helpless infant on their lap,
> and who sustained their tender love,
> although they received from him in return
> nothing but his many naughty pranks?
>
> Who on earth, even an enemy,
> could possibly bear to go away and leave behind
> those suffering, unprotected, miserable beings
> in whose womb he found an occasion to stay,
> and who bore him when he was weak,
> their hearts overcome with love?[83]

Here, the particularistic love associated with one's own mother is intentionally diffused onto the universal category of "all sentient beings" and is thus both invoked and simultaneously undercut. While Candragomin does not elaborate any further, in the Tibetan tradition, this same basic idea was fully developed into a specific form of meditation involving a number of concrete steps. In Tsong kha pa's *Lam rim chen mo*,[84] for example, we get a long series of instructions in which the meditator is told to imagine his mother clearly in front of him, remember all of the kindnesses she bestowed on him (such as using her mouth to remove mucus from his nose and her hand to wipe away his excrement), become aware that all sentient beings have served as his mother in innumerable lifetimes, and then cultivate the wish to repay his infinite mothers' kindness by freeing them from samsara, as well as the realization that he alone, as their son, is fully obligated to do so. Though the meditation begins by harnessing the meditator's emotions toward his own, particular mother, its ultimate purpose is to redirect these emotions toward the category of sentient beings at large. Once again, then, the category of "mother" is here extended to infinity, and the particularity of a single mother is ultimately erased. The universality of the son's compassion for his infinite "mothers" stands in stark contrast to the particularity of the mother's love for her "own and only" son.

We should also pause to take notice here of the highly ambiguous role that mother-love plays within this form of meditation. On the one hand, mother-love is clearly the emotion that fuels the entire exercise, for it is by remembering this love that the son first gives rise to compassion. (As Tsong kha pa puts it, "If you do not develop [the idea that all beings are your mothers], you will have no basis for remembering their kindness.")[85] But on the other hand, the mother herself serves merely as the *object* of the son's compassion, rather than the *agent* whose love models compassion for him. As Rita Gross puts it, mothers here serve "not as models of compassion, but as models of the recipients of compassion."[86] Thus, instead of a technique in which the love of the mother is *imitated* by her son—which seems at least theoretically feasible—we have a technique in which the suffering of the mother arouses the son's compassion *in response*. In fact, far from serving as a worthy model for the son, the mother is best imagined as *one who suffers for her sins and wrongdoings*, thus making her an appropriately pitiful object of the son's compassion. In Tsong kha pa's description, for example, the mother is imagined as one who "engag[es] in wrongdoing and receiv[es] ill repute,"[87] is possessed by "the madness of the afflictions,"[88] is "crazed" and "unable to remain composed," and is "blind" and "stumbl[ing] with every step" because "[her] wrongdoing cripples [her] at each moment."[89] The Buddhist tradition thus depends on maternal love to motivate the son's cultivation of compassion—yet it does not consider that love itself to be a worthy model for the state being cultivated. This technique thus deals with maternal love wholly "from the child's point of view" and "*does not* valorize parenting as a spiritual discipline from the parents' point of view."[90] Why, for example, is there no corresponding form of meditation (as far as I know) in which the bodhisattva reflects on the fact that he himself has served, at one time or another, as the *mother* of all sentient beings? This, after all, would seem to be a natural extension of the canonical metaphor that describes the bodhisattva's love for all beings as being similar to "a mother's love for her only son." The fact that this extension was *not* made—that, in fact, the metaphor had to be *reversed* before it could become an appropriate form of meditation—once again suggests the particularity attached to mother-love, and, thereby, its limitations as a metaphor.

By citing these examples of the idealized son's proper attitude toward the mother, I do not mean to suggest that Buddhist sons were *not* encouraged to love and care for their mothers—clearly they were (as we have already seen), and this obligation was adhered to even by the Buddha himself (as we will see in later chapters). Nevertheless, the existence of multiple contexts in which Buddhism's idealized sons are encouraged to cultivate emotional attitudes that involve some kind of eradication, diffusion, or universalization of the category of "mother" brings into higher relief the Buddhist tradition's standard (and opposing) perception of the mother's particularistic love for the son. While the ideal son is consistently depicted as one who can rise above and transcend his particular tie to his mother, the same is not true for the mother herself—for she is defined wholly in terms of the particular love she bears for her son.

The contrast between mother-love and father-love, the contrast between mother-love and son-love, and the ultimate equivalence of *all* mothers, whether "good" or "bad," all point in the same direction: In all of these contexts, we can see that despite its positive uses as a metaphor, mother-love is finally judged to be a form of selfish attachment that stands opposed to the perfect detachment of the arhat and the universal compassion of the Buddha. It binds the mother to the realm of samsara, impedes her spiritual progress, and makes her vulnerable to loss, grief, mindlessness, and suffering. So much is this the case, in fact, that the mother comes to serve as a paradigmatic embodiment or privileged symbol of such states. And perhaps nowhere is this more true than in the iconic figure of the mother in grief.

2

"*Whose Heart Was Maddened by the Loss of Her Child*"

MOTHERS IN GRIEF

ONE OF THE most fundamental Buddhist teachings (enunciated, for example, in the "Four Noble Truths" that constituted the Buddha's first sermon) is the claim that suffering (Skt. *duḥkha*) is omnipresent, that it originates in desire or attachment (Skt. *tṛṣṇā*), and that the primary goal of the Buddhist path is to eliminate all suffering by eliminating all attachment. This is the basic rationale behind the Buddhist call to world-renunciation: The monk or nun renounces all the components of an ordinary, worldly life (such as sexual activity, familial relationships, and material possessions) not because they are inherently "sinful," but because they foster desire and attachment. By minimizing and eventually eradicating all such attachment, the monk or nun also eradicates the suffering that inevitably comes in attachment's wake—and the complete cessation of all suffering is equivalent to the attainment of nirvana.

If, as we have seen, mother-love is perceived as a pernicious form of attachment keeping us bound within the realm of samsara, and if all attachment inevitably leads to suffering, then it stands to reason that the mother who has lost her child to death would serve as a particularly potent manifestation of suffering. Once again, it is the intensity of maternal love that makes the corresponding maternal grief such an effective image: The anguish of the bereaved mother whose dearly beloved child has been cruelly snatched away by the jaws of death—particularly in infancy or childhood—constitutes an especially dramatic illustration of the omnipresent suffering that envelops all unenlightened beings within samsara. In premodern India, where women derived significant social status by successfully producing legitimate children, yet child fertility and mortality rates were both very high, the mourning mother must have been a fairly common sight, and a figure strongly associated with intense grief and suffering. From the Buddhist point of view, moreover, there is nothing noble or beneficial about such suffering. In fact, Buddhism holds that a modicum of happiness and comfort is essential for making any progress in overcoming suffering; those who are mired too deeply within suffering (such as animals or hell-beings) lack the presence of mind that makes spiritual progress possible. In this sense, the grieving mother shares the spiritual status of lowly creatures such as animals. In fact, Buddhist literature is full of bereaved mothers whose intense suffering drives them into actual madness, and the madness of the mother in grief is consistently cited as an example of the type of mindless distraction that *prohibits* any spiritual advancement: Thus, the *Mahāprajñāpāramitā Śāstra* cites the famous bereaved mother Kisā Gotamī as such an example of "madness caused by grief";[1] the *Abhidharmakośabhāṣya* cites another famous bereaved mother, Vāsiṣṭhā, in a similar context;[2] and the *Kalpanāmaṇḍitikā*, in the course of listing a series of contrasting pairs (such as rich and poor, virtuous and wicked), opposes Vāsiṣṭhā, "whose heart was maddened by the loss of her child," to the venerable monk Revata "and others who rejoice in practicing samādhi."[3] The hysterically grief-ridden mother is thus the very opposite of the mindful and dispassionate Buddhist monk.

In a short sūtra cited by Diana Paul (now extant only in Chinese),[4] this opposition between the grieving mother and the mindful monk is depicted in a particularly poignant manner: An eight-year-old Buddhist novice who has attained nirvana and can recall his previous lives remembers four different mothers who grieved over his death in infancy during four different previous lives, as well as his current mother, who is grieving over his renunciation of the world (a kind of "social death," as it were). He poignantly describes these five sorrowful mothers "who, day and night, lament and grieve for me, constantly saying to themselves: 'Son, I will never forget you.'"[5] Rather than recalling only their grief, however, he also emphasizes the manner in which the intensity of their grief prevents them from becoming liberated, and he contrasts these helpless, grieving mothers with himself—a mere eight-year-old boy:

> Because I have renounced the world, I have left my parents to seek the path. . . . I have the care of my teacher and have accepted the discipline in the Buddhist sutras. Now, because I am liberated, I remember my five mothers who were unable to be free because they grieved over me. I vow that they all will finally end [their grief].

> People in the world grieve for each other in their minds. When there is no rest [from grief and other attachments], the body is only reborn. . . . The bliss of Nirvana is what my teacher has explained.[6]

The grieving mother is thus contrasted with the mindful monk, and the maternal love that is spiritually impotent (for both mother and son) is contrasted with the spiritual guidance of the Buddhist teacher, which effectively leads his young disciple to nirvana.

The mother in grief thus stands as a potent symbol of intense suffering—a heightened version of the suffering that entraps all deluded beings within samsara. In this, she is once again frequently contrasted with an idealized, nongrieving father. Buddhist literature, in fact, sometimes seems to exult in depicting ideal fathers with absolute hearts of stone. In one episode from the *Therīgāthā,* for example, a woman named Cāpā desperately tries to prevent her husband Upaka from renouncing the world by threatening to stab and kill their only son: "Now I will knock this son of yours down to the ground with a stick or a knife," she says to him, "and out of grief for your son (P. *putta-sokā*), you will not go!"[7] But Upaka is completely unfazed: "You can give our son to the jackals or the dogs, you miserable woman, and you still won't turn me back again for the boy's sake!"[8] Even harsher is the *Nidānakathā*'s depiction of a father—a previous life of the Buddha—who gives his own children to a cannibalistic demon and is completely unmoved by the sight of the demon devouring them and vomiting up their blood: "Even upon seeing this, he did not give rise to any grief (P. *domanassa*), not even to the extent of a single strand of his hair."[9] The complete *lack* of grief displayed by such highly idealized fathers brings into sharper relief the excessive grief and its attendant madness ordinarily attributed to the mother. These two figures are contrasted perhaps most effectively within a single scene in the famous *Vessantara Jātaka* (*Jātaka* No. 499). Here, when the exiled prince Vessantara (a previous life of the Buddha) demonstrates his great generosity by giving his two children away to an evil and greedy brahmin, his wife Maddī begins grieving and lamenting on page 66 (of the English translation of Cone and Gombrich) and does not stop until the bottom of page 73, in what is surely one of the most beautiful and evocative Buddhist depictions of a grieving mother ever composed.[10] Though Vessantara, too—somewhat unusually—is said to be full of grief and heartache upon giving away his children, he remains stoic and silent, refusing to tell his wife where the children are and even accusing her of infidelity in order to deflect attention from himself. Maddī and Vessantara thus fulfill their assigned Buddhist roles as the hysterical, grieving mother and the stoic, dispassionate father.

Yet in spite of the iconic manner in which the grieving mother embodies suffering and spiritual impotence, Buddhism is ultimately an optimistic tradition which holds that even suffering of such intensity might still be overcome, for if given the proper resources—that is, the Buddhist teachings themselves and the charisma of the one who delivers them—even a mother overcome by hysterical grief *is* capable of turning the corner and eventually attaining nirvana. But exactly how does this occur? How can a paradigmatic embodiment of attachment and suffering be transformed into a detached and saintly ideal?

In order to understand some of the ways in which this transformation is depicted, and what further light these alternatives might shed on the Buddhist depiction of motherhood, it will be useful to first consider some of the implications child death might have for the religious lives of women. In an article that appeared over a decade ago,[11] Susan Starr Sered drew attention to the strong association that exists cross-culturally between women's religious involvement and the deaths of their children, observing that child death seems to be "an extremely salient theme in the religious lives of many women,"[12] whereas the same association does not appear to hold true for men. Citing numerous examples from around the world, she observes that because women, in most cultures, are more heavily immersed and invested in the raising of children than are men, "the death of a child tends to have a greater impact upon women,"[13] leading not only to more profound and prolonged grieving, but also to a greater confrontation with compelling existential questions that often leads such women into greater religious involvement.

One persistent pattern of this involvement, moreover, is that many women become dissatisfied with the interpretations of child death offered to them by the dominant, patriarchal religions of the cultures in which they live, and instead become leaders and members of various alternative religious traditions dominated by women—such as the *zar* spirit possession cults of North and East Africa, the Afro-Brazilian cults of Umbanda and Candomblé, or the spirit cults of Northern Thailand. According to Sered, what many of these traditions have in common—and what makes them so appealing to mothers in grief—is the possibility they offer of reestablishing contact with deceased children and maintaining regular, ongoing relationships with them, thereby denying the finality of death and the complete severance of the mother/child bond. In general, this stands in contrast to the tendency of dominant, patriarchal religions to interpret child death in abstract and universal terms—terms that sever the interpersonal mother/child relationship and erase the identities of specific, deceased children. It is for this reason, Sered speculates, that child death is so strongly correlated not only with greater religious involvement for women, but often with their involvement in alternative, women-dominated traditions. In other words, these traditions, more so than those traditions dominated by men, seem to recognize and accommodate the mother's continuing need to love and grieve for her own, particular children.

As Sered further points out, however, it is precisely this emphasis on specific, interpersonal relationships that has caused such women-dominated traditions to be interpreted by scholars in terms of "magic" or "superstition," rather than in terms of "religion." For conceptual models prevalent since the time of Sir James Frazer have convinced us that whereas "religion" speaks of ultimate concerns (such as death) in abstract and transcendent terms, "magic" is a lower pursuit concerned only with the private, the personal, and the particular. Thus, bereaved mothers who show concern "for particular dead babies and not for dead babies in the abstract"[14] are engaging in "magic" rather than "religion." Sered compares this bias to a similar bias existing in the field of moral development (as critiqued by Carol Gilligan),[15] according to which women are generally "stuck" in a "lower" stage of moral development, in which morality is defined through interpersonal relationships, whereas men generally succeed in attaining a "higher" stage, in which morality is defined through universal principles of justice. In both cases, she points out, "women's modes . . . somehow end up as inferior to men's modes simply because the 'man-made' model posits that the male mode is superior."[16] As a feminist scholar, however, Sered strives to overcome such models that automatically hierarchize the abstract over the specific (and men over women), and she ends her article by encouraging us "to see the link between child death and women's religion for what it really is—an expression of the primacy of love and care, and a legitimate existential grappling with what is surely one of the most incomprehensible facets of human experience."[17]

Sered's analysis—in particular, its invocation of the conflict between the particular and the universal—clearly intersects with my own discussion of mother-love and provides us with a useful context in which to consider the following questions: How do Buddhist texts depict the religious transformation of the mother in grief? Must the mother's particular grief over one specific dead baby be eradicated in favor of a concern for "dead babies in the abstract" in order to conform to Buddhist ideals, and in a way that erases her status as mother? Or can such particularistic grief be accommodated and perhaps even recognized as a legitimate basis for developing valued Buddhist qualities such as empathy, love, and compassion? Finally, how are these questions further complicated by the complex interaction between popular, local traditions and the translocal ideology of Buddhism so characteristic of South Asian religions? Is there any evidence of Buddhism, as a dominant, patriarchal tradition, struggling to accommodate various "lower" forms of religion—such as women's religion, folk religion, or local, popular traditions—that were perhaps more compatible with mother-love?

The De-mothered Nuns of the Therīgāthā

The religious transformation of the mother in grief is a consistent theme throughout the *Therīgāthā*, an important Theravāda canonical collection of seventy-three poems attributed to the nuns of the earliest Buddhist community. When read in conjunction with Dhammapāla's sixth-century CE commentary (which provides the traditional background stories that contextualize each poem), we see that five of these seventy-three poems exhibit a similar pattern: A mother loses her child to death and is driven completely insane by her grief. She then encounters the Buddha (or one of his disciples), who gives her a teaching that snaps her out of her grief and allows her to regain control of her wayward mind, whereupon she becomes a Buddhist nun and goes on to attain nirvana. Two of these poems, in fact, are attributed to Kisā Gotamī and Vāsiṭṭhī (the Pali equivalent to Vāsiṣṭhā), the two bereaved mothers mentioned above. Two more poems are attributed to two further bereaved mothers, Ubbirī and Paṭācārā, while the fifth poem is attributed collectively to a group of five hundred grieving mothers who were converted directly by Paṭācārā. In these five poems,[18] we see a dramatic transformation take place: The hysterical, grieving mother mired in suffering is turned into her very opposite—a calm, dispassionate, and fully liberated Buddhist nun.

It is striking to note, in the first instance, that the grieving mother seems to constitute a particular "type" of Buddhist renunciant in a way that the grieving father does not. In fact, as noted by Kathryn Blackstone, in the *Theragāthā*, a companion collection of poems attributed to the monks of the earliest Buddhist community, "none of the *theras* report the deaths of family members, nor do they record feeling grief"[19]—even though this collection is much larger (containing 264 poems altogether) than the corresponding collection for nuns. Clearly, the grieving mother who becomes a nun was a more compelling, instructive, or commonly seen figure than the grieving father who becomes a monk. In line with Sered's argument, this in itself already suggests that in premodern India—as in the various contemporary contexts Sered discusses—mothers were believed to be more affected by the deaths of their children than were fathers, and more likely to turn to religion as a direct result of such emotional crises.

What I am interested in emphasizing, however, is exactly *how* the religious transformation of these women takes place—and it is here that we can return to some of Sered's insights. If Buddhism can be described as one of the dominant, patriarchal traditions (mentioned by Sered) that tend to speak of ultimate concerns such as death in wholly abstract and universal terms, then we might speculate that the mother's continuing need to love and grieve for her own, particular child could not be accommodated by the canonical scriptures of such a tradition. From this perspective, the only spiritually successful grieving mother would be one whose particularistic grief over one specific dead baby has been eradicated in favor of a concern for "dead babies in the abstract"—in other words, one whose maternal grief has been properly universalized into a general understanding of the inevitability of death, impermanence, and suffering.

And this is, indeed, precisely what we find in four of these five poems: Narratives from the *Therīgāthā* in which grieving mothers become nuns and then arhats consistently emphasize this movement from the particular to the universal, from the personal emotion of grief to the abstract truths of death and suffering, from the death of one particular child to the endless cycle of death and rebirth that characterizes the entire universe. Only when the mother's very personal grief has been transformed into an impersonal and analytical understanding of suffering (P. *dukkha*) is she able to regain her mind and eventually attain nirvana. This transformation is made possible, however, only by erasing the specific identity of her deceased child, permanently severing the mother/child bond, and eradicating her status as "mother." The violence inherent in this move is further suggested, perhaps, by the fact that she becomes a nun—one who has renounced all familial relationships, no longer engages in sexual intercourse that might lead to the birth of more children, and is androgynous even in her physical appearance. This is a transformation, in other words, that *eradicates the woman's motherhood*—in other words, wholly "de-mothers" her—because it sees motherhood itself as being fundamentally incompatible with the highest Buddhist ideals. From Sered's perspective, then, the bereaved mothers of the *Therīgāthā*—with the single exception of Vāsiṭṭhī, whom I will address later—perhaps represent those women who reject and transcend the particularistic nature of motherhood and wholly internalize the viewpoint of the dominant, patriarchal tradition. These women succeed in becoming Buddhist nuns and in attaining Buddhism's very highest ideals—yet only at the expense of their motherhood.

A brief review of each of these four accounts will help to demonstrate the striking consistency of this pattern—that is, the movement from particularistic grief to universal insight, and the violence inflicted on motherhood in the process.

Ubbirī

Ubbirī is described as a privileged and beautiful woman who becomes the wife of a king and gives birth to a daughter named Jīva. When her daughter suddenly dies, Ubbirī is overcome with grief; she goes to the cremation ground every day, crying and lamenting for her lost child. She only comes to her senses when the Buddha confronts her in the cremation ground, tells her, "Get a hold of yourself, Ubbirī!," and informs her that within her previous lives, "eighty-four thousand [daughters], all of them named Jīva, have been consumed in this cremation ground—for which among them do you mourn?"[20] By placing one particular dead daughter named Jīva within the context of eighty-four thousand dead daughters named Jīva, the Buddha forces Ubbirī to universalize her grief, and it is this that finally brings her to her senses. Moreover, as K. R. Norman has pointed out,[21] *jīva*, as a noun, means "living being." Thus, even the eighty-four thousand daughters specific to Ubbirī are themselves universalized into generic "living beings"—subject (as all living beings are) to death, impermanence, and suffering. Ubbirī's particularistic grief over one specific "Jīva" is thus transformed into a detached appreciation for the impermanence of all *jīvas*. She describes this transformation, moreover, with the sharp imagery of an arrow being pulled from her heart: "Overcome by grief, I had an arrow stuck in my heart. Surely, he has pulled it out! He has expelled that grief for my daughter."[22] As the commentary on this verse makes clear, however, this "arrow" is not only maternal grief (P. *soka*) but also maternal love (P. *taṇha*).[23] And it is only by eradicating this love "with nothing left over" (P. *anavasesato*)[24] that Ubbirī has been saved.

The motif of the mother whose grief must be universalized in order for spiritual progress to occur can be further illuminated by comparing Ubbirī's story to another, seemingly very similar story, this time involving a father and his son. In the *Upasāḷha Jātaka* (*Jātaka* No. 166),[25] a father asks his son to make sure that the father, on death, is cremated at a particular spot where he claims nobody else has ever been cremated. The son doubts this is true, and his suspicions are confirmed by a wise ascetic (a former birth of the Buddha):

> Young man, there is no limit to those who have been cremated at this very spot! Your own father, reborn in this very [city of] Rājagaha, in this very brahmin family, and bearing this very name Upasāḷhaka, has been cremated at this very spot in the mountains in fourteen thousand previous births! For on this earth, it is not possible to find a spot where cremations have not occurred, or that has not served as a cremation ground, or that has not been covered with human heads.[26]

Thus, much as we see in the story of Ubbirī, the death of one particular individual named Upasāḷhaka is here universalized through the fact that fourteen thousand other rebirths of the same individual (all of them similarly named) have been cremated in the very same spot.

But although the lesson conveyed by this story is identical to that conveyed by the story of Ubbirī, the differences are equally instructive: Instead of a parent going mad with grief over the death of a child, we have a child calmly preparing for the anticipated death of his parent. There is no question here of parental loss and the resulting experience of grief, but only a rational and detached analysis presented by the ascetic for the benefit of the son—a son, moreover, who already suspects that there is nothing singular about the death of his father. The hysterical mother, plunged into grief, who must be dramatically changed and transformed is thus replaced by a wise and capable son, who merely needs to confirm that which he already suspected. In addition, this more dispassionate version of the same basic message seems to demand that the mother and her daughter be replaced by a father and his son. The differences between Upasāḷhaka's story and Ubbirī's story thus further highlight the distinctive nature of the grieving-mother motif—an impression further confirmed by the other grieving-mother narratives of the *Therīgāthā*.

Paṭācārā

Paṭācārā is a privileged woman who pursues an illicit sexual relationship with one of her household servants (who later becomes her husband), and suffers mightily as a consequence of her sinful karmic deeds: While she is pregnant with her second child and traveling toward her parents' home, along with her husband and young son, she goes into labor and gives birth along the road. An enormous storm suddenly kicks up, whereupon her husband goes off to look for shelter but is killed by a poisonous snake. She spends the whole night using her body to shelter her two sons from the raging storm, only to discover her dead husband the next morning. She then attempts to carry her sons, one at a time, across a swollen river, but in the midst of this process, the newborn is carried off by a hawk, and the older boy falls in and drowns. As she approaches her parents' village, a man informs her that the previous night's storm caused her parents' house to cave in, killing both parents, as well as her brother. She goes mad with grief, wandering the streets naked and babbling incoherently, while people throw rubbish and dirt on her in contempt. She then encounters the Buddha, and, in this case, all that is required for her to come to her senses is a quick command: "Sister, get a hold of yourself!"[27]

His very next words, however, once again place her own, particular grief within a universal context: "For just as you are now shedding tears, on account of the death of your sons and others, so also, the tears that have been shed within this round of rebirth, without beginning or end, on account of the deaths of sons and others, is greater than the water of the four great oceans."[28] Here, we get the physical image of a single woman's tears being lost within an enormous ocean of water—thereby losing any specific identity. The same water imagery is also evident in two other versions of Paṭācārā's story, in which Paṭācārā, in the midst of her tremendous grief, believes that the rainstorm *fell on her alone*. Thus, in the *Dhammapada Commentary*, she tells the man coming from her parents' village, "All night long, it rained on me alone, not on anybody else,"[29] while in the Sinhalese *Saddharmaratnāvaliya* (a later adaptation of the *Dhammapada Commentary*), she asks him: "Did that rain fall elsewhere too or did it rain just for me?"[30] What Paṭācārā needs to learn, of course, is that the rain of suffering experienced by her falls on all living beings without exception.

Later on in her life, after becoming a Buddhist nun, Paṭācārā succeeds in attaining arhatship, and the specific experience that propels her to this attainment once again involves water and further demonstrates the universalization of her grief: As she is washing her feet with a pot of water, she sees that some trickles of water go a little distance, others go a further distance, and yet others go further still—just as living beings might die in youth, middle age, or old age. She thinks to herself: "Just as this water is subject to destruction and loss, so too are the conditions resulting in life for beings." "Thinking this," she tells us, "I perceived the characteristic of impermanence, and as a result of that, the characteristics of suffering and no-self, and I deepened my insight."[31] The abstract, doctrinal, and disembodied language used in this enlightened statement forms a stark contrast to the more personal words she had earlier uttered while still in the midst of her grief: "My sons are both dead. My husband is dead on the road. My mother, father, and brother have been cremated in a single heap."[32] Clearly, the specific identities of her sons, husband, and parents have been replaced by a detached analysis of "the conditions resulting in life for beings" that come to destruction in either youth, middle age, or old age. Her family has become an abstraction, and her own status as a mother has been eradicated.

Five Hundred Nuns under Paṭācārā

Having gone through this experience herself, it seems that Paṭācārā subsequently became something of an expert at preaching to other bereaved mothers. For tradition tells us of a nameless group of five hundred women, all of whom were overcome with grief after the deaths of their children, and all of whom were brought to their senses by a single, stark series of verses uttered by Paṭācārā—verses that encourage these mothers to view their dead children with utter detachment and indifference:[33]

> You cry out "My son!" for him whose way you do not know,
> neither his coming nor his going,
> for that being who came from who knows where.
> But you wouldn't grieve for him whose way you knew,
> whether coming or going,
> for such is the nature of living beings.
> Without being asked, he came from there.
> And without being permitted, he left from here,
> after coming from somewhere, I suppose,
> and living for just a few days.
> He left from here by one [way],

and he'll leave from there by another.
Dying with a human form, he'll go wandering on again.
As he came, so he left.
What reason for lamenting is that?[34]

In his commentary, Dhammapāla explains the significance of these somewhat enigmatic verses: Within the context of the endless cycle of death and rebirth, "mother" and "son" are really nothing more than strangers meeting on a road; therefore, for the mother to grieve for a son as if he had some special relationship to her is nothing more than "utter selfishness" (P. *kevalaṃ mamattaṃ*).[35] If she truly understood that birth and death ("coming and going") were simply the "nature of living beings," then she would have no reason to grieve—even over one who was "agreeable to [her] as a son" (P. *tava puttābhimata*).[36] Dhammapāla thus seeks to place the particular and the universal in proper relationship to each other: Yes, he might be your own, beloved son within this particular life, but don't lose sight of the larger picture—within the cosmological context of death and rebirth, everyone is just a stranger passing through. It is only by learning to see their sons in such a detached manner that the five hundred women are saved. And once again, using the same verses as were spoken by Ubbirī, the five hundred women refer to this as having an "arrow pulled out" from their very hearts.[37]

Kisā Gotamī

It is the justly famous story of "Kisā Gotamī and the Mustard Seed"—cited repeatedly in introductory textbooks on Buddhism—that perhaps illustrates more concretely than any other story the bereaved mother's transition from particularistic grief to universal understanding. Kisā Gotamī is described as a poor woman who is treated shabbily by her in-laws until she gives birth to a son, whereupon her status within her husband's family rises (a typical feature of traditional Indian family structure). But when her young son suddenly dies, she is driven mad with grief and carries the baby's corpse from door to door, asking for medicine that will cure him. A wise old man finally realizes that only the Buddha "will know the medicine for her,"[38] so he tells Kisā Gotamī to go to the Buddha and ask for medicine. When she does, the Buddha tells her that he will give her such medicine, but only if she will bring to him some white mustard seed from any household that has never experienced death (Figure 2.1). She goes from house to house, but of course there is no household that has not been touched by death; as the very first

FIGURE 2.1 The grieving mother Kisā Gotamī asks the Buddha for medicine to cure her dead son. Illustration by U Ba Kyi, from *The Illustrated History of Buddhism,* published in Rangoon by the Young Men Buddhist Association of Burma in 1951. Image courtesy of Young Men Buddhist Association.

household puts it, "Who can count those who have died here?"[39] Her wandering from house to house—at first desperately and then with a sense of acceptance—might be seen as a physical representation of the process by which her particularistic grief is gradually universalized into an analytical understanding of the omnipresence of death and suffering. After realizing that "this very thing will be true for the whole city,"[40] Kisā Gotamī finally comes to her senses, lays her son's corpse down in the cremation ground, and goes to the Buddha to be ordained as a nun. She then speaks a verse that explicitly demonstrates her transition from the particular to the universal: "This is not the law of a [single] village, the law of a [single] town, nor the law of a single family. This alone is the law for the entire world, together with its gods: [Everything is] impermanent."[41] Once again, she describes this realization as having "my arrow cut out, my burden laid down."[42] Another version of her story from the *Dhammapada Commentary*, moreover, makes it clear to us what this "arrow" or "burden" consists of, for it tells us that "as she was thinking thus, her heart, which had been tender (P. *muduka*) with love for her son, became hard (P. *thaddhabhāvaṃ agamāsi*)."[43] Much like Ubbirī, Paṭācārā, and the five hundred other nuns, Kisā Gotamī has come to embody the highest Buddhist ideal by inflicting violence on her own motherhood.[44]

Visākhā

One more woman who might loosely be seen as a member of the same sisterhood—although she functions as a grandmother rather than a mother, and her story does not appear in the *Therīgāthā*—is the famous laywoman Visākhā, whose grief over the death of a granddaughter is related in both the *Udāna* and the *Dhammapada Commentary*.[45] In both versions, Visākhā is driven mad by her grief and approaches the Buddha in an unseemly manner, whereupon the Buddha universalizes her emotions by asking her if she would like to have as many children and grandchildren as there are inhabitants in Sāvatthi. When Visākhā replies in the affirmative, the Buddha points out that because of the great number of people who die in Sāvatthi every day, "there wouldn't be time enough for you to grieve; you would wander around day and night, doing nothing but crying and lamenting."[46] Visākhā thus comes to realize the universality of death and the futility of grief, and once again makes a statement that clearly demonstrates her movement from the particular to the universal: "[My granddaughter], Venerable One, is no different from the [other] human beings who die in Sāvatthi."[47] Much like the mothers of the *Therīgāthā*, then, Visākhā is transformed by eradicating any sense of particularistic, familial ties. And the moral of the story, according to the *Dhammapada Commentary*, is verse 213 of the *Dhammapada*: "From love comes grief; from love comes fear. He who is free of love has no grief—and how could he fear?"[48] Visākhā has not only eradicated her grief; she has also eradicated the love from which her grief derives.

From a certain kind of feminist viewpoint, these stories are worthy of celebration, for in all of these stories, the Buddhist tradition expresses genuine concern for the life experiences of young women, sympathy for grieving mothers, and a sincere belief in the ability of such women to transcend their suffering and realize their potential beyond the function of motherhood. It is instructive, in fact, to take note of the stark contrast between the fate of these women and the fate of those found in the standard South Asian cultic complex I described in chapter 1, in which women whose motherhood is cruelly frustrated morph into vengeful mother-goddess spirits requiring appeasement and pacification by their devoted worshippers. In the *Therīgāthā*, by contrast, we discover that for Buddhism, frustrated motherhood is not only the pivot that turns a "good" mother into a "bad" mother who requires appeasement; it is also, when dealt with in a skillful manner, a spiritual *opportunity* to transcend maternal attachment altogether in favor of Buddhist detachment and compassion for others. Just as good motherhood and bad motherhood are really two sides of the same coin, so too is the frustration of motherhood double-sided: It can cause the "good" mother to flip directly into the "bad" mother, thus demonstrating their ultimate equivalence, *or* it can present one with the opportunity to escape forever from the selfish attachment to children that both good and bad mothers share. In this sense, rather than condemning Buddhism for its failure to idealize mother-love consistently, we should recognize that this ambivalence is directly related to the Buddhist tradition's willingness to allow women to pursue roles other than that of the idealized mother. It indicates a Buddhist willingness to view women as individualized human beings, rather than as the embodiments of an idealized maternal function. Buddhism resists the tendency to fetishize or sanctify motherhood, thereby leaving open other possibilities for women to pursue. Buddhism also maintains that, despite the intensity of maternal attachment, women are fully capable of renouncing and rejecting the strongest emotional tie of all—a powerful testament to their spiritual capabilities.

Nevertheless, within these stories, it is also clear that mother-love is incompatible with the idealized state of enlightened detachment, and the particularistic love of the mother stands in stark opposition to the universal compassion espoused by the Buddha. Within these poems, maternal love must be *eradicated* rather than *extended* or *transformed*. Unlike the contemporary Kashmiri nun quoted by Kim Gutschow, who maintains that "nuns are fortunate . . . [because] they can be mother to many children" and can "love all children equally,"[49] Kisā Gotamī does not *extend* her love for her son to encompass other beings; instead, her heart must "become hard." Maternal love is depicted not as a possible *basis* for something higher, but instead as its greatest impediment. This is why I would maintain, following Sered, that within these four poems, we see the voice of women who have fully internalized the values of Buddhism as a dominant, patriarchal tradition. Brooking no concession or compromise, this is a confident voice that firmly upholds an ultimate scale of values—a scale along which motherhood must finally be condemned as incompatible with Buddhism's highest soteriological goals. The mothers of the *Therīgāthā* thus speak with a "patriarchal" voice—"patriarchal" not in the sense that these women have been subordinated or suppressed by men but, rather, in the sense that they have adopted without question the universal and abstract values typical of patriarchal, male-dominated religions and have fully made such values their own. Here I draw on the idea that a "feminist" viewpoint, as Catherine MacKinnon puts it, "not only challenges masculine partiality but questions the universality imperative itself . . . as a strategy of male hegemony."[50] It is in this sense, I believe, that Bernard Faure has spoken of the discourse of nuns as often approaching "a kind of male ventriloquism."[51]

Vaḍḍhamātā and Vāsiṭṭhī: Spiritual Mothers?

Two further poems from the *Therīgāthā*, however, begin to suggest the possibility of other alternatives. In both cases, a mother becomes a nun and goes on to attain arhatship, but she does not leave her motherhood behind. Instead, she continues to love and show concern for her own, particular children. Her maternal love, moreover, far from being eradicated, matures and deepens to encompass a soteriological dimension. In these two poems, I contend, we see the Buddhist tradition struggling to accommodate maternal love and make it more compatible with Buddhist soteriological goals.

Vaḍḍhamātā[52] is described as a wife and mother who hears the dhamma, becomes full of faith, places her son Vaḍḍha in the care of relatives, becomes a Buddhist nun, and goes on to attain arhatship. Nevertheless, when her son Vaḍḍha later becomes a monk himself, she seeks him out and gives him instruction, whereupon her son confirms her spiritual attainment by proclaiming: "O Mother, you speak to me about this with confidence. Indeed, I believe, dear Mother, that there is no craving in you."[53] The commentary, moreover, glosses the word "craving" (P. *vanatha*) with the phrase "even mere worldly love for me"[54]—that is, her son—thus going out of its way to suggest that Vaḍḍhamātā has indeed lost any selfish attachment toward her own, particular son. Nevertheless, she does instruct her son, and her instruction is fully effective, for Vaḍḍha himself attains arhatship and proclaims this in three verses that emphasize his mother's role in his attainment:

> My mother, so compassionate,
> has surely prodded me with an excellent goad—
> verses bringing about the highest goal.
> I heard her words, my mother's instruction,
> and I became anxious for the dhamma,
> so that I could attain rest from [all] exertion.
> Resolved on exerting myself,
> not resting day or night,
> urged on by my mother,
> I attained the highest peace.[55]

The poem as a whole thus suggests that Vaḍḍhamātā has indeed eradicated all craving—but without losing the maternal love that is directed specifically toward her own son. In contrast to the *ineffective* love so often attributed to ordinary mothers, moreover, Vaḍḍhamātā's love is fully effective and results in her son's achieving the highest soteriological goal.

But although Vaḍḍhamātā's poem poses a possibility that the other narratives seem to exclude, it is, for several reasons, finally unsatisfactory. Since we do not witness Vaḍḍhamātā's attainment of arhatship, we do not see the process by which her particularistic love for her son is gradually universalized into something greater, and, correspondingly, we also do not see how this universalization can still accommodate Vaḍḍhamātā's continuing concern for her own son. For if she *has* truly eradicated *all craving*—"even mere worldly love for [her son]"—then why does she still seek him out and give instruction specifically to him? And because Vaḍḍhamātā is not a *grieving* mother, we do not witness the profound religious transformation by means of which overwhelming personal grief is transmuted into a detached analysis of the nature of samsara, nor do we gain any understanding of how this enlightened condition might still be compatible with maternal concern. Vaḍḍhamātā's poem, in other words, seems to assert a possibility without doing much to illuminate it.

For a more satisfactory alternative, I will end with the story of Vāsiṭṭhī[56] because it is significantly different from all of the previous accounts and serves as a transition to the discussion that follows. The Pali tradition surrounding the figure of Vāsiṭṭhī is somewhat garbled and confused. Within the *Therīgāthā* and its commentary, Vāsiṭṭhī is described as a young woman who loses her only son to death and then spends three years in madness, wandering the streets naked and with disheveled hair and dwelling on rubbish heaps and in cremation grounds. She is brought to her senses on encountering the Buddha and later becomes a nun and attains arhatship, but we are not told what kind of teaching brings her around. Elsewhere in the *Therīgāthā*, however, another woman, who seems to be equivalent to Vāsiṭṭhī except that she has lost seven children rather than one, is briefly described as having helped a grief-stricken man named Sujāta get over the death of his son.[57]

In Sanskrit and Chinese sources examined in detail by Hubert Durt,[58] on the other hand, we get a slightly different story that allows us to make sense of the garbled Pali tradition. Here, Vāsiṣṭhā (as she is known in Sanskrit) is a mother who loses six children in a row, goes insane, and then regains her mind through an encounter with the Buddha, who makes her realize the inevitability of death and suffering. At this point, she becomes a laywoman (rather than a nun), and later she gives birth to a seventh child, who also dies in infancy. This time, however, she feels no grief, due to her enlightened understanding of reality. Her husband, Sujāta, himself overcome by grief, is surprised by his wife's detachment, but on being instructed by her about the omnipresence of suffering, he becomes a Buddhist monk and attains arhatship, whereupon Vāsiṣṭhā and her single surviving daughter do likewise. The Sanskrit and Chinese sources thus bring the Pali fragments together into a single, coherent tradition.

None of these sources provide much detail about what kind of teaching the Buddha gave to Vāsiṣṭhā, and none of them displays the typical movement from the particular to the universal that I have been concerned to demonstrate above. Nevertheless, the story itself, I believe, has a distinctive point to make that distinguishes it from the others: In contrast to those accounts, in which grieving mothers universalize their grief in a way that completely eradicates their status as mothers (which is further embodied by their becoming nuns), Vāsiṣṭhā's story offers us the example of a grieving mother whose grief is universalized, but who also continues to be a mother and goes on to have another child. More important than just her continuing biological motherhood, however, is the role she then plays in relation to her husband and surviving daughter: Having learned to overcome her own grief by universalizing it, she then serves as a model for her husband and daughter, directly teaching Buddhist doctrine to her husband, and encouraging her daughter to renounce the world (along with herself). Her exalted status within the family is emphasized by the fact that here—in sharp contrast to all the other stories I have recounted—we have a *father* driven mad by his grief, and brought to his senses only by the wise words of his wife, words he refers to as "extraordinary" (P. *abbhuta*).[59] The story thus suggests that not only can the grieving mother universalize her grief and still continue to be a mother who shows special concern for her own family, but in addition, this concern is now spiritual in nature, superior to and more effective than the concern she showed before. The worldly mother can develop into a spiritual mother, using her own experience as a grieving mother to help lead the rest of her family to nirvana (through the mother's naturally nurturing and educative role). Motherhood is compatible with arhatship, and mother-love can serve as a foundation for the spiritual love of buddhas, bodhisattvas, and arhats, rather than its strongest impediment.

None of this is made explicit within the story itself; instead, it is my own interpretation, teased out from the story's narrative details. Nevertheless, this interpretation raises a number of interesting questions: Are there Buddhist traditions in which maternal love and maternal grief directed toward one's own, particular children are more fully accommodated than in the *Therīgāthā*? Can maternal love and maternal grief be viewed positively as a legitimate basis for developing valued Buddhist qualities such as empathy, love, and compassion, rather than as particularistic attachments that must be wholly eradicated? And do such traditions betray any evidence of Buddhism, as a dominant, patriarchal tradition, struggling to accommodate various "lower" forms of religion—perhaps those that were particularly appealing to women?

Accommodation of Mother-Love in the Story and Cult of Hārītī

One prominent Buddhist tradition that seems to answer some of these questions is that surrounding the figure of Hārītī, who has left many traces on Indian Buddhist texts, art, and cultic practices.[60] The fullest version of her story can be found in the Chinese translation of the *Mūlasarvāstivāda Vinaya*, the monastic disciplinary code for the Mūlasarvāstivāda school.[61] Here, we are told that Hārītī is a *yakṣiṇī* (female demon) who lives in the city of Rājagṛha at the time of the Buddha. She is married to the male demon Pañcika, and together they have five hundred sons, the youngest of whom is Priyaṅkara, who is the favorite of his mother. Although Hārītī comes from a family of virtuous and benevolent demons, because of "a criminal vow formed in a previous existence," she (with the help of her sons) engages in the habit of stealing and devouring all of the human children of Rājagṛha. As more and more of their children die, the people of Rājagṛha finally turn to the Buddha for help. He responds by going to Hārītī's abode while she is out and hiding her youngest son Priyaṅkara under his begging bowl. When Hārītī returns and cannot find her youngest child, she is overwhelmed with grief. "Beating her breast, shedding tears of sorrow, her lips and mouth dry and burning, her spirit troubled and lost, her heart torn by suffering," she searches the entire kingdom but cannot find him. She rips off her clothes, lets her hair fly loose, crawls around on her elbows and knees, and then searches the entire world, the four quarters of the universe, the heavens, and the hells. She finally ends up at the abode of the god Vaiśravaṇa, who takes pity on her miserable condition and tells her to go to the Buddha, for only he can restore her son.

Up to this point, the story bears a striking resemblance to the stories of the *Therīgāthā*. Once again, we have a mother who loses her child and is plunged into grief. Much like Paṭācārā and Vāsiṭṭhī, she rips off her clothes and lets her hair fly loose, and much like Kisā Gotamī, she is finally led to the Buddha by someone who takes pity on her. The Buddha, moreover, once again brings the bereaved mother to her senses by encouraging her to universalize her grief (though in less doctrinal terms than we find in the *Therīgāthā*). "Hārītī," he says, "because you no longer see one of your five hundred sons, you experience such suffering; so what will be the suffering of those whose only child you take and devour?" When she admits that their suffering must be even greater than her own, he replies: "Hārītī, you know well now the suffering of being separated from what one loves. Why, then, do you eat the children of others?" In another version of the story, he further points out that "others love their children, just as you do," and they, too, "go along the streets and lament just like you."[62] And in yet another text, he states: "It is because you yourself love your own son that you eagerly run around, demanding to see him. Why, then, with such cruelty, do you continually devour the children of others? Realize . . . that your feelings are instructing you: No longer kill, no longer torment."[63] Hārītī takes the Buddha's words to heart, understands the inherent connection between her own, particular grief and the suffering experienced by others, and, as a consequence, promises to give up her child-snatching ways. Like the nuns of the *Therīgāthā*, Hārītī succeeds in universalizing her grief and is spiritually transformed in the process.

Despite these similarities to the stories of the *Therīgāthā*, however, the remainder of Hārītī's story goes in a significantly different direction. Once Hārītī has made the transition from particularistic grief to universal insight, the Buddha *restores her beloved son to her*, and she becomes a loving mother once more—she takes refuge in the Three Jewels and accepts the five precepts, and thereby becomes a laywoman rather than a celibate nun. Moreover, continuing to show a mother's concern for her own children, she then asks the Buddha how she will feed her five hundred children if they can no longer devour human babies, whereupon the Buddha strikes her a bargain: Every day, throughout all of the monasteries of India, Buddhist monks will make food offerings to her and her children after finishing their own meal. They will keep her and her children fed, but in exchange for this, she must agree to do two things: protect all Buddhist monasteries from harm, and respond to the pleas of childless parents by allowing them to have offspring.[64] The ritual cult of Hārītī described in these texts does, indeed, seem to have existed throughout India; the Chinese pilgrim Yi Jing (who traveled throughout India in the late seventh century CE) tells us that "the image of Hārītī is found either in the porch or in a corner of the dining-hall of all Indian monasteries," and "every day an abundant offering of food is made before this image."[65] Surviving shrines dedicated to Hārītī have been found at various Buddhist monastic sites, with Hārītī generally depicted as a benevolent mother figure holding one baby in her arms and having another three to five children around her knees (Figure 2.2).

If we consider Hārītī's story against the background provided by the *Therīgāthā*, then it seems to me that what we see in the case of Hārītī is a complicated negotiation between the particularistic love of the mother and the universal ideals espoused by the Buddhist tradition. On the one hand, Hārītī's grief over her own child must be universalized into an analytical appreciation of suffering in order for her to become a good Buddhist (rather than a cannibalistic demon). On the other hand, however, once this

FIGURE 2.2 The *yakṣiṇī* Hārītī, surrounded by her children. Gandhāra, 2nd–3rd c. CE. British Museum, London. Photograph © The Trustees of the British Museum.

occurs, she is allowed to have her child returned and her motherhood restored. Henceforth, she manifests the Buddhist ideal of universal compassion by giving children to other women and allowing them too to experience maternal love—while still continuing to love and protect her own children as well. Also significant here is the complicated interdependence between Hārītī and the Buddhist Saṃgha: The Saṃgha is full of those who have rejected all familial ties, yet they depend for their health and safety on the protective "mothering" of Hārītī herself. Hārītī's maternal love for her own children thus becomes the foundation not only for her protection of other mothers and their children, but even for the protection of those who embody Buddhism's highest and most universal ideals. And the protection she grants now clearly extends beyond the worldly limits of maternal love, for in some texts she is even referred to as "a great bodhisattva,"[66] one who leads "male demons and female demons en masse, along with their male and female descendants," to the Buddhist teachings[67]—yet not at the expense of her own motherhood.

Within this complicated negotiation, the detached and passionless monks, too, take on a somewhat "motherly" role. Not only do they feed Hārītī's children every day (as a mother generally does); they also undertake another "maternal" task as well. For we are further told that once Hārītī becomes a Buddhist, the other demons torment her, causing her to give her sons to the Saṃgha for safekeeping. When the women of Rājagṛha see this, they, too, give their sons to the Saṃgha temporarily, paying for their upkeep while they are there and later bringing them home. Richard Cohen sees this as "a myth that charters Buddhist monasteries to act as schools," noting, for example, that the Chinese pilgrim Yi Jing speaks of many monks in India taking on students for a time and instructing them in secular subjects.[68] The nourishing and educative functions natural to the mother are thus assumed by renunciant Buddhist monks—just as the universal compassion and insight espoused by Buddhist monks are embodied by the mother Hārītī. The concept of "motherhood" seems to be broadened, such that a mother's "mothering" can extend to those besides her own children (without compromising her special love for them), while those who are not mothers themselves can "mother" society at large. The line between particularistic mother-love and universal Buddhist values such as detachment or compassion is not such a strict line, after all—something indicated, in visual terms, by depictions of Hārītī in her most motherly aspect located within the Buddhist monastic compound itself.

This willingness to accommodate mother-love characteristic of the traditions surrounding Hārītī finds perhaps its most intriguing expression in the *Mahāmāyā Sūtra* (extant only in Chinese and most likely a Chinese composition), a text that focuses on the figure of Māyā, the biological mother of the Buddha.[69] It is a well-established tradition that the Buddha himself, in loyalty to his own mother, Māyā, once spent an entire monsoon season up in heaven, where his mother had been reborn as a deity, in order to teach her the dharma. In one passage from the *Mahāmāyā Sūtra*, Māyā (as a deity in heaven) praises her son for the compassion he has shown toward all beings, citing his compassion toward Hārītī (whom she refers to only as "the Mother-of-demons") as one specific example. She relates the story of Hārītī in verse, and then ends with a rather startling admonition to her son:

> Just as this Mother-of-demons,
> because she loved her own son,
> extended [her love] to other men,
> and finally stopped killing forever,
> I ask you, O Venerable One of Great Pity,
> that you do the same now.
> Through your compassion for the mother who gave birth
> to you,
> extend [this compassion] to all other beings;
> I ask you to open in haste the right path,
> and cause all to hear and receive it.

In this intriguing Chinese passage, the Buddha's own mother, Māyā, praises and celebrates Hārītī's particularistic love for her son—because it was precisely this love that became the *basis* for the love and protection she now showers on all beings. Even more startling is the fact that she then goes on to ask her son, the Buddha, to *follow Hārītī's example*—taking his own love for his mother (and his mother's love for him) as the basis for extending his compassion toward all living beings by teaching them the dharma. The Buddha's mother thus states explicitly what the Buddha himself perhaps cannot see: Maternal love is the *foundation* for the Buddha's love, not its very opposite; the particular forms the *basis* for the universal, not its strongest impediment. The bold nature of this statement is visually intensified by the fact that throughout this monologue, Māyā is said to be breastfeeding the fully grown Buddha; in fact, even though he is supposed to be absent from the earth for only one monsoon season, the *Mahāmāyā Sūtra* describes this period of time as "eons without number during which he drank no other milk than from her." Perhaps in no other passage that I am aware of is mother-love so fully accommodated, and so seamlessly integrated with the highest of Buddhist ideals. Granted, the *Mahāmāyā Sūtra* is a Chinese text, and there is no evidence to suggest that it is based on an Indian original. Nevertheless, the fact that this text's authors chose to connect the greatest possible accommodation of mother-love specifically to the figure of Hārītī strongly suggests that Hārītī had such significance already, even within her Indian context.

Buddhism and "Women's Religion"

What is it, historically speaking, that might account for such willing accommodation of mother-love? Here we might consider the probable origins of Hārītī and return to some of Sered's insights about the difference between dominant, patriarchal religions and alternative religious traditions (such as those popular among women) in dealing with the mother/child bond. Several scholars have recognized that Hārītī, like the several "bad mothers" discussed in chapter 1, must originally have been a goddess of smallpox or some other childhood disease—one of the many disease goddesses existing throughout South Asian religious history and still worshipped on the subcontinent today, particularly at the village level.[70] Such goddesses are treated ambivalently by their worshippers, for on the one hand, they afflict children with illness and cause them to die, while on the other hand, if properly worshipped and appeased, they can also spare sick children and return them to life, as well as granting children to those who are childless. In modern Hinduism today, the cults surrounding such goddesses are generally not the "women-dominated religions" that constitute Sered's particular focus; nevertheless, since they frequently deal with the health of children, they certainly do appeal to young mothers. Moreover, such cults do generally belong to the "little" tradition of Hinduism, rather than the "great" or "Sanskritic" or pan-Indic tradition, with each individual goddess having a primarily local identity.

What we are seeing, then, in the story of Hārītī is the complicated process by which Buddhism, as an elite and translocal ideology, appropriates a local, popular cult and brings it under Buddhism's control.[71] Thus, the fearful goddess Hārītī is "converted" to Buddhism; under the influence of Buddhist teachings, Hārītī's positive, child-granting functions can continue, while her negative, child-snatching qualities can abate. This is appealing to the surrounding public, of course, but it is also beneficial to the Buddhist Saṃgha—for sacrificial offerings once made directly to Hārītī are now redirected (as almsfood) toward the Buddhist Saṃgha (since they are the ones responsible for keeping Hārītī and her children fed). Hārītī's shrine earns a place within the Buddhist monastic compound, yet Hārītī herself is clearly subordinated to the Buddha and his monks: She is fed last in the order of seniority, and she is seen primarily as a "protector" of Buddhism rather than a primary cultic focus. In this way, Buddhism is domesticated within the local landscape, while Hārītī's traditional worshippers can continue uninterrupted in their devotions.

The polemic involved in asserting Buddhism's superiority to such a cult has left obvious traces within the story of Hārītī itself. In the Chinese *Mūlasarvāstivāda Vinaya*, for example, when Hārītī is devouring the children of Rājagṛha, the people of Rājagṛha first make all kinds of traditional offerings to the demons—but the text makes it clear to us that such offerings *do not work*. Only by bringing Hārītī's cult under the direct control of *Buddhism* can the children of Rājāgṛha be saved. This polemic is even clearer in another version of the story, where the Buddha castigates Hārītī not only for her habit of devouring children but also for the behavior of her one thousand sons[72]—who are said to disguise themselves as all kinds of different spirits and minor deities, bring trouble and suffering to the people, and then force them to respond with costly animal sacrifices that will only lead them to hell. This text thus implicitly suggests that when these sons (along with their mother) are later converted to Buddhism, Buddhism's displacement of one thousand different popular cults is assured.

This process of appropriating popular, local cults is typical of the Buddhist tradition and does not apply to Hārītī alone; indeed, as Buddhism moves throughout India, we find evidence of a similar process occurring in connection with a multitude of different *yakṣas* (demons), *nāgas* (serpent-deities), and other divine creatures.[73] Two features, however, seem to distinguish Hārītī from the rest. In the first place, although Hārītī may have originated as a purely local figure—perhaps native to the area around Rājagṛha—it is clear that her character changes once the Buddha commands that Hārītī should be installed in *all* Buddhist monasteries throughout India. As Richard Cohen has pointed out, Hārītī, in a sense, became "a portable local deity, a ready-made, institutionalized, translocal basis for localization."[74] We can thus view Hārītī as perhaps *the* paradigmatic model for Buddhism's struggle to appropriate popular forms of religion.

It is from this perspective that the second distinctive feature of Hārītī's story becomes particularly interesting to consider—that is, its emphasis on the themes of maternal love and maternal grief. It is only the story of Hārītī in which these themes are developed at length, and it is only the story of Hārītī that seems to recall, in some way, the grieving mothers of the *Therīgāthā*. It is instructive, in fact, to compare Hārītī's story to another, quite similar story (from the Sanskrit *Mūlasarvāstivāda Vinaya*) involving a male demon named Gardabha:[75] The demon Gardabha is in the habit of devouring the children of Mathurā. The people of Mathurā ask the Buddha for help, the Buddha commands Gardabha to stop devouring Mathurā's children, and Gardabha promises to do so if only the citizens of Mathurā will construct a Buddhist monastery and dedicate it in his name. Thus, once again, we have a child-devouring demon, his "taming" by the Buddha, and a bargain struck between the demon and the affected citizens—but gone are all of the themes that the story of Hārītī is so concerned to develop: There is no attention paid to the grieving parents of Mathurā, no ruse employed by the Buddha to cause the demon himself to grieve over a child, no realization of the connection between one's own suffering and that of others, no restoration of the child taken away, and no promise that the demon will henceforth bring children to others. It is against the background of the story of Gardabha (and many other demon-taming stories that could be cited) that the distinctiveness of Hārītī's story comes to the fore.

What I am suggesting, then, is that the story of Hārītī is not merely concerned with asserting Buddhism's dominance over various "lower" forms of religion, but is instead particularly concerned with facing head-on one of the most fundamental conflicts between itself and those "lower" forms: the intensity of the love between mother and child, the mother's continuing need to love and grieve over her own, particular children, and the possibility that this love might be seen as a legitimate basis for cultivating more transcendent and universal Buddhist ideals. And what I further suggest, following Sered, is that this willing accommodation of mother-love is directed, perhaps first and foremost, to an audience of *women*, offering women a more palatable model of female religious involvement than the asexualized and de-mothered nuns of the *Therīgāthā*, and thus avoiding the potential loss of women to smaller, more woman-centered forms of religion.[76]

Historically, I will admit, there is perhaps little evidence for this latter suggestion concerning Hārītī's particular appeal for women. I will content myself, therefore, with citing only a single, suggestive example. At the back of Cave 2 at the Buddhist cave site of Ajaṇṭā, there is a central shrine dedicated to the Buddha, flanked by two subsidiary shrines, of which the shrine on the right contains images of Hārītī and her husband, Pañcika.[77] This is a reflection of Hārītī's ambiguous status: On the one hand, she is enshrined within the monastic dwelling, but on the other hand, she is made subordinate to the Buddha. The sculpted image of Hārītī itself, however, is also flanked on both sides by two painted murals, and it is these that interest me here. In the mural on the right, we see women and their children bringing offerings to Hārītī, placing them before her, and paying homage at her feet. And in the mural on the left, according to Richard Cohen's interpretation of the scene,[78] we see Hārītī herself, along with two of her children, granting a vision of herself to these same female devotees. Her right hand is holding another child but is also forming the *varada mudrā* or symbolic gesture of gift-giving, while her left hand is forming the *śrī mudrā* or symbolic gesture of wealth and good fortune. The mural on the right thus depicts a ritual dedicated to Hārītī, while the mural on the left depicts its hoped-for result—the gift of children and other good blessings.

It is striking to me that these murals focus solely on *female* devotees and seem to reflect, first and foremost, their concern for their *children*. In fact, these murals seem to be depicting what Sered might describe as a typical example of "women's religion"—in other words, a cultic complex in which women are dominant, in which women are free to express their concern for their own, particular children, and in which the deity responds by protecting their children's health or granting children to those who are childless. The particularistic "women's" concerns embodied within these paintings are made subordinate, however, to the sculpted image of Hārītī herself—who might be described as mediating between the particular and the universal—while Hārītī herself is made subordinate to the transcendent Buddha. The physical layout of the cave is thus a graphic illustration of how such a "women's cult" might be related to the dominant, patriarchal tradition of Buddhism.

If we consider the women depicted in the murals, the figure of Hārītī herself, and the de-mothered nuns of the *Therīgāthā*, then perhaps we can see that Buddhism in India offered mothers a variety of different avenues for reconciling their commitment to universal Buddhist ideals with the intensity and partiality of their love for their own children. There was no single model for being both a mother and a Buddhist; rather, there were various different models for such women to choose from—to the degree, of course, that they consciously considered the matter at all. It is the very multiplicity of these models, in fact, that perhaps contributes to Buddhism's general ambivalence toward mother-love (celebrating it at one moment and reviling it at the next). For no religious tradition—even the most dominant or most patriarchal—is ever monolithic and uniform in its messages. Ultimately, I believe, Buddhist monastic authors in India were indeed adhering to Sered's suggestion that we recognize and take seriously the enormous power of both maternal love and maternal grief.

"Don't Cry, Children, I Am Listening to the Dharma"

I conclude my discussion by returning to the figure of Hārītī and citing a theme that appears in connection with her in several different texts—a theme that I believe most poignantly captures the complexity of the issues raised by the mother's fierce love of her children.[79] In several different Pali, Sanskrit, and Chinese texts, a demoness who is referred to variously as "Hārītī," "the mother of Priyaṅkara," "the mother of Punarvasu," or simply "the mother of demons"—all of whom can be loosely identified with Hārītī herself—tries to listen as the Buddha or one of his disciples preaches the dharma, but is disturbed by the crying of her two children, a son referred to as either Priyaṅkara or Punarvasu and a daughter referred to as Uttarā. She shushes her children, telling them that she wishes to hear the dharma, and further promises them that once she has benefited from the dharma, she will cause them to benefit, too. "You, Uttarā," she says in the *Mahāprajñāpāramitā Śāstra*, "don't cry; don't cry any longer, Punarvasu. I am listening to the Dharma; when I have obtained the way, you will surely obtain it too."[80]

Though Hārītī's exact words vary from one version to another, they always follow the same twofold sequence of first shushing her children so that she can hear the dharma, and then holding out the possibility that they might be enlightened, too, perhaps through their own mother's encouragement. Hārītī's response to the situation, in other words, always displays the double-sided nature of motherhood: On the one hand, children monopolize a mother's attention, distract her from other concerns, and drain her of life and energy. Thus, in a sūtra from the (Chinese) *Saṃyuktāgama*, she is very much the harried mother who realizes all of the frustrations and limitations imposed by familial ties:

> Let me listen to the dharma preached by the Tathāgata. Neither father nor mother can make their children escape from suffering. It is by listening to the dharma preached by the Tathāgata that one obtains deliverance from suffering. . . . At this moment, I want to hear the dharma; you, you must be quiet.[81]

On the other hand, however, she truly loves her children, and she *does not leave them behind*. And in this, she is akin to the Buddha himself: The mother's love for her children and her natural inclination to want whatever is best for them could be seen as perhaps *the* paradigmatic and original model for the Buddhist belief that only one who teaches others out of compassion really qualifies as a fully enlightened Buddha. Thus, in the *Mahāvibhāṣā Śāstra*, she says to her children, "When I have seen the truths, I will cause you to see them too"[82]—and what could be a more Buddha-like statement than that?[83] As full of attachment and clinging as she might be, moreover, the mother's words here are also fully effective, for her children do stop crying and begin listening to the dharma. "Excellent!," they say to their mother in the *Saṃyuktāgama*, "we too are happy to listen to the dharma"—whereupon their mother responds with delight: "Marvelous! What intelligent children!" She then concludes with an utterance of joy that seems to celebrate the possibility of *both* her freedom from all forms of bondage *and* her eternal tie to her children: "You, Punarvasu, and you, Uttarā, my daughter, give rise to joy along with me; I have seen the noble truths!"[84]

It is *this* vision of the relationship between mother-love and Buddha-love that finally makes the most sense, I believe, if we consider carefully just what it means to "love all beings just as a mother loves her only child." "Universal" love, in other words, cannot simply be an abstraction; instead, it must be seen as the *union of all possible particulars*—beginning with the most original particular of all, the mother's love for her child. Indeed, it is difficult to imagine what "universal" compassion would be if it were *not* simply the union of all particulars. This is well recognized by the Buddhist tradition itself—for example, in the *Visuddhimagga*'s admonition that one should develop universal compassion by first cultivating compassion for a dear friend, and only gradually working up toward compassion for a stranger or an enemy, thus moving from one "particular" to another, until universality itself has been established. Similarly, in the Mahāyāna tradition, the bodhisattva is celebrated for his great "skill in means" (Skt. *upāya-kauśalya*)—which is universally applied, yet always applied *in light of particular circumstances*, and which is, in fact, valued precisely for its skillful attention to the particular. The thousand-armed image of Avalokiteśvara also calls to mind the idea of universal compassion being constituted out of an infinite number of particular, saving deeds (otherwise, as my friend Julie put it, "why all the hands, when a single disembodied Mind would do?").[85] The Buddhist tradition thus agrees with Iris Murdoch that "the moral task is not to generate action based on universal and impartial principles but to attend and respond to particular persons,"[86] and with Alasdair MacIntyre that "without those moral particularities to begin from there would never be anywhere to begin; but it is in moving forward from such particularity that the search for the good, for the universal, consists."[87] Nevertheless, it seems that certain strands of the Buddhist tradition have been reluctant to connect this recognition to the image of mother-love, preferring instead to pose an outright *opposition* between the particularistic love of the mother and the universal compassion of the Buddha.

3

"Whose Womb Shall I Enter Today?"

MĀYĀ AS IDEALIZED BIRTH-GIVER

I TURN NOW to the Buddha himself, who figures in Buddhist literature not only as a perfectly awakened buddha, but also as the adored son of two different mothers. The Buddha's relationships with his mothers have been used to explore not only the depictions of mother-love discussed in chapter 1 and the motif of the grieving mother discussed in chapter 2, but several other issues surrounding motherhood—such as the debt the son owes to his mother and his guilt and anxiety over its repayment, the continuing emotional bond between mother and son even after the son has renounced the world, the very nature of birth from a woman's body, and the special questions raised when this birth finds its fulfillment in a perfectly awakened buddha. In order to work out these ideas, the Buddhist tradition was not content with giving the Buddha a single mother, but felt compelled to provide him with two: Queen Māyā or Mahāmāyā, the biological mother who conceived and gave birth to the bodhisattva but died just seven days later, and her sister Mahāprajāpatī Gautamī, who became the bodhisattva's foster mother and lovingly raised him to young adulthood, as well as playing a crucial role in the early history of the Saṃgha by asking the Buddha to institute an order of nuns. Māyā and Mahāprajāpatī, in addition to being sisters, are also co-wives of King Śuddhodhana, the Buddha's father. Yet as mothers to the Buddha, they function in very different ways.

Indeed, the very fact that the Buddha has two mothers has never adequately been considered before, nor has the relationship between them been explored at any length. My own position is that while it is quite possible that the historical figure Siddhārtha Gautama actually had both a biological mother who died and a foster mother who raised him, whether or not this is true is finally irrelevant, once we recognize the several ways in which these two mothers came to be shaped as a contrasting pair in

Buddhist discourse. In fact, the biggest problem with existing scholarship on Māyā and Mahāprajāpatī, in my view, is that despite its relative abundance, it has consistently failed to consider these two figures in relation to each other.[1] By contrast, my discussion will weave its way back and forth between them, pursuing the argument that the Buddhist tradition has consciously shaped these two mothers into a contrasting pair, using this pair to explore the nature of motherhood in a highly nuanced, imaginative, and complex fashion.

Perhaps it will be useful, at the outset, to summarize the analysis I pursue in this and the following two chapters. Māyā, in my view, is an idealized embodiment of the Maternal Function—she is Woman as Mother and Birth-Giver, and nothing else whatsoever. As such, she is virtuous, pure, and perfect; she surpasses all ordinary women, escapes from all of the faults normally associated with the female sex, and sets an unattainable ideal that no real human mother could ever fulfill. Despite this idealization, however, Māyā is finally reduced to little more than an appropriate "fetal container."[2] She gives birth to the bodhisattva in a highly idealized and supernatural manner, then quickly exits the scene through her early and preordained death. I will argue that as a result of this early death, she spares her son both the *guilt* that he would otherwise feel for abandoning her when he later renounces the world, and the sense of an unresolved *debt* that he is obligated to repay but whose repayment is complicated by his renunciation of worldly life. This means that in relation to Māyā, the Buddha can express his lingering tie to his mother in a free and affectionate manner, while also avoiding all of the consequences that one's relationship with any actual mother would ordinarily involve. In all of these ways, Māyā might be described as the ultimate "good" mother—one who fulfills her birth-giving function in a clean and pleasant manner and then quickly gets out of the way.

Mahāprajāpatī, on the other hand, might be seen as the reality that underlies this ideal: She embodies the realization that women *cannot* be reduced to nothing other than the Maternal Function; they are not just Mothers and Birth-Givers, but also individual, complicated human beings, with their own desires and demands. Mahāprajāpatī nurtures and raises the bodhisattva—which, on the one hand, makes her the object of great affection and gratitude, but, on the other hand, also creates an enormous *debt* within her son that demands to be repaid. And unlike Māyā, she does not "get out of the way." Instead, she sticks around long enough to grieve over her son's renunciation of the world—thereby causing him considerable *guilt*—and to demand repayment of the debt her son has incurred, through the establishment of an order of nuns. Indeed, I will argue that the very existence of female monasticism—something about which the Buddhist tradition has often been highly ambivalent—can be directly linked to the debt the Buddha owed to Mahāprajāpatī for her mothering and his anxiety over its repayment. In all of these ways, Mahāprajāpatī is—not exactly the "bad" mother—but at least the problematic mother, the focus of much ambivalence. Consequently, the Buddha's lingering tie to Mahāprajāpatī is expressed not freely and lovingly, but with a certain amount of anxious calculation. It finds expression through the economic language of debt and repayment, and is sometimes surrounded with the negative emotions of guilt, anxiety, and subconscious hostility.

There is also, however, a crucial flip side to this contrast between Māyā as the "good" mother and Mahāprajāpatī as the "problematic" mother. This flip side becomes apparent when we consider each mother in terms of her *grief*. Both of them, at different points in their lives, are presented as mothers in grief, yet they differ from each other in what they do with their grief. Because Māyā dies so quickly and is immediately reborn as a deity living in heaven, she is permanently "frozen" into the role of Mother and Birth-Giver and is unable to spiritually benefit from confronting her grief. Unlike the mothers of the *Therīgāthā*, who confront their grief and universalize it, transcend their motherhood, and go on to attain nirvana, Māyā's loss of human status limits her spiritual capability, leaves her incapable of capitalizing on her grief, and forever paralyzes her in the role of Mother. Mahāprajāpatī, on the other hand, precisely because she "sticks around," does have the opportunity to overcome and transform her grief, and much like the mothers in the *Therīgāthā*, she *is* able to become a nun and go on to attain nirvana. In fact, she is the very one who makes this course possible for other women.[3]

Thus, what at first appears to be a straightforward case of "splitting" the mother into two—Māyā as the "good" mother, Mahāprajāpatī as the (not-quite) "bad" mother—reveals itself to be something rather more complex. On the one hand, Māyā may be highly idealized and celebrated as a pure embodiment of Motherhood, but on the other hand, it is also recognized that a woman thus reduced to her motherhood is a spiritually stunted creature. Conversely, Mahāprajāpatī may be treated ambivalently and sometimes negatively for being an autonomous individual, rather than an idealized embodiment of Motherhood, but on the other hand, it is also recognized that only someone who *is* such an individual can attain the highest goal. In short, Māyā is idealized, but at the expense of her spiritual potential; Mahāprajāpatī is treated ambivalently, but as a consequence of granting her her spiritual potential. The two mothers together thus allow the Buddhist tradition to reflect on both idealized motherhood and actual human mothers; on Woman-as-Mother and Woman as something that transcends the role of mother; on the enormous appeal of allowing women such transcendence; and on the resulting fear and repugnance, as well.

Buddhist thinking about Māyā and Mahāprajāpatī covers a span of many centuries and involves multiple schools, genres, texts, and authors. It would be unreasonable, therefore, to expect all of the traditions surrounding them to conform to the analysis I have presented above—and, indeed, not all of them do. Nevertheless, I hope to demonstrate through the remainder of this chapter and the following two chapters that this analysis does give us a coherent and useful way of understanding these two figures and interpreting many of the traditions surrounding them. My argument here is not that the "Buddhist tradition" was some kind of omniscient author who carefully constructed stories about Māyā and Mahāprajāpatī in the service of this particular analysis. Rather, what I seek to suggest is simply that once the basic notion of a *mother who dies* and a *mother who survives* was set into place, these two figures became natural vehicles for considering the contrast between a woman *reduced* to her birth-giving function and a woman who *surpasses* her birth-giving function—and, subsequently, all of the other consequences that might flow from that basic distinction.

Māyā as Idealized Birth-Giver

Depicting the birth of Siddhārtha Gautama, the future Buddha, presented the Buddhist tradition with a difficult conceptual problem:[4] The Buddha, by definition, is a sacred and highly valued figure—a perfectly pure and transcendent being who is free of all corruption, impurity, and defilement. And even though this is true only of the fully enlightened Buddha, these qualities tend to be projected backward in time to his many lives as a bodhisattva as well, thus requiring him to have a pure and undefiled origin even before he has become a buddha. At the same time, however, the Buddha is also a human being—not a deity—and therefore must be depicted as being born from a human woman's womb, which was generally understood in Indian thought (both Buddhist and non-Buddhist) to be a disgusting, filthy, and impure place.

Indian descriptions of the "suffering of the womb" (Skt. *garbha-duḥkha*) and the "suffering of birth" (Skt. *janma-duḥkha*) describe the mother's womb as a dark, cramped, and airless space in which the fetus constantly suffers, being submerged in feces and urine and experiencing torment whenever his mother moves.[5] Birth itself is depicted as an extremely painful passage through the narrow canal of the vagina and a violent expulsion into the cold air outside, with the startled infant dropping "like a worm . . . which falls down upon the ground from a foul-smelling sore."[6] Birth, in fact, is repeatedly cited in Buddhist literature as one of the foremost examples of the omnipresence of suffering. In the *Visuddhimagga*, for example, Buddhaghosa compares the embryo to "a worm in rotting fish or rotting curds or a cesspool," trapped within a womb that is "exceedingly loathsome and full of foul odors and fetid smells," where he undergoes "extreme suffering, being cooked like a pudding in a bag by the heat produced by his mother's womb, being steamed like a lump of dough, unable to bend, stretch, etc."[7] Thus, the basic problem, common to many religious traditions: How could the purest and most excellent being in the universe be born from a human woman's filthy womb?[8] The *Lalitavistara* puts the question succinctly: "So how, indeed, could the bodhisattva, who rises above all worlds, who is pure and free from any foul odors, who is a jewel among beings—how could he descend from the realm of the Saṃtuṣita gods and remain for ten months in a foul-smelling human body, in the womb of his mother?"[9]

The key to resolving this problem, of course, lies precisely in the mother. It is only by depicting Māyā as a highly idealized birth-giver, completely unlike any other birth-giver—while still maintaining her human status—that this quandary can be resolved. In Pali canonical sources (such as the *Acchariyabbhuta Sutta* and *Mahāpadāna Sutta*) and in Buddha biographies (such as the *Nidānakathā*, *Mahāvastu*, *Lalitavistara*, and *Abhiniṣkramaṇa Sūtra*), the features of Māyā as an idealized birth-giver are given elaborate and extended description.[10]

In the first place, the status of Māyā as the birth-giver of the bodhisattva is neither a random accident nor a result brought about by ordinary karmic processes. Instead, it is a conscious choice on the part of the bodhisattva, one of the four or five considerations he makes—"mindful and deliberate"[11]—at the end of his penultimate life as a deity in the Tuṣita Heaven about when and where he will take his final rebirth. In the *Mahāvastu*, for example, he asks himself:

> Now, which woman delights in tranquility and moral restraint, comes from a prominent family, speaks well, and is generous, beautiful, and kind? Which [woman] is dignified, free of ignorance, passion, and hatred, supremely beautiful, excellent in conduct, and abundant in merit? Who is capable of bearing me for ten months, and who is worthy of such happiness? Who, now, should be my mother? Whose womb shall I enter today?[12]

In other biographies, such as the *Lalitavistara* and the *Abhiniṣkramaṇa Sūtra*, we are given daunting lists of thirty-two specific qualities that such a woman must possess,[13] again including features of both physical and moral perfection, as well as the fact that "she is free from all of the faults of womankind."[14] It is only after determining that "she alone is fit to be the mother of the Great Sage and has served as the bodhisattva's mother in no fewer than five hundred births"[15] that Māyā's status as the birth-giver is assured. The fact that this status is the result of the bodhisattva's conscious deliberation rather than automatic karmic processes places Māyā's motherhood completely outside the ordinary workings of samsara. Moreover, the fact that Māyā *alone* meets all of the necessary qualifications also places her motherhood completely beyond the reach of ordinary Womanhood.

The depiction of Māyā as an idealized birth-giver continues through the bodhisattva's conception, gestation, and birth. The description of these events seems to combine, on the one hand, an extreme idealization of Māyā, in both physical and moral terms, and, on the other hand, a simultaneous desire to largely ignore Māyā's moral virtue, erase and elide her physical body, turn her into nothing more than a transparent fetal container, and avoid any association whatsoever between the bodhisattva and the ordinary physiological processes surrounding conception, gestation, and birth. Thus the conception, in most biographies, is not associated with the sexual act, for "bodhisattvas certainly don't come from their mothers and fathers, but are, in fact, self-produced (Skt. *upapādukā*) and originate from their own qualities (Skt. *svaguṇanirvṛttā*)."[16] Instead, the conception is generally depicted as taking the form of an auspicious dream Māyā has, in which deities come down from the heavens and transport her up into the Himalayas, bathe her with celestial waters "to remove her human imperfections,"[17] clothe her in heavenly garments, and anoint her with divine perfumes. The bodhisattva, in the form of a noble, six-tusked white elephant, then comes to her and appears to enter into her right side (Figure 3.1). As soon as this

FIGURE 3.1 Māyā dreams of a white elephant and conceives the future Buddha. Medallion from the Bharhut Stūpa, 1st c. BCE. Indian Museum, Calcutta. Photograph by John C. Huntington, courtesy of the Huntington Photographic Archive at The Ohio State University.

magical conception has occurred, the earth trembles, the whole world fills with light, throngs of deities come to stand guard over mother and son, and thirty-two miracles occur—for example, the blind can see, the deaf can hear, and the lame can walk. Throughout this entire sequence, Māyā, being asleep, is wholly passive, and actions are performed *upon her* rather than her actively engaging in them. In the *Lalitavistara*, in fact, the bodhisattva almost appears to conceive himself, for on the night of his conception, he is said to ingest a drop of nectar that contains within itself "whatever constitutes the essence, the pith, or the vitality here in this million-billion-fold world-system."[18] This drop of nectar is given to him by the great deity Brahmā and results from the maturation of the bodhisattva's own meritorious deeds. Once again, Māyā herself seems almost irrelevant.

The singular nature of the bodhisattva's birth continues with the description of Māyā's pregnancy. Throughout the pregnancy, the bodhisattva inhabits the auspicious right side of Māyā's womb and never moves over to the left. He entertains multitudes of deities and supernatural beings every day, yet his movements cause his mother no discomfort, nor do her movements cause any discomfort to him. Unlike other embryos, which develop gradually over time, the bodhisattva is "complete with all major and minor limbs and not lacking any of his faculties"[19] from the very beginning—perhaps a way of emphasizing that even his very body receives no substantial contribution from her. Even more remarkable, Māyā can *see* the bodhisattva within her womb, "just as if a pure and genuine lapis lazuli jewel, beautifully cut into an octagon, clear, bright, flawless, and perfect in every way, were strung on a blue, yellow, red, white, or orange thread," and a man with good eyesight could determine the color of the thread.[20] Māyā's womb, in other words, is as perfectly transparent as a crystal. Just as contemporary feminist scholars have argued that the greater visibility of the fetus through modern advances in sonographic technology has resulted in a corresponding erasure of the mother—casting the fetus as "primary and autonomous, the woman as absent or peripheral"[21]—so too the transparency of Māyā's womb serves to indicate that she lacks any autonomy of her own, and her only purpose is to serve as a fetal container for her illustrious son. This is also suggested by the metaphor that consistently describes Māyā as a *vessel* or a *vase*: Thus, in the *Lalitavistara*, a throng of goddesses, on seeing Māyā, proclaims: "Just as a jewel might be placed in a beautiful vessel (Skt. *bhājana*), so also will the queen be a vessel for the god of gods!"[22] It is because Māyā is such a "fit vessel" (Skt. *pratirūpabhājanaṃ*), in fact, that the bodhisattva can "shine forth illustriously" (Skt. *paramaṃ virājate*),[23] once again suggesting the vessel's transparency.

The reduction of Māyā to the vessel-like functioning of her womb is further reinforced by the subordination of her own thoughts and deeds to the will of the embryo she is carrying. Hubert Durt has carefully studied both the five pregnancy cravings (Skt. *dohada*) experienced by Māyā in the Sanskrit *Mūlasarvāstivāda Vinaya* and related texts, and the three supernatural powers of healing she possesses while pregnant in the *Lalitavistara* and related texts.[24] These studies have shown that both her pregnancy cravings and her powers of healing are the direct result of the embryo she carries within her womb and a perfectly transparent reflection of its qualities and powers. It thus appears that the physical transparency of Māyā's womb extends to the remainder of her person as well, encompassing her thoughts, feelings, and even actions. Māyā acts not as an autonomous individual, but only as a mediator for the will and power of her son.

Yet despite the reduction of Māyā herself to the carrying functioning of her womb, there is still considerable anxiety over the nature of the womb itself and thus an attempt to isolate the bodhisattva from the womb's impurities. This is done in a number of ways. The *Mahāpadāna Sutta* is content to state that it is a rule for all bodhisattvas to emerge from their mothers' wombs "perfectly clean, unsoiled by water, mucus, blood, or any other impurity, pure and clean," just as "when a jewel is laid down upon muslin from Benares, the jewel does not soil the muslin, nor does the muslin soil the jewel . . . because of the purity of both"[25]—which seems to suggest that the womb itself might be pure. For the *Mahāvastu*, on the other hand, the bodhisattva's cleanliness on birth requires further explanation: "And, moreover, while the bodhisattva is in his mother's womb, he is not smeared with bile, mucus, blood, or any other impurity, but remains clean. For while the bodhisattva dwells in his mother's womb, his body is anointed with oils and washed clean."[26] The *Lalitavistara*, however, finds that even this is insufficient: When Ānanda expresses amazement that the bodhisattva could ever have inhabited "a foul-smelling human body" (Skt. *manuṣyāśraye durgandhe*), the Buddha replies by revealing to Ānanda and the assembled audience the magnificent "jeweled sanctum" (Skt. *ratnavyūha*) in which the bodhisattva was encased while inhabiting his mother's womb.[27] The problem posed by birth from a woman's womb is thus solved by surrounding the bodhisattva with an extra layer of protection.

If we consider all of these texts together, we can plot the trajectory of an ever-increasing tendency to undermine the real existence of Māyā: First, she is highly idealized and made unlike any other woman; then, despite her ideal nature, she is reduced to the vessel-like functioning of her womb; then her womb is made transparent and virtually invisible; and finally, actual walls are erected between the womb and the bodhisattva who inhabits it. This erasure of Māyā, and especially of her physical body, continues with the birth itself. The birth has many wonderful qualities that, according to the *Mahāpadāna Sutta*,[28] are common to all bodhisattvas in their last existences: For example, the mother carries the baby for exactly ten months, she gives birth standing up, the baby is received by deities rather than falling onto the ground like a worm, and although he is perfectly clean, two streams of water fall from the sky to bathe him. Most significant, however, is the fact that the bodhisattva does not emerge from his mother's vagina; instead, "mindful and deliberate, the bodhisattva, without injuring his mother, appears from her right side"[29] (Figure 3.2). This ensures not only that the bodhisattva can avoid the impurity of the

FIGURE 3.2 Māyā gives birth to the future Buddha from her right side. Gandhāra, 2nd–3rd c. CE. Freer Gallery of Art, Smithsonian Institution, Washington, DC: Purchase, F1949.9.

mother's vagina—and the association with sexuality that the vagina will immediately call to mind[30]—but also that he is spared from the harrowing and painful passage down the vaginal canal. As Minoru Hara has noted,[31] according to many Hindu texts, it is precisely because of the enormous suffering experienced during this passage that the ordinary infant is said to lose the knowledge of karma and the memory of his previous lives that he was believed to have possessed as a fully developed fetus. Thus, such an infant is born as a *bāla* (both "fool" and "child") who "does not know who he is, whence he has come, to whom he belongs, by what form of bondage he has been bound, what he should do, what he should not do, what he should eat, what he should not eat, what he should drink, what he should not drink, what is truth, what is falsehood, what is knowledge, what is ignorance."[32] Because passage through the mother's vagina is associated with ignorance, the bodhisattva, "mindful and deliberate," passes through his mother's right side. And once again, the physicality of his mother's body is further diminished, for various texts make it clear that there is no resulting wound. According to the *Mahāvastu*, for example, Māyā's body is "uninjured and unscarred," her womb is "unobstructed and whole,"[33] and her side is not rent by the bodhisattva passing through: "When she gives birth to the most excellent of men, why does the side of the Conqueror's mother not split open, and why does she have no pain? Because Tathāgatas appear in a form that is made of mind; thus, her side does not split open, nor does she have any pain."[34]

Although it is the bodhisattva, rather than Māyā, who is here described as being "made of mind" (Skt. *manomaya*), this ghostly quality seems equally true of Māyā herself. As Obeyesekere has put it, "She who begets an illusion must herself be an illusion"[35]—a suggestion further reinforced by Māyā's very name. The term *māyā* has a range of meanings running from "illusion" to "magical creation" to "deceptive appearance" and might suggest that Māyā herself is just an illusion. This meaning of the term is invoked in connection with Māyā in the *Lalitavistara*, which states that she was given the name Māyā (or Māyādevī) because "she seemed like an image created through magic" and because "she ravishes the mind like a magical creation."[36] The erasure of Māyā's physical body evident throughout the entire pregnancy process is thereby completed in her name.

The *Abhiniṣkramaṇa Sūtra* adds one final detail that further suggests the illusory nature of Māyā as birth-giver. After Māyā has given birth, Mahānāma, the minister of King Śuddhodhana, compares the wonderful birth of the bodhisattva to several other highly auspicious births of the past—including the births of various legendary figures who are described as having been born from a flower, the father's head, the father's hand, the father's stomach, the father's arm, and a stalk of sugar cane.[37] Thus we see that the auspicious births to which Māyā's birth-giving can best be compared are those that occur *through the father alone*, or in some other manner that excludes any mother. Here, as throughout the entire birth-narrative, the ideal birth-giver is one who is illusory, transparent, or barely present at all.

Birth as Illusory Arising: Māyā in the Gaṇḍavyūha Sūtra

The illusory quality of Māyā as an idealized birth-giver, though already present in the earliest biographical sources, finds its fullest and most elaborate expression in a Mahāyāna context—more specifically, in two passages from the *Gaṇḍavyūha Sūtra*. This text, which takes place in a magical and ephemeral Mahāyāna landscape with no real connection to historical time or space, traces the journey of the bodhisattva-pilgrim Sudhana as he encounters and receives Buddhist teachings from a series of over fifty different religious teachers. Throughout the course of his pilgrimage, Sudhana encounters two figures who have much to say about the birth of the bodhisattva. One of these figures is a goddess named Sutejomaṇḍalaratiśrī, who presides over the Lumbini grove where the bodhisattva was born and who witnessed the birth itself. And the other figure is none other than the bodhisattva's mother Māyā, now a deity in heaven. Both figures describe the birth of the bodhisattva from Māyā's body in a highly elaborate, magical, and cosmic manner that bears no resemblance whatsoever to ordinary birth-giving.[38]

Sutejomaṇḍalaratiśrī, for example, in recounting the birth of the bodhisattva, describes ten auspicious omens that appeared in the Lumbini grove, ten omens involving great light (by which Māyā's body outshone all the light existing in the billion-world universe), and ten miracles that attended the birth itself. These miracles include such things as the reflection of everything existing in all universes within Māyā's single abdomen, the complete vision of the bodhisattva's entire, eons-long bodhisattva career within every one of Māyā's pores, and the birth from Māyā's womb not only of the bodhisattva himself but also of "bodhisattvas equal in number to the atoms and dust-particles in inexpressible tens of hundreds of thousands of millions of billions of buddha fields."[39] Not surprisingly, these births are described not as ordinary, literal birth-givings but, rather, as taking place "by way of the manifestation of illusory form, by way of non-coming, by way of appearing in the world without arising or ceasing."[40] Later on, when Sudhana goes to visit Māyā herself, the same type of mind-bending description continues. Māyā emerges from the ground seated on a magnificent lotus throne, and her physical body is elaborately described as "transcending the three worlds," "going beyond all states of existence," "penetrating the sphere of reality at every instant," and so on.[41] Her description of her pregnancy with the bodhisattva makes it clear that during that time too all ordinary physical laws were held in abeyance: "My body rose above all worlds, and my womb became as vast as the realm of space, yet it did not exceed a normal human size."[42] Billions of bodhisattvas and buddhas inhabited her womb simultaneously, and "all of them walked around with strides as big as three thousand world-systems, with strides as big as world-systems equal in number to the atoms and particles of dust in an inexpressible number of buddha-fields . . . and yet, even receiving so many multitudes, my womb did not grow any larger, nor did my body become any different from a regular human body."[43] In addition to such physical impossibilities, Māyā herself, as a personality, loses all historical specificity and location in time—for just as she gave birth to Śākyamuni, so also she gave birth to the previous buddhas Krakucchanda, Kanakamuni, and Kāśyapa, and so also in the future will she give birth to the future buddha Maitreya. In fact, she will be the mother "of all the Tathāgata Arhat Saṃyaksambuddhas of this eon . . . within this million-billion-fold world-system . . . [and also] for millions of eons in the future, in all Jambudvīpas in all world-systems, in all multitudes and assemblies of world-systems, throughout this entire ocean of world-systems."[44] Clearly, with such descriptions, we have moved as far away as one could possibly go from the ordinary process of giving birth.

In her analysis of these remarkable passages, Miranda Shaw has correctly observed that their real concern lies not so much with describing the bodhisattva's birth but, rather, with giving imaginative expression to the Mahāyāna philosophical notion of emptiness and its endless creativity—or, in other words, the idea that "all phenomenal arising is miraculous, spontaneous, and illusory. All things are born out of emptiness, take form in empty space, . . . shimmer momentarily like a magician's illusion, and then dissolve. . . . In this prevalent Mahayana view, the world of appearances shares in the purity . . . of its ontological matrix, emptiness, the womb of reality."[45] The birth of the bodhisattva is used to convey these ideas simply because birth is perhaps a natural image for this illusory arising, while the womb is a good metaphor for emptiness. In the process of this image-making, however, both birth and the womb are wholly purified: "No stigma attaches here to the process of birth, and Māyādevī's womb is glorified without reservation."[46] Thus, the same idealization we have seen operating throughout the entire birth-giving sequence here reaches a kind of perfect fulfillment through its connection with the notion of emptiness.

The crucial point to emphasize here, however, is that although this particular text's description of Māyā stands somewhat apart from that of the other sources and has some unique philosophical concerns, it is, in the final analysis, merely a logical extension of the idealization and erasure of Māyā already present within the earliest biographical tradition. In that sense, it represents not so much a unique take on Māyā as another manifestation of the underlying impulse that motivates her depiction throughout. At the very least, one could say that it would be difficult—if not impossible—to imagine Mahāprajāpatī ever being invoked in a similar manner.

The Short Life-Span of the Ideal Mother

ĀNANDA: "It is wonderful, Venerable One, it is marvelous, Venerable One, how short-lived was the Blessed One's mother!"
BUDDHA: "This is true, Ānanda! For short-lived are the mothers of bodhisattas."[47]

One final feature of Māyā's depiction as an ideal embodiment of the maternal function is her very short life span—which, at ten months and seven days from the time of the bodhisattva's conception, is just long enough for her to give birth, as well as to avoid the suspicion that giving birth has killed her. In the *Mahāpadāna Sutta* (as in the passage from *Udāna* 5.2 cited above), it is said to be a rule for all buddhas that their biological mothers must die seven days after giving birth,[48] while in both the *Nidānakathā* and the *Mahāvastu*, the mother's short life span is included in the four or five "considerations" the bodhisattva makes when deciding when and where to be reborn. In the *Mahāvastu*, consideration of the mother's life span falls under the larger category of choosing the appropriate "family," and it is specified that the mother must be "short-lived, whose remaining lifespan was only ten months and seven nights."[49] In the *Nidānakathā*, on the other hand, the mother's life span itself constitutes one of the bodhisattva's five considerations (the others being the time, the country, the family, and the mother).[50] The biographical tradition thus asserts fairly strongly that Māyā's short life span is a preordained fact and that the same rule applies equally to the mothers of all buddhas.[51]

Why is the ideal mother one who dies seven days after giving birth? The Buddhist tradition itself provides us with several possible answers. One prominent reason for the mother's premature death—which is in line with many of the concerns surrounding female anatomy we have already seen above—is that once such a mother has served the exalted function of giving birth to the bodhisattva, it would be wholly inappropriate for her ever again to be engaged in the polluting processes of sexual intercourse and ordinary childbirth. The unseemliness of the mother engaging in sex is cited, for example, in the *Mahāvastu*:

> Now, why is it that the mothers of Omniscient Ones die so quickly after giving birth to the Best of Men? . . . [The Blessed One says:] "Because it would not be appropriate for one who has carried an

> excellent [being] like me to engage in sexual intercourse later on." . . . Indeed, the Blessed One speaks constantly about the faults of sensual pleasures, so how can the Lord of the World's [own] mother enjoy [such] sensual pleasures?[52]

Along with sexual intercourse, pregnancy with an ordinary embryo would be similarly inappropriate. Here, the vessel-like functioning of Māyā's womb is again invoked by comparing the womb to a relic chamber, which, once inhabited by holy relics, should not be polluted by anything more mundane. Thus, the *Nidānakathā* asserts: "Since a womb inhabited by a bodhisatta is, indeed, like the relic chamber of a shrine, and cannot be inhabited or enjoyed by anyone else, the mothers of bodhisattas die seven days after the bodhisattas are born . . ."[53]

In addition to polluting physical processes such as sexual intercourse and ordinary pregnancy, it would also be unbecoming for such an exalted mother to be placed in any kind of inferior or servile social position, and the only way to ensure this, once we leave behind the perfect world of the birth narrative, is by having the mother die. Thus, in the commentary to *Udāna* 5.2, we are told that "it would not have been proper if she, the Buddha's mother, who carried in her womb for ten months the foremost being in the world, the Teacher, who is indeed of such great majesty, had become a servant to anyone else"—instead, "it was perfectly in keeping with the qualities of the Teacher that she, the Blessed Mother, died seven days after he was born."[54] Later on, the same text further specifies that the mother must die because "it is not possible for the bodhisatta's mother to be removed from the position of Chief Queen and another [woman] installed in her place."[55] Once Māyā has been elevated above the reach of all other women, in other words, she cannot be subjected to any further development that might threaten to sink her back down.

Whether pertaining to physical or social processes, all of these reasons share the basic recognition that the depiction of Māyā as an idealized womb-vessel becomes completely unsustainable once she is returned to the ordinary human world. Once she has been reduced to her birth-giving function and her birth-giving function has been fulfilled, there is nothing else one could narrate about her without undermining her role as a birth-giver. Any further events one might narrate about her would only suggest that she was an actual woman, not just a perfect vessel for the delivery of her son. Thus, the only way to keep Māyā in the picture at all is by having her die and be reborn as a deity in heaven. Once she becomes a deity who has been removed to the sphere of heaven, her daily life requires no specific narration, and the tradition can thus invoke her solely in contexts in which she continues to function *as the Buddha's mother*. It is in this sense that Māyā's early death permanently "freezes" her in the role of Mother, by disallowing any further narrative development of her character. This "freezing" is evident in an interesting passage from the *Abhiniṣkramaṇa Sūtra*. Here, it is said that Māyā died because she was "unable to . . . recover the joy she experienced whilst the child dwelt in her womb," but that once she became a deity in heaven, she returned to King Śuddhodhana to "assure him that her joy was now equal to that she experienced during the period of her gestation."[56] Death and removal to heaven have thus frozen Māyā into the permanent status of birth-giver.

As necessary as Māyā's almost-immediate death may be, however, it is also important to avoid any suggestion that giving birth to the Blessed One is what killed her. This, I believe, is the rationale behind quantifying Māyā's short life span as being exactly ten months and seven days (although there is, as far as I know, no text that states this explicitly). Since all bodhisattvas are born after exactly ten months of gestation, this life span is just long enough to allow for the bodhisattva's birth, while also separating it from the mother's death by a period of seven days. Nevertheless, there seems to have been some anxiety over the possible suggestion of death-in-childbirth, for several Buddhist texts go to extra lengths in order to deny it. In the *Lalitavistara*, the Buddha states: "Now, Monks, it may occur to you that Māyādevī died through the fault of the bodhisattva, but this is really not the way to see it. And why? Because it was merely the end of her lifespan."[57] Similarly, in his commentary to *Udāna* 5.2, the commentator Dhammapāla emphasizes the fact that the mothers of all bodhisattvas "die merely through the exhaustion of their lifespan, as stated previously, and not because of giving birth."[58] The fact that Māyā is predestined to die immediately after fulfilling her birth-giving function strongly suggests that this function is what defines her—whereas depicting a mother killed in childbirth might suggest that birth-giving was merely an unfortunate event that cut short the life of a woman otherwise destined to engage in many other life-events. The length of Māyā's life-span, its preordained nature, and the reasons offered for its necessity thus all work together to reinforce Māyā's status as the idealized birth-giver, one who performs her function perfectly and then quickly exits the scene.

I conclude this consideration of Māyā's death with one final reason offered for its necessity—one that appears less often than some of the others but plays a larger role in my own analysis. The *Lalitavistara*, after speaking of Māyā's early death, notes that this is true of the mothers of all other bodhisattvas as well: "And why? Because if a bodhisattva were to grow up, become fully mature, and leave home to become an ascetic, his mother's heart would break [Skt. *sphuṭet*]."[59] Here we gain a sense of some of the problems caused by allowing the birth-giver continued life. Instead of fulfilling her function and then departing, the mother who survives becomes an autonomous human being—one with whom the son has an intimate relationship and whose emotions must be considered. The survival of this mother, moreover, might lead to conflict when the son later decides to renounce the world: She brings him into life and suffers endlessly on his behalf, yet he chooses to pursue his own spiritual goal, renounce the world, leave behind the life of the household, and reject his relationship with her. Although we know from various kinds of evidence (to be discussed in chapter 8) that Buddhist monks in India did not necessarily sever all ties with their families on renouncing the world, there is still plenty of evidence in Buddhist literature for the significant sense of guilt some monks must have felt for their formal renunciation of familial ties, as well as anxiety over the debt still owed to their mothers for their nurturance and care. One significant feature of Māyā as an idealized mother, therefore, is that, through her early death, she spares her son both debt and guilt—by neither raising him nor grieving over his renunciation of the world. The physical erasure of Māyā we have seen throughout the entire birth-giving sequence thus continues in the form of her emotional erasure from the remainder of the Buddha's life.[60] In all of these ways, as we will see, Māyā's character stands in stark contrast to that of Mahāprajāpatī.

Māyā and Mary: Alone of All Their Sex

> She . . . had no peer
> Either in our first mother or in all women
> Who were to come. But alone of all her sex
> She pleased the Lord.
> —Caelius Sedulius (on the Virgin Mary)[61]

The logic that governs Māyā's depiction as an idealized birth-giver who alone is capable of giving birth to the holy one can be further clarified by considering how similar it is to the logic governing the depiction of the

Virgin Mary as the mother of Jesus Christ. The details are significantly different, of course, but the underlying imperatives are much the same: Just as the Buddha had to be portrayed as both a human being and a superhuman buddha, so Jesus had to be portrayed as both fully human and fully divine. In both cases, much of the burden of these portrayals fell upon the bodies and persons of their mothers.

The comparison begins at the moment when each mother is "chosen": Just as Māyā becomes the bodhisattva's mother through a careful and conscious deliberation (on the part of the bodhisattva) that removes her maternity from the ordinary workings of karma and samsara, so Mary experiences the Annunciation, the revelation by the Angel Gabriel that she will conceive the Son of God. In the Gospel according to Luke, Mary's singularity and uniqueness are emphasized by describing her as one who is "blessed . . . among women" (1: 42) and has "found favor with God" (1: 30)—such that *she alone* is fit to become the mother of Jesus.[62] Both women are singled out as the only appropriate vessels, yet both women remain wholly passive in the act of designation itself (which is instead undertaken by male figures). In both cases, conception itself occurs in a wholly purified manner, without any sexual intercourse, and attention is deflected away from the mother's vagina toward other parts of their bodies: Māyā conceives the bodhisattva when he enters into her right side, while Mary conceives Jesus through the words of the Angel Gabriel, which was sometimes interpreted to mean that she conceived Jesus through her ear. Thus, in a sixth-century Latin hymn attributed to Venantius Fortunatus, it is said that "the angel bore the seed, the virgin conceived through her ear, and, believing in her heart, became fruitful."[63] In both cases, conception is separated not only from the sexual act, but also from those parts of the mother's body associated with the sexual act.

One stark and obvious difference between these two conceptions, of course, is the insistence, in Christianity, on Mary's virginity at the time of conception. No such claim is made of Māyā, who is said to have conceived the bodhisattva fairly late in life, after many years of marriage to King Śuddhodhana; thus, presumably, she was not a virgin at the time of conception, and there seems to have been no motivation to claim that she was.[64] In spite of this difference, however, once the baby has been conceived, both traditions seem equally intent on ensuring the physical integrity and purity of the mother's body from that point onward—both during the birth process itself and forever after. Thus, just as giving birth leaves Māyā's body "uninjured and unscarred" and her womb "unobstructed and whole,"[65] so Christians came to assert much the same of Mary. According to the thirteenth-century work *The Meditations on the Life of Our Lord,* Mary (much like Māyā) gave birth painlessly and standing up, and "the Son of the eternal God came out of the womb of the mother without a murmur or lesion, in a moment";[66] similarly, the sixteenth-century Jesuit theologian Francisco Suarez declares: "That troublesome weariness with which all pregnant women are burdened, she alone did not experience."[67] The early fathers of the church routinely assert that even during the process of giving birth, Mary's womb remained "closed" and her virginity intact. How this could be possible remains a divine mystery best explained through evocative imagery: In one hymn from the thirteenth century, Jesus's birth is compared to "the sun enter[ing] and pass[ing] back through a windowpane without piercing it"[68]—once again invoking the *transparency* of the ideal mother's womb (and thus the erasure of the mother herself in favor of the fetus she is carrying).

This physical integrity of the mother's body, moreover, continues to be preserved long after the birth itself. In the case of Māyā, it is preserved by having the mother die and be removed to the sphere of heaven before any further violation of her body can occur. This reasoning is made explicit by the tradition itself: As we saw earlier, the unseemliness of such a body either engaging in sexual intercourse or enduring another pregnancy after bearing such a holy one is cited as the very reason why Māyā (and all mothers of buddhas) *must* die shortly after giving birth. Mary, on the other hand, survives for many years, thereby raising the question of her continuing physical purity after Jesus's birth—a question made more problematic by the New Testament's several suggestions that Mary and Joseph did indeed consummate their marriage and conceive other children after Jesus was born. Nevertheless, the inherent logic of the idealized mother seems to have ensured that the doctrine of Mary's perpetual virginity would quickly take hold, with prominent Christian thinkers throughout the centuries asserting fervently that Mary remained a virgin throughout her entire life and that the siblings of Jesus mentioned in the New Testament should be interpreted as cousins, other relatives, or children of Joseph from a previous marriage.[69] This view of Mary as *virgo intacta* throughout her life is still prevalent today among Catholics, Eastern Orthodox, and Lutherans. The significant energy expended over the centuries in defending Mary's perpetual virginity against its detractors demonstrates one of the problems with allowing such an idealized birth-giver continued life—a problem Buddhism avoids altogether by killing the mother off.

Two additional beliefs about Mary that came to be asserted as dogmas within the Roman Catholic Church further suggest the difficulty of maintaining the idealized nature of a birth-giver who survives long beyond the context of the birth itself. The Immaculate Conception of Mary, declared as official church dogma by Pope Pius IX in 1854 after many centuries of reflection and debate, holds that Mary herself was conceived without any stain of original sin and was therefore wholly perfect and wholly pure, incapable of sinning in any way from the very moment of her birth.[70] This purity from the moment of birth leads directly to a corresponding purity at the moment of death: The Assumption of Mary, declared as official church dogma by Pope Pius XII in 1950 but described in apocryphal Christian sources since at least the fourth century, holds that "the immaculate Mother of God, the ever Virgin Mary, having completed the course of her earthly life, was assumed body and soul into heavenly glory."[71] In other words, Mary's body was not subject to putrefaction in the grave, but was taken up into heaven at the moment of her death. So great is the pressure of maintaining the birth-giver's purity, in other words, that if the birth-giver is to live out an entire life, then not only must the conception, pregnancy, and birth-giving be pure, but in addition, the mother's own inherent purity from the moment of birth up to the moment of death and beyond must also be dogmatically asserted—even if such assertions threaten to undermine the essentially *human* status of the mother herself. Taken together, Mary's Immaculate Conception and Assumption are functionally equivalent to Māyā's death shortly after giving birth, for both have the effect of "freezing" the idealized mother in the purified moment of birth-giving.

The similar logic underlying the depictions of Māyā and Mary as idealized mothers who are reduced to their status as purified vessels for the delivery of their sons will become yet clearer as we turn to a very different vision of motherhood—that embodied in the figure of Mahāprajāpatī.

4

"Who Breastfed the Blessed One after His Mother Had Died"

NURTURANCE, GUILT, AND DEBT IN THE TRADITIONS SURROUNDING MAHĀPRAJĀPATĪ

I TURN NOW to the Buddha's other mother, the woman who raised him into young adulthood and whose relationship with the Buddha presents us with a very different depiction of motherhood. Mahāprajāpatī Gautamī (P. Mahāpajāpatī Gotamī), as Māyā's sister and co-wife, is the most obvious choice to become the bodhisattva's foster mother once Māyā herself has died. Nevertheless, several texts depict Mahāprajāpatī's status as foster mother to again be the result of a conscious and careful deliberation. In the *Lalitavistara*, for example, as soon as Māyā has passed away, King Śuddhodhana's advisers gather together and ask themselves: "Who indeed is capable of protecting, caring for, and cherishing the bodhisattva, with a heart that is benevolent, affectionate, good, and gentle?"[1] And although fifty different women all clamor for the job, the eldest royal adviser concludes: "All of these women are young, tender, and immature, intoxicated by pride in their own youth and beauty. They won't be able to look after the bodhisattva day after day. But the prince's mother has a sister, Mahāprajāpatī Gautamī. She is capable of raising the prince properly and with happiness. And she can also support King Śuddhodhana."[2] The *Buddhacarita* further notes that Mahāprajāpatī "was equal to [Māyā] in majesty and indistinguishable from her in love and affection."[3] Thus Mahāprajāpatī is designated as the bodhisattva's official foster mother (though she is aided by thirty-two nurses).

Since most biographies of the Buddha pay little attention to his life as a child, we do not see much of the relationship between Mahāprajāpatī and her son as the boy is growing up. Nevertheless, the literature as a whole consistently emphasizes her role as the mother who breastfeeds,

FIGURE 4.1 Mahāprajāpatī nursing the future Buddha. (As far as I know, no such image of Mahāprajāpatī nursing has been found in South Asia.) Chinese, Yuan dynasty, early 14th c. CE. Ink and color on silk. Wang Zhenpeng, Chinese, active about 1280–1329. Museum of Fine Arts, Boston, Special Chinese and Japanese Fund. Photograph © 2012 Museum of Fine Arts, Boston.

nurtures, and raises him (Figure 4.1). As Ānanda points out in the *Dakkhiṇāvibhaṅga Sutta*, "Mahāpajāpatī Gotamī, Venerable Sir, has been very helpful to the Blessed One; she was his maternal aunt and foster mother, and she nourished him, gave him milk, and breast-fed him when his mother had died."[4] Buddhaghosa, commenting on this passage, further elaborates with some intimate details:

> "Foster mother" means that she brought him up. When his hands and feet were incapable of doing what they were supposed to do, she attended to his hands and feet and took care of them—this is the meaning. "Nourished him" means that two or three times every day, she bathed him, fed him, made him drink, and nourished him. Regarding "breast-fed him": It is said that Prince Nanda [i.e., Mahāpajāpatī's own biological son with King Suddhodhana] was younger than the bodhisatta by several days, but when he was born, Mahāpajāpatī gave her own son over to wet-nurses, and herself performing the duties of a wet-nurse for the bodhisatta, she gave him her own breast.[5]

So committed was Mahāprajāpatī to the task of mothering the bodhisattva that she even gave up caring for her own newborn son—a powerful indication of the many sacrifices she must have endured on the bodhisattva's behalf. In the *Abhiniṣkramaṇa Sūtra*, moreover, Mahāprajāpatī's tireless care is directly related to the successful growth and health of the young prince:

> Thus she sedulously attended him without intermission, as the sun tends on the moon during the first portion of each month, till the moon arrives at its fulness. So the child gradually waxed and increased in strength; [just] as the shoot of the Nyagrodha tree gradually increases in size, well-planted in the earth, till [it] itself becomes a great tree, thus did the child day by day increase, and lacked nothing.[6]

In addition to Mahāprajāpatī's physical nurturance of the bodhisattva, the *Lalitavistara*—the only traditional biography to pay significant attention to the bodhisattva's childhood—offers us a few fleeting glimpses of the emotional connection between mother and son. When the baby Siddhārtha is brought to the Śākyas' temple to pay honor to the traditional gods, for example, Mahāprajāpatī dresses him up and tells him where they are going, and he informs her what will happen when they get there: the gods will honor him instead.[7] When five hundred sets of jewels are made for the young bodhisattva, Mahāprajāpatī is described as holding him in her arms while the jewels are being put on (whereupon they immediately lose their luster).[8] And when Siddhārtha, as a child, travels to a farming village and engages in his first meditative experience under a rose-apple tree, Mahāprajāpatī and Śuddhodhana are described as searching for him, with Mahāprajāpatī urgently imploring Śuddhodhana that her son must be found.[9] Despite the relative lack of attention paid to the bodhisattva's childhood, then, it is clear that Mahāprajāpatī is a nurturing and caring mother who is both physically and emotionally invested in her son. It is also clear that the bodhisattva, as a human child, depends on this mother for her many services. The mutual reciprocity characteristic of this relationship sets the background for what is to follow.

We do not hear much more about Mahāprajāpatī until the time comes for the bodhisattva to perform his Great Renunciation. It is at this point that Mahāprajāpatī's extreme attachment to her son becomes clear in the significant attention paid in the biographies to her enormous grief on seeing her son depart the world. In fact, throughout this episode, Mahāprajāpatī is consciously depicted as a grieving mother quite similar to the grieving mothers of the *Therīgāthā*. Although her son has not actually died, renunciation does constitute a kind of "social death," as it were, and the texts make it all too apparent that Mahāprajāpatī's grief is no less than that of Ubbirī, Paṭācārā, or Kisā Gotamī. In several passages, moreover, Mahāprajāpatī's long care of the bodhisattva and the grief she will experience on his renunciation are used by other characters to argue *against* the bodhisattva's decision to renounce. It is thus my contention that although the bodhisattva's guilt over abandoning his mother is never explicitly addressed or stated, it is nevertheless strongly suggested through the depiction of Mahāprajāpatī's great suffering. It is here that we begin to see the complex emotions of guilt, anxiety, and indebtedness that result when the mother survives.

In the *Buddhacarita*, for example, when Siddhārtha is first embarking on the Great Renunciation, his charioteer Canda urges him to reconsider, for if he does renounce the world, he will be abandoning his father, Śuddhodhana; his mother, Mahāprajāpatī; his wife, Yaśodharā; and his newborn son, Rāhula, as well as Canda himself. Each affected person is the subject of a separate verse, and the verse devoted to Mahāprajāpatī explicitly mentions her long-suffering care of the bodhisattva: "You should not forget the queen, your second mother, who completely exhausted herself bringing you up, like an ungrateful man forgets kind treatment."[10] Clearly, Canda is attempting to induce a sense of guilt within Siddhārtha, hoping that it will prevent him from leaving the world. Interestingly enough, Siddhārtha answers Canda's argument, in part, by using his *other* mother, Māyā, as an example of the impermanence of all such relationships: "The mother who bore me in her womb with great desire and much suffering—her efforts have been fruitless. What am I to her and what is she to me?"[11] Reading between the lines, we might say that Canda cites the "problematic" mother, Mahāprajāpatī, and her nurturance of the bodhisattva as a tie that binds Siddhārtha to the world, whereas Siddhārtha counters by citing the "good" mother, Māyā, and her early death as the permission he needs to depart.

Later on, after discovering that the bodhisattva has indeed left home, Mahāprajāpatī is presented as the very picture of the mother in grief: "Then Gautamī, the king's chief queen, as full of love for her son as a buffalo-cow who has lost its calf, flung her arms [into the air] like a golden plantain tree with its leaves shaking, and fell down [to the ground] weeping."[12] With a "tear-strewn face and eyes trembling with despair, suffering like a female osprey who has lost its young," she "lost her self-composure and cried out loud, gasping for air."[13] The comparison of Mahāprajāpatī to both a buffalo-cow and an osprey suggests the animal-like nature of the mother driven mad with grief. This suggestion is made yet again when King Śuddhodhana's chief minister and chief priest are sent into the forest to convince the fledgling ascetic Siddhārtha to return back home, and they do so, in part, by again invoking his mother's enormous suffering: "Consider the queen, who brought you up . . . who is weeping pitifully and constantly suffering, like a loving mother cow longing for its lost calf."[14] Mahāprajāpatī's grief over the departure of her son has thus reduced her to the state of a helpless and pitiable animal.

A similar picture of Mahāprajāpatī as a mother in grief emerges from the same scene, as depicted in the *Lalitavistara*. Here, however, Mahāprajāpatī herself actively attempts to prevent the bodhisattva's departure. When she learns of his intention to renounce the world, she instructs the women of his harem: "Use singing and dancing, and stay awake and alert throughout the night! Guard the prince, so that he does not leave without anyone knowing!"[15] Even further, she tells them that they should close and lock all of the doors; arm themselves with daggers, swords, and javelins; surround his bed to prevent him from leaving home; keep constant guard over him; and help each other not fall asleep. Here we are reminded of the way in which the grieving mother becomes a privileged emblem of the bonds of samsara: If samsara is indeed a "man-trap" and "women are the agents of incarceration,"[16] then the prospect of abandonment by her son has driven Mahāprajāpatī to become the very embodiment of the clutches of samsara. Moreover, once Siddhārtha has succeeded, despite these measures, in escaping from the palace unseen,

Mahāprajāpatī is predictably plunged into grief: She collapses and rolls on the ground, moaning to her husband: "Great King, quickly get me back my son!"[17] When Canda returns to the palace with the royal ornaments the prince has renounced, the sight of them causes Mahāprajāpatī such torment that she demands they be thrown into a pond. In this way, the *Lalitavistara*'s earlier glimpses of the loving relationship between Mahāprajāpatī and the young boy Siddhārtha now find their unhappy fulfillment in the form of a delusional and grief-stricken mother abandoned by her beloved son.

A comparison of two passages taken from two additional biographies will further solidify the contrast between Mahāprajāpatī as the mother who grieves over her son's departure, and Māyā as the mother who has already exited the scene. It is a well-established tradition that on the night of the bodhisattva's Great Renunciation, the gods magically put everyone in the palace to sleep so that he could escape from the city unseen. As this is happening, according to the *Mahāvastu*, Siddhārtha's charioteer Canda wonders why nobody is waking up to intervene—including Māyā (as a deity in heaven), who must surely be asleep:

> Even the goddess [Māyā], after being awake for a very long time . . . lies blissfully asleep in the excellent city of the gods . . . at the very moment when the Best of Men is leaving home. She, the queen and the mother of the Lord of Men, whose lovely eyes are [usually] wide with affection, is now overpowered by sleep and does not hear me as I speak to her mournfully and look upon [her] separation from a loved one.[18]

Māyā's blissful ignorance of her son's renunciation can be contrasted with Mahāprajāpatī's anxious foreboding. In the *Abhiniṣkramaṇa Sūtra*, Mahāprajāpatī, as a member of the palace compound, has also magically been put to sleep—yet her sleep is troubled by an inauspicious dream: "She thought she saw a white ox-King in the midst of the city going on in a wistful way bellowing and crying, whilst no one in the place was able to get before it to stop or hinder it."[19] The contrast between Māyā's deep slumber and Mahāprajāpatī's fitful sleep—between Māyā's blissful ignorance and Mahāprajāpatī's anxious dread—again reminds us that Mahāprajāpatī, through her survival, is destined to grieve and suffer over her son's abandonment of worldly life, whereas Māyā, through her death, has been "frozen" into the blissful state of Birth-Giver.

Although the passages discussed above give us ample evidence of Mahāprajāpatī's long nurturance of the bodhisattva, her grief when he renounces the world, and the use of this grief by other characters to argue against his renunciation, we have not seen any indication yet of a resulting sense of *guilt* on the part of her son. I would argue, however, that in another episode from the *Mahāvastu*, this guilt is strongly suggested.[20] Here we learn that when the fully enlightened Buddha returned home to Kapilavastu (six years after becoming a buddha) and performed the "Twin Miracle," Mahāprajāpatī was unable to witness it because "at the time when the Blessed One left home, Mahāprajāpatī Gautamī's eyes, because of her crying and grieving, seemed to be covered over by membranes, and she had become blind."[21] Clearly, there is some suggestion of *guilt* here, the son's renunciation of the world and abandonment of his mother being directly responsible for her extreme grief and resulting blindness. There is also, however, a kind of magical resolution, for the Buddha's ex-wife Yaśodharā, wishing for Mahāprajāpatī to see the miracle, "filled her cupped hands with water gathered from the five hundred streams flowing from the Blessed One's body as he performed his miracle, and bathed Mahāprajāpatī's eyes. And through the power of the Buddha, the membranes [covering her eyes] broke apart, and now, her sight became clear and faultless, just as before."[22] Thus, the abandonment of the mother is erased, the guilt caused by the mother's suffering is erased, the indebtedness toward the mother for her care is erased—and all of this occurs through a sort of *reverse breastfeeding*, where the *son* showers the *mother* with a nourishing and healing liquid rather than the other way around. The son's guilt over abandoning his mother is thus expressed through a fanciful story that denies and reverses it.

Even this willful fantasy is not enough, however, for we then learn that the Buddha similarly cured Mahāprajāpatī's blindness in a previous life as well, when the two of them were mother and son elephants. This *jātaka* appears in both prose and verse[23] and depicts the bodhisattva as exactly the kind of dutiful son that he would later fail to be. Thus the son elephant dutifully and intimately cares for his mother even when he is an adult himself:

> When he grew up, he served his mother with great respect and affection. He gave food and drink to her before enjoying them himself, and from time to time, he bathed and wiped clean his mother's tall body with a forest vine. In this way, the young elephant attentively served his mother at all times with kindness, affection, and respect.[24]

Moreover, instead of leaving his mother willingly (as Prince Siddhārtha would later do), the son elephant is captured by a king completely against his will, and while in the king's possession, he is so overcome by worry about his mother that he "sighed deeply, let his tears fall, languished, and withered away."[25] When the king learns the reason for his constant brooding, he is deeply impressed:

> How wonderful it is that this young elephant should honor his mother so much and be so righteous and noble that he has not accepted food or had anything to drink for so many days, because of his grief for his mother! Very few are the men who possess the virtues that this young elephant has. It would not be proper or fitting for us to harm such noble beings as him.[26]

The king thus decides to set the elephant free, and the elephant rushes back home to find that "his mother, weeping with grief and not seeing her dear son, had become blind."[27] He responds as only a dutiful son would do:

> Then the young elephant broke off a tender forest vine and used it to wipe his mother clean and remove the dust from her body. Pleased, satisfied, and delighted, full of joy and happiness, he filled his trunk with water from a pool and bathed his mother. And once she had been bathed, her eyes washed clean, all dirt rubbed away, and all impurities removed, her sight became clear and spotless.[28]

Thus, the bodhisattva, as an elephant, does everything that the bodhisattva, as a human prince, fails to do: He takes care of his mother, he does not willingly leave her, he is focused only on her welfare, and he repays the debt that he owes.

I would argue that this *jātaka* constitutes a sort of fantasy—displaced into a previous lifetime—meant to eradicate the son's underlying guilt over abandoning his mother. The experiences of grief and suffering, in fact, are here subject to a complete reversal: Emphasis is placed on the *son's* grief and suffering over not being there for his mother, rather than on the *mother's* grief and suffering over being abandoned by the son. What happened between the Buddha and Mahāprajāpatī in their previous lifetimes as elephants thereby helps the tradition to ameliorate whatever guilt may have been incurred in the present. Interestingly enough, in addition to the mother and son elephants being identified as previous births of Mahāprajāpatī and the Buddha, the king who sets the elephant free to return to his mother is further identified as a previous birth of Mahāprajāpatī's biological son Nanda. Reading between the lines, this suggests the further eradication of any lingering guilt that may have been felt toward the son Mahāprajāpatī abandoned as well.[29]

The traditions surrounding Mahāprajāpatī's motherhood of the bodhisattva thus weave together into a complex web the mother's nurturance of the son, the son's abandonment of the mother, the mother's intense grief, and the son's resultant guilt. What emerges is a rich portrait of the emotionally fraught relationship between mother and renunciant son—a relationship attributed to the Buddha himself, but perhaps equally reflective of the actual relationships experienced personally by the monastic authors who created and preserved these traditions. The translatability of this relationship to other situations is facilitated, moreover, by the fact that Mahāprajāpatī herself is depicted in a highly realistic manner. There is nothing unique about her physical or moral character, and although she is described as being virtuous and good, she is in no way set apart from the species of ordinary women. At the very least, this is a far cry indeed from the short-lived Māyā and her crystalline womb.

Indebtedness, Anxiety, and the Order of Nuns

Mahāprajāpatī's nurturance of the bodhisattva throughout his childhood is connected not only to the emotions of grief for the mother and guilt for the son, but also to the sense of an unresolved *debt* that demands to be repaid and whose repayment is explicitly linked to the Buddha's establishment of an order of nuns—which, according to Buddhist tradition, did not happen until five years after he had attained buddhahood, and then only at the request of Mahāprajāpatī herself. Although the connection drawn between Mahāprajāpatī's mothering and the establishment of an order of nuns has gone virtually unnoticed in previous scholarship, it is quite evident in the relevant texts themselves and therefore deserves to be examined at some length.[30]

The traditional story of the founding of the nuns' order is oft-repeated and well-known: According to the *Vinaya Piṭaka* of the Theravāda school,[31] in the fifth year after his enlightenment, the Buddha is dwelling among his own people, the Śākyans, in the city of Kapilavastu, when Mahāprajāpatī approaches him to make a request. At the time, Mahāprajāpatī has been recently widowed by the death of the Buddha's father, King Śuddhodhana, and she comes to the Buddha not only for herself but also on behalf of a large group of Śākyan women, most of whom have also been "widowed" by their husbands' ordination as Buddhist monks. Approaching her son, the Buddha, in humble submission, she states: "It would be good, Lord, if women were allowed to go forth from the home to the homeless life under the doctrine and discipline proclaimed by the Tathāgata."[32] The Buddha, however, without explicitly refusing her request, issues a sort of warning: "Stop, Gotamī! Don't set your mind on women going forth . . . !"[33] Mahāprajāpatī then makes the same request and receives the same reply a second and a third time. Then, "miserable" and "depressed" because the Buddha will not allow women to renounce the world, she departs, "crying, her face full of tears."[34] The Buddha then travels from Kapilavastu to Vaiśāli (said to be a distance of several hundred miles), followed all the way by Mahāprajāpatī and her companions, who have now shaved their heads and donned orange-colored monastic robes in an effort to prove their seriousness. She stands outside of the monastery hall in which the Buddha is staying, "her feet swollen, her body covered with dust, miserable, depressed, and crying, her face full of tears"[35] (Figure 4.2). The Buddha's attendant Ānanda encounters her there and learns the reason for her distress, whereupon he agrees to intercede on her behalf. He goes to the Buddha and makes exactly the same request another three times, but once again, the Buddha answers him with a similar warning. Clearly, the Buddha has no intention, at this point in the narrative, of establishing an order of nuns.

FIGURE 4.2 Mahāprajāpatī standing outside the monastery after the Buddha has refused to institute an order of nuns. Illustration by U Ba Kyi, from *The Illustrated History of Buddhism*, published in Rangoon by the Young Men Buddhist Association of Burma in 1951. Image courtesy of Young Men Buddhist Association.

It is at this juncture that Ānanda decides to take another approach:

> Then the Venerable Ānanda thought to himself: "The Blessed One will not allow women to go forth. . . . But suppose I were to ask the Blessed One in some other manner. . . ?"
>
> Then the Venerable Ānanda said to the Blessed One: "Lord, are women who have gone forth . . . capable of realizing the fruit of Stream-Entering, or the fruit of Once-Returning, or the fruit of Non-Returning, or Arhatship?"
>
> "Yes, Ānanda, women who have gone forth . . . are capable of realizing [all four fruits]."
>
> "Since, Lord, women who have gone forth . . . are capable of realizing [all four fruits], and, Lord, Mahāpajāpatī Gotamī was very helpful (P. *bahūpakārā*) to the Blessed One—serving as his aunt, foster-mother, caregiver, and giver of milk, who breastfed the Blessed One after his mother had died—it would be good, Lord, if women were allowed to go forth . . ."
>
> "If, Ānanda, Mahāpajāpatī Gotamī will agree to abide by eight strict rules, that itself will constitute her ordination."[36]

He then proclaims the eight "strict rules" (P. *garu-dhamma*) incumbent on all nuns, which Mahāprajāpatī willingly accepts, and the order of nuns is thus initiated. This is followed by the Buddha's famous prediction that although the Buddhist dharma would have lasted for one thousand years, it will now last for only five hundred years because of women's entrance into the Saṃgha, which he compares to such things as mildew attacking a field of rice and disease attacking a field of sugar cane.

Previous scholarship devoted to this much-discussed account has focused solely on the first of Ānanda's two arguments in favor of women's ordination—that is, the fact that women are fully capable of realizing the fruits of Stream-Entering, Once-Returning, Non-Returning, and Arhatship—often using this argument as evidence for the Buddhist tradition's inherent belief in women's spiritual equality with men. Virtually no attention has been paid, on the other hand, to the fact that Ānanda clearly offers up a second argument as well: *Mahāprajāpatī was the Buddha's mother and did such-and-such on his behalf.* Moreover, it is only after both arguments have been made that the Buddha suddenly relents. The question then becomes: Did the Buddha, as this passage presents him, agree to institute an order of nuns because of women's spiritual capability, or did he do so in order to repay Mahāprajāpatī for her mothering? Did he institute an order of nuns for all women, or did he do so for his mother in particular? I would argue that although this passage does not explicitly answer this question for us, at the very least it suggests that the two arguments were of equal importance in the Buddha's final decision and that those who composed and preserved this account felt it necessary to include both.

It is interesting to note, as well, that once Mahāprajāpatī has been ordained directly by the Buddha, the Buddha specifies that future nuns may henceforth be ordained by his monks. This causes the other nuns to later raise questions about the legitimacy of Mahāprajāpatī's ordination: "Our lady is not ordained," they claim, "but we are ordained, since the Blessed One declared that nuns should be ordained by monks."[37] The Buddha is then forced to clarify that Mahāprajāpatī has indeed been ordained: "As soon as Mahāpajāpatī Gotamī accepted the eight strict rules, that itself was her ordination."[38] This episode, though somewhat puzzling, seems to suggest that the other nuns may have been wary about any possible distinction being drawn between Mahāprajāpatī, as the Buddha's mother, and everyone else—for if female ordination had been established as a special favor for the Buddha's mother, then what did this imply about their own legitimate status as Buddhist nuns? Their questioning of the legitimacy of Mahāprajāpatī's ordination might simply reflect a defensive desire to make certain that ordination for *all women* had indeed been established, not merely ordination for the Buddha's mother.

The importance of Mahāprajāpatī's mothering in the establishment of the order of nuns is suggested yet again in another section of the Theravāda *Vinaya*. Here, shortly after the Buddha's death, the other monks are censuring Ānanda for five different offenses he committed throughout his life as a monk. The fifth offense concerns Ānanda's role in the establishment of the nuns' order and once again causes Ānanda to invoke Mahāprajāpatī's mothering:

[MONKS]: "Venerable Ānanda, this, too, is an offence committed by you: You worked hard so that women could go forth. . . . Confess to this offence!"

[ĀNANDA]: "Yes, Venerable Ones, I did work hard so that women could go forth . . . because it was Mahāpajāpatī Gotamī who served as the Blessed One's aunt, foster-mother, caregiver, and giver of milk, who breastfed

> the Blessed One after his mother had died. I do not see this as an offence, but out of faith in the Venerable Ones, I confess to it as an offence."[39]

Here, on the one occasion on which Ānanda is depicted explaining the motivation behind his actions, the reference to women's spiritual capability is nowhere to be found, and it is only Mahāprajāpatī's mothering that is cited: He worked hard on behalf of women's ordination *because Mahāprajāpatī mothered the Buddha*, not because women are capable of attaining nirvana. Moreover, Mahāprajāpatī's mothering of the Buddha also constitutes the reason why his efforts do not constitute an offense—a clear suggestion that this mothering, at least in the mind of Ānanda, rightfully deserved some sort of *repayment*. At the very least, this secondary and supporting passage suggests that we ought to pay some attention to the role Mahāprajāpatī's mothering plays within the original episode itself.

Nor is the reference to Mahāprajāpatī's mothering unique to the Theravāda version of these events alone. As Ann Heirman's thorough analysis of "all the different versions" of this story makes clear, it is a standard element in virtually every surviving version—appearing not only in the Theravāda *Vinaya* (and the identical passage found in the *Aṅguttara Nikāya*), but also, for example, in the accounts found in the *Mahīśāsaka Vinaya*, the *Mahāsāṃghika-Lokottaravāda Bhikṣuṇī-Vinaya*, the *Dharmaguptaka Vinaya*, the (Chinese) *Mūlasarvāstivāda Vinaya*, the *Sūtra on Gautamī* of the Sarvāstivādin *Madhyamāgama*, and a sūtra extant only in Chinese, the *Sūtra on the Bhikṣuṇī Mahāprajāpatī* (*Da ai dao bi qiu ni jing*).[40] Though the motherhood argument appears in a number of different manifestations, it is clearly an essential element of the story—which makes its utter neglect by the surrounding scholarship all the more surprising.

If we are to take this element seriously, I believe, then we must be led to posit the possibility that the Buddha, as this tradition presents him, did not institute an order of nuns for all women; instead, he did it because his mother Mahāprajāpatī asked him to, because he owed an enormous *debt* to Mahāprajāpatī for everything she had done on his behalf, and because despite his renunciation of the world and all social and familial ties, the tie to the mother—unlike the ties to father, wife, and son—was one that could not be broken. The debt the son owed to the mother had to be repaid, and this repayment was explicitly linked to the establishment of female monasticism—something depicted in highly negative terms as being akin to mildew invading a healthy crop and as a legitimate reason for the censuring of Ānanda. Indeed, throughout its history, the Buddhist tradition has proven itself to be highly ambivalent about the existence of an order of nuns.[41] Now we see the manner in which this ambivalence is intentionally connected by the Buddhist tradition to the Buddha's lingering debt toward Mahāprajāpatī as his mother.

Buddhist literature, in fact, gives us plenty of further evidence for ongoing, creative engagement with this "debt to the mother" theme, both in other versions of the same story and in other Buddhist texts. Let me begin with the version of the story found in the *Mahāsāṃghika-Lokottaravāda Bhikṣuṇī Vinaya* (hereafter abbreviated as *MLBV*) preserved in Buddhist Hybrid Sanskrit.[42] This version of the story has the same basic narrative structure as the Theravāda *Vinaya* account, but also many minor differences. Mahāprajāpatī makes her request only two times (rather than three), for example, and follows the Buddha to Śrāvasti rather than Vaiśāli. It is in Ānanda's arguments on behalf of women's ordination, however, that we find the most substantial differences. The crucial passage reads as follows:

> "Blessed One, how many assemblies did previous . . . fully enlightened buddhas have?"
>
> . . ."Previous . . . fully enlightened buddhas, Ānanda, had four assemblies—monks, nuns, laymen, and laywomen."
>
> . . ."Blessed One, can even a woman, if she dwells alone, attentive, zealous, and observant, realize the four fruits of the monastic life—the fruit of Stream-Entering, the fruit of Once-Returning, the fruit of Non-Returning, and the ultimate fruit of Arhatship?"
>
> . . ."Yes, Ānanda, even a woman, if she dwells alone, attentive, zealous, and observant, can realize these four fruits of the monastic life. . . ."
>
> . . ."Since, Blessed One, previous . . . fully enlightened buddhas had four assemblies. . ., and since even a woman, if she dwells alone, attentive, zealous, and observant, can realize these four fruits of the monastic life. . ., it would be good, Blessed One, if women were allowed to go forth under the doctrine and discipline proclaimed by the Tathāgata and receive ordination as nuns. Moreover, Mahāprajāpatī Gautamī performed some difficult deeds for the Blessed One; she nourished him, cared for him, and suckled him when his mother had died—and [for this] the Blessed One is grateful and appreciative."[43]

Here we find *three* arguments presented on behalf of women's ordination, rather than the usual two, the third argument being that all previous buddhas had such an order of nuns. More significantly for our purposes, however, we also find that a new element is added to Ānanda's motherhood argument: Not only does he describe what Mahāprajāpatī did on behalf of the Buddha, he also states rather bluntly that the Buddha is "grateful and appreciative" (Skt. *kṛtajño kṛtavedī*). This extra phrase has the effect of heightening the force of the motherhood argument, since it not only refers to the Buddha's debt, but also hints at the necessity for some form of repayment.

As if to rise to this additional challenge, however, in this version Ānanda's motherhood argument does not go unanswered by the Buddha (as it does in the Theravāda *Vinaya*). For now the Buddha, saying nothing at all about the first two arguments, addresses the motherhood argument alone:

> This is true, Ānanda, Mahāprajāpatī Gautamī did perform some difficult deeds for the Tathāgata, and she did nourish him, care for him, and suckle him when his mother had died—and [for this] the Blessed One is grateful and appreciative.
>
> Nevertheless, the Tathāgata, too, Ānanda, has also performed some difficult deeds for Mahāprajāpatī Gautamī. For it is thanks to the Tathāgata, Ānanda, that Mahāprajāpatī Gautamī has taken refuge in the Buddha, taken refuge in the Dharma, and taken refuge in the Saṃgha. It is thanks to the Tathāgata, Ānanda, that Mahāprajāpatī Gautamī has undertaken a life-long abstention from killing, stealing, sexual misconduct, lying, or drinking liquor, wine, or spirits. It is thanks to the Tathāgata, Ānanda, that Mahāprajāpatī Gautamī has grown in faith, grown in moral discipline, grown in learning, grown in generosity, and grown in wisdom. It is thanks to the Tathāgata, Ānanda, that Mahāprajāpatī Gautamī understands suffering, understands the arising [of suffering], understands the cessation [of suffering], and understands the path [leading to the cessation of suffering].[44]

Here we find a remarkable new twist: The Buddha explicitly acknowledges his debt toward Mahāprajāpatī, but proceeds to point out that Mahāprajāpatī is also indebted to him. It is not merely the case that she did much for him; instead, the Buddha makes it clear that he also did much for her. The indebtedness between mother and child moves in both directions and includes not only the mother's maternal care of her child, but also the child's spiritual care of his mother.

While the exact significance of this passage is difficult to determine, it seems to me that two different interpretations are possible. The more charitable interpretation might consider this passage merely as an exploration of the complex and lingering bond between parent and child—a mutual, loving, and beneficial bond that persists throughout time and continues to flow in both directions despite the son's supposed renunciation of familial ties. In this interpretation, there is no concern with debt and repayment as such, but only with paying respect to the continuing tie between mother and son. A less charitable interpretation, however, is also possible: Perhaps, under the surface, this passage is really concerned with the economics of *debt* and *repayment*. In other words, perhaps what the passage really wishes to suggest is that the mother's indebtedness toward her son so far exceeds the son's indebtedness toward his mother that the son's debt is effectively canceled out, and he stands fully exonerated of any obligation toward her. Thus, not only does the son *not* owe a debt to his mother, but in truth, it is the other way around: It is the *mother* who owes an incalculable debt to the *son*.

These two interpretations are not mutually exclusive; indeed, I believe the passage is complex in its significance, and both interpretations can be equally brought to bear. Nevertheless, it is the less charitable interpretation that seems to be supported by the Buddha's subsequent words, for immediately after this statement, he continues:

> Ānanda, when one person, thanks to another person, takes refuge in the Buddha, takes refuge in the Dharma, and takes refuge in the Saṃgha, it is not easy for the former to repay the latter. Even if she were to serve that person for her entire life—for example, [by providing him] with the standard monastic requisites of robes, almsfood, furnishings, and medicine to cure the sick—even then, it would not be easy to repay him.
>
> Ānanda, when one person, thanks to another person, undertakes a life-long abstention from killing . . . [etc.], . . . even then, it would not be easy to repay him.
>
> Ānanda, when one person, thanks to another person, grows in faith . . . [etc.], . . . even then, it would not be easy to repay him.
>
> Ānanda, when one person, thanks to another person, understands suffering . . . [etc.], . . . even then, it would not be easy to repay him.[45]

This is quite a remarkable passage placed into the mouth of the Buddha (even in the highly abbreviated form in which I have provided it). The crucial Sanskrit phrase used repeatedly here by the Buddha is *na supratikaraṃ bhavati*, "there would be no easy repayment," with *pratikaram* being derived from the verb *prati + kṛ*, meaning "to return, repay, requite, pay back (a debt)."[46] The passage thus makes explicit the Buddha's overriding concern with the issue of *repayment*, and has the Buddha state explicitly and repeatedly that such "repayment" would be virtually impossible for Mahāprajāpatī to accomplish, so indebted is she to her son. In just a few sentences, then, the text has moved from Ānanda's initial suggestion that the Buddha is indebted to Mahāprajāpatī to the diametrically opposed position that Mahāprajāpatī herself is so crushingly indebted to her son that any form of worldly repayment would be insufficient. The obvious discomfort that any notion of a "debt to the mother" causes for this text is revealed by the Buddha's overeagerness in downplaying it.

The kind of anxiety that I believe lies behind this passage can be further demonstrated, perhaps, by comparing it to another passage that is quite similar in its subject matter but very different in its emotional tone. In a passage from the *Aṅguttara Nikāya* (part of which we have already seen in chapter 1), the Buddha says:

> Monks, I say that there are two [people] whom it is not easy to repay (P. *na suppatikāraṃ*). Which two? One's mother and one's father. Monks, if a man were to carry his mother on one shoulder and his father on the other shoulder for as long as he lived, for a full one hundred years, and if he were to anoint and massage their bodies, bathe them, and knead them, and if they were to piss and shit all over him, even so, Monks, he would not repay or requite his mother and father.
>
> Moreover, Monks, if he were to establish his mother and father in kingship and lordly sovereignty over this [entire] great earth abounding with the seven treasures, even so, Monks, he would not repay or requite his mother and father. Why is that? Because, Monks, mothers and fathers do much for their children; they take care of them and nourish them and show them this world.[47]
>
> However, Monks, he who incites, exhorts, and establishes his unfaithful parents into the blessing of faith[,] . . . his immoral parents into the blessing of morality[,] . . . his stingy parents into the blessing of generosity[, . . . and] his foolish parents into the blessing

of wisdom—by doing just that much, Monks, he does repay, requite, and more than pay back his parents.[48]

This passage is striking in terms of its contrast with the Buddha's words in the *MLBV*. Whereas the Buddha of the *Aṅguttara Nikāya* emphasizes the enormity of the child's debt toward his parents, the Buddha of the *MLBV* emphasizes the enormity of the parent's debt toward the child. And, whereas the Buddha of the *Aṅguttara Nikāya* asserts confidence that the child's gift of the dharma might constitute a sufficient repayment for all of the nurturance provided to him by his parents, the Buddha of the *MLBV* expresses doubt that the parent could ever do anything sufficient to repay the child's gift of the dharma. It is interesting to note, as well, that the *Aṅguttara Nikāya* passage focuses on both parents, whereas the *MLBV* passage focuses on the mother alone. The two statements are polar opposites, and it is against the calm confidence of the Buddha's generic statement in the *Aṅguttara Nikāya* that we can see more clearly the high anxiety surrounding his words in the *MLBV*—an anxiety explicitly connected to Mahāprajāpatī as his mother. In the former passage, he speaks as a buddha, whereas in the latter passage, he speaks as his mother's son.

The argument I am pursuing here might be pushed even further by citing yet another Theravāda text—one that bears many similarities to the *MLBV* account we just looked at, but also some subtle and significant differences. This text is not a version of the story that establishes female monasticism, but seems to be closely related to it. The *Dakkhiṇāvibhaṅga Sutta* (*Majjhima Nikāya* No. 142) is well known for its detailed exposition of different types of gifts and the amount of merit deriving from each type, depending on such things as the worthiness of the recipient, the mental state of the donor, and so forth.[49] But although this sūtra is frequently cited in discussions of generosity and merit, virtually no attention has been paid to the fact that the opening section of the sūtra seems to have a close relationship to the story establishing female monasticism. For before engaging in its detailed exposition on gifts, the sūtra opens with Mahāprajāpatī making an unsuccessful request of the Buddha and Ānanda interceding on her behalf—and although Mahāprajāpatī's request has nothing to do with women's ordination, in every other manner the two accounts are quite similar.[50]

At the beginning of the sūtra, Mahāprajāpatī comes to the Buddha with a new pair of golden robes and says: "Lord, I have cut and woven this new pair of robes by myself, especially for the Blessed One. Lord, please let the

Blessed One, with compassion, receive and accept them from me."[51] The Buddha, however, refuses this request. "Give them to the Saṃgha, Gotamī," he says, "if you give them to the Saṃgha, both I and the Saṃgha will be honored."[52] Mahāprajāpatī then makes the same request a second time and a third time, but receives the same reply.[53] Perhaps there is already the suggestion of a mother/son dialectic at work here: Mahāprajāpatī has woven a pair of golden robes especially for her son and is pressing her particularistic claims on him, whereas the Buddha tries to deflect this claim by assimilating himself to the Saṃgha as a whole—he is merely a monk, like any other monk in the Saṃgha, and she has no particular claim on him. Buddhaghosa's commentary on this passage, in fact, supports this interpretation of a mother/son dialectic at work, for according to him, Mahāprajāpatī makes her request three times with the intention of driving home to her son this message: "Venerable Sir, because we have a storehouse full of clothing, I am capable of giving cloth robes to a hundred monks, to a thousand monks, and to a hundred thousand monks. But *this* [set of garments] has been cut and woven by me [specifically] on account of the Blessed One!"[54] Even if one does not accept this loaded reading, however, this text's similarity to the story establishing female monasticism in terms of basic narrative structure is obvious already.

It becomes yet more obvious when Ānanda then suddenly intercedes on Mahāprajāpatī's behalf. Here, of course, women's spiritual capabilities are irrelevant to the discussion, and it is only the motherhood argument that appears, with Ānanda asking the Buddha to accept the golden robes, since "Mahāpajāpatī Gotamī, Lord, was very helpful to the Blessed One—serving as his aunt, foster-mother, caregiver, and giver of milk, who breastfed the Blessed One after his mother had died."[55] In this case, however, instead of merely invoking the son's debt toward his mother, Ānanda now immediately continues with an enumeration of the mother's significant debt toward her son, in much the same terms as we saw the Buddha use in the *MLBV*: "And the Blessed One, too, Lord, has been very helpful to Mahāpajāpatī Gotamī, for it is thanks to the Blessed One, Lord, that Mahāpajāpatī Gotamī has gone for refuge to the Buddha . . ."—and so on, with a similar enumeration as we saw before.[56] In spite of this similarity, however, we again see a subtle intensification: This text is not content merely to have the *Buddha* downplay the son's debt toward his mother by also citing her significant debt toward him; now it is *Ānanda himself* who does this. Far from reminding the Buddha that he is "grateful and appreciative" (as before), Ānanda himself now deflates his own argument.

Now, in other words, we have a neutral and independent witness—someone other than the son himself—weakening the force of the son's indebtedness.

This intensification is subtle, no doubt, but it is further confirmed by the Buddha's reply, for unlike the Buddha of the *MLBV*, the Buddha of the *Dakkhiṇāvibhaṅga Sutta* does not even bother to acknowledge his debt toward Mahāprajāpatī (let alone the notion that he is "grateful and appreciative"). Instead, he ignores this aspect of Ānanda's comments completely and focuses solely on the impossibility of Mahāprajāpatī ever being able to repay him: "This is true, Ānanda, this is true! For when one person, Ānanda, thanks to another person, has gone for refuge to the Buddha . . . I say that it is not easy for the former to repay the latter . . ."—and so on, just as we saw in the *MLBV*.[57] Completely aside from the question of whose debt overshadows whose, the Buddha's comments here leave it unclear whether he owes his mother any debt whatsoever. Thus, although these two texts are quite similar in their narrative structure and phraseology, there are subtle differences between them that cause the *Dakkhiṇāvibhaṅga Sutta* to be an even stronger refutation of the son's debt toward his mother. In fact, without addressing the question of their precise historical relationships, it is clear that we can place the texts examined thus far onto a continuum of increasing discomfort with the son's debt toward his mother—a continuum proceeding from the grudging but implicit acceptance of this debt (Theravāda *Vinaya*), to the weakening of this debt by overshadowing it with Mahāprajāpatī's even greater debt toward the Buddha (*MLBV*), to the final refusal to acknowledge any debt whatsoever (*Dakkhiṇāvibhaṅga Sutta*).

What, then, might constitute the final point on this continuum? How could one go yet farther? While the *MLBV*, as we have seen, uses the Buddha to refute this debt, and the *Dakkhiṇāvibhaṅga Sutta* uses Ānanda, perhaps it would be even more remarkable if the *mother herself* were to do this: What if Mahāprajāpatī herself made it clear to us that the Buddha owes her nothing? This is precisely what we find, in fact, in yet another Theravāda text, the *Gotamī Apadāna* from the *Apadāna* collection.[58] In this biography of the life of Mahāprajāpatī, spoken largely by Mahāprajāpatī herself, we find a clear and explicit refutation of this debt addressed directly by Mahāprajāpatī to the Buddha: "You do not owe any debt to me!"[59] Now the mother herself, in other words, explicitly releases her son from any debt. Moreover, by *apologizing* to the Buddha for requesting an order of nuns, she makes it clear that there was no obligation on his part to establish one: "Chief of the World, women are indeed believed to be full of all sorts of faults. If there is any fault in me, forgive it, Mine of Compassion! I asked you over and over again to allow women to go forth. If I'm at fault for this, please forgive it, Bull Among Men!"[60] In fact, not only does Mahāprajāpatī acknowledge that it is *she* who owes an incalculable debt to *him*, but in addition, going beyond either Ānanda or the Buddha, she explicitly describes this debt through the metaphor of *parenting*. "I might be your mother," she states, "but you are my father, Hero . . . Gotama, I've been born from you! Well-Gone One, I may have nourished your physical body, but my faultless dharma-body was nourished by you. For I fed you the milk that quenches thirst for just a moment—but you fed me the dharma-milk that is perpetually tranquil."[61] Here we see yet another intensification: Not only does the mother herself acknowledge her indebtedness to her son, but this debt itself is now described as a *child's debt to her parent*, thus completely reversing the expected debt/repayment equation. The Buddha's spiritual "mothering" of Mahāprajāpatī is so superior to Mahāprajāpatī's mere worldly mothering of him that any notion of the son's debt toward his mother would seem ridiculous. In fact, it is the other way around: It is the *son* who constitutes the *true mother*, and the *mother* who constitutes the *indebted son*.

If we return for a moment to the *Dakkhiṇāvibhaṅga Sutta*, it is interesting to note that this same strategy—of inverting the parent/child relationship, so that the child becomes the "true" parent and the parent becomes the "true" child—is also apparent in two contexts loosely related to the *Dakkhiṇāvibhaṅga Sutta*, though not invoked within the sūtra itself. In the fifty-third dilemma of the *Milindapañhā*,[62] King Milinda expresses his confusion to the monk Nāgasena concerning the events portrayed in the *Dakkhiṇāvibhaṅga Sutta:* If the Buddha is the most supreme being in the world, the king asks, then Mahāprajāpatī would clearly have derived more merit from giving the golden robes to him than she would from giving them to the Saṃgha. So why did the Buddha instruct her to give them to the Saṃgha? Clearly, the correct, doctrinal answer to this question would be for Nāgasena to tell the king that his basic assumption is mistaken—for, in fact, a gift given to the Saṃgha is always more meritorious than a gift given to an individual, even if that individual is the Buddha (indeed, this point is made in the *Dakkhiṇāvibhaṅga Sutta* itself).[63] But this is not how Nāgasena responds. Instead, Nāgasena gives a completely different reason that the Buddha redirected these robes to the Saṃgha: He did it out of compassion for the Saṃgha, Nāgasena replies, because he knew that his statement would exalt the Saṃgha, make it worthy in the eyes of the public, and ensure its future prosperity—*just as a father exalts his son's virtues in public,* which does not necessarily mean that the son is more worthy than the father. Not only does this answer constitute an outright refutation of the *Dakkhiṇāvibhaṅga Sutta*'s own exposition of gifts and merit; it also executes a rather remarkable parent/child reversal: A scenario in which the Buddha is a child who is obligated to accept a gift from his parent has now been reinterpreted by Nāgasena in such a way that it is the Buddha himself who becomes the parent, graciously passing gifts directed toward him on to his children—the Saṃgha. The mother has been replaced by the father, and the Buddha himself has become the parent toward whom a debt of gratitude is owed, rather than being the indebted son. Nāgasena's choice of this particular simile is no coincidence, I believe, but constitutes an intentional rejection of the "debt to the mother" suggested by Mahāprajāpatī's attempt to give her son the golden robes.[64]

The same type of reversal, in which the Buddha's spiritual fatherhood takes clear precedence over Mahāprajāpatī's worldly motherhood, is also subtly invoked in another context related to the *Dakkhiṇāvibhaṅga Sutta*—a later but well-established tradition concerning the future destiny of these golden robes. This tradition (discussed at some length by Étienne Lamotte)[65] holds that these very same robes were subsequently given by the Buddha to one of his disciples as a marker of his prediction that this young man, in the far distant future, would one day become the next fully enlightened buddha, Maitreya. Thus while Mahāprajāpatī, as a worldly mother, fails in her effort to give these robes to her son, he, as a spiritual "father," succeeds in giving these very same robes to his spiritual "son" and successor, Maitreya. Spiritual fatherhood trumps worldly motherhood, and the spiritual lineage existing between past and future buddhas is seen to take precedence over the worldly lineage existing between mother and son. The fact that there are two separate traditions that both seem to execute the same kind of parent/child reversal in connection with the *Dakkhiṇāvibhaṇga Sutta* suggests to me that the tradition itself is grappling with the "debt to the mother" theme inherent within this text.

We have now come full circle in our analysis, and the debt/repayment equation between mother and son has become the very opposite of where we began, even though this has required me to venture away from the founding story of female monasticism to look at several other Buddhist texts. Let me conclude this discussion by returning to the original story itself and briefly considering two additional versions—versions that perhaps contain further suggestions of the relevance of the "debt to the mother" theme. The fragmentary *Bhikṣuṇī Karmavācanā* manuscript preserved in Sanskrit and deriving from the Mūlasarvāstivāda school[66] contains a version of the story establishing female monasticism in which Ānanda offers neither the spiritual-capability argument nor the motherhood argument; instead he simply repeats Mahāprajāpatī's original request, whereupon the Buddha suddenly agrees to institute an order of nuns. In this sense, it is irrelevant to the discussion I have undertaken here. Nevertheless, there is one unusual element of this version that perhaps pertains to the "debt to the mother" theme. For at the beginning of this version, when Mahāprajāpatī first asks the Buddha to allow women to be ordained, the Buddha answers that *Mahāprajāpatī alone* should be permitted to do so: "Just you alone, Gautamī, should practice, for your entire life, the monastic career which is perfectly pure and clean, with your head shaved and wearing the robes of a nun, just as you said. This will result in your welfare, benefit, and enjoyment for a very long time!"[67] Mahāprajāpatī is not satisfied by this, however, and continues to put forth the same request a second time and a third time, each time being told by the Buddha that she alone should be permitted to become a nun. It is only when Ānanda intercedes on her behalf that the Buddha finally agrees to allow women in general to go forth into the renunciant's life.

Not a word about motherhood is uttered, nor does any version of the motherhood argument appear. Nevertheless, this element of the story is highly unusual and would seem to demand some sort of explanation: Why on earth would the Buddha first decide that *only* Mahāprajāpatī should be allowed to ordain? If all women are capable of attaining nirvana, then why not extend the same right to all women? And if, on the other hand, "there should be no renunciation, ordination, or nunhood for women!"[68]—as the Buddha exclaims—then why make an exception for Mahāprajāpatī alone? It is only the "debt to the mother" theme, I would argue, that can make sense of this puzzling element: Women should not be permitted to ordain, yet the Buddha felt compelled to make an exception for his mother—and the force of this compulsion was nothing other than the debt he owed to her as her son. Though there is nothing explicitly stated to confirm this interpretation, the associated literature we have already examined suggests, at the very least, its potential—a possible subtext to the story that has heretofore been ignored.

Another such possible subtext can be detected in one final version of the story establishing female monasticism that might be brought to bear on this discussion. This is the version of the story found in the (Chinese) *Sūtra on the Bhikṣuṇī Mahāprajāpatī* (*Da ai dao bi qiu ni jing*, T. 1478), which, according to Heirman, was perhaps translated in the first half of the fifth century, though Akira Hirakawa suggests that it might be a purely Chinese compilation.[69] As Heirman notes, this version of the story, like many of the others, has Ānanda argue for women's ordination using both the spiritual-capability argument and the motherhood argument. It distinguishes itself from all other versions, however, by a significantly sharpened spirit of misogyny and hostility toward women. Thus women are compared to venomous snakes that people fear even after they have been killed; they are described as "a threat to all living beings, including plants," because "they all have 84,000 bad attitudes";[70] and so on. In fact, according to Heirman, in this version, "femininity itself is the cause of failure," and women are viewed as a dangerous "threat to the goals of Buddhist men personally."[71]

What Heirman fails to notice, however, is that this new element of severe misogyny seems to coincide with one additional new element in this account: a particular emphasis on *mothers*. Whereas most versions of the story state that Mahāprajāpatī is accompanied in her quest to become a nun by "many Śākyan women" or "five hundred Śākyan women," this version states explicitly that she is accompanied by "several old mothers."[72] It is thus a group of *mothers* who wish to renounce the world who provoke the Buddha's misogynistic statements. Moreover, when the Buddha refuses Mahāprajāpatī's request, it is specifically the ordination of *mothers* (not women in general) to which he objects and the negative qualities of *mothers* that he cites as his justification.[73] Finally, when Ānanda puts forth the spiritual-capability argument, he reminds the Buddha not that women can attain the four fruits of the monastic life but, rather, that *mothers* can do so.[74] It is at this point that he also makes use of the motherhood argument itself—thus implicitly linking the mother's ability to attain religious goals to the fact that she is owed an enormous debt by her son.

The extreme misogyny of this account is thus explicitly and consistently linked with a new emphasis on the theme of motherhood. Might this confluence be more than just a coincidence? I would speculate that within this text, it is specifically the *mother's* dogged determination to pursue a religious life, the *mother's* extreme persistence in seeking this opportunity, the *mother's* spiritual potential (which has to be admitted), and the *mother's* inherent right to demand this opportunity from her indebted son that are being struggled with—and it is the discomfort and hostility surrounding these things that perhaps result in the text's sharpened misogyny concerning the dangerous and deleterious effects of all women (but especially mothers). Again, as far as I can tell, there is nothing explicitly stated to substantiate this claim—but I do believe it becomes plausible once we learn to recognize and acknowledge the "debt to the mother" theme.

We have now traced the existence, sometimes explicit and sometimes only suggested, of a "debt to the mother" theme not merely in the Theravāda *Vinaya*'s version of the founding story of female monasticism but also in several other versions of the story and related Buddhist texts. Although each text offers us a slightly different resolution, all of them are dealing with the same basic problem: the son's indebtedness toward the mother who raised him and the possible relationship this indebtedness had with the existence of female monasticism and the troubling presence of women within the Saṃgha. I now conclude with some general comments on the historical and sociological background that might help to account for such a theme.

The basic structure of the Indian family is one very general phenomenon that would tend to support the existence of a "debt to the mother" theme, as well as some of the anxieties surrounding its expression. The original North Indian homeland of Buddhism is, and always has been, characterized by a predominantly patriarchal, patrilineal, and patrilocal culture—one in which descent, inheritance, and official status are passed down from father to son, leaving the mother as the natural focus of a son's love and affection. Moreover, as wives are brought into the patriline from the outside to produce male heirs, and marriages are a family matter arranged by the parents and demanding obedience from the son, the son continues, throughout much of his life, to be more strongly associated with his parents than with his newly acquired wife, the mother (rather than the wife) perhaps constituting his primary female object of affection. At the same time, the status of the wife within her husband's family is relatively low until she proves herself by producing a male heir. This causes her status within the family to rise and makes her heavily invested in and emotionally attached to her son, thereby further reproducing and reinforcing the mother/son bond from one generation to the next. Indian familial structure is thus characterized by a strong attachment between mother and son, and male Indian authors throughout history have glorified and exalted the mother's status. As with any intense relationship, however, the flip side of such love and attachment might very well be ambivalence, guilt, submerged hostility, and the overbearing burden of indebtedness. And in a patriarchal and patrilineal culture, whereas one's indebtedness to one's father has a recognized method of repayment in the form of producing one's own son to successfully continue the patriline, one's indebtedness to one's mother is inchoate and free-floating in nature and has no recognized outlet, thus resulting in anxiety about its repayment. Both the son's debt toward his mother and his anxiety about its repayment are thus well accounted for by Indian familial structure.

The men who composed and preserved Indian Buddhist texts, moreover, were not only the sons of their mothers. They were also the adherents of an elite religious tradition that often denigrates women and encourages the repudiation of all familial ties. Guilt and anxiety over repaying the debt to the mother must have been heightened in their case (one thinks of Mahāprajāpatī going blind with grief after her son renounces the world), while at the same time combined with a socially recognized identity—that of the renunciant—that perhaps encouraged them to deny the existence of any such lingering tie. Bernard Faure, in an East Asian context, has similarly argued that "monks cared so much about their mother precisely because they had lost (or abandoned) her, and because of their ambivalent feeling toward a person to whom they were deeply indebted, but whom they saw as (physically and sometimes morally) defiled."[75] I would speculate, then, that the son's unresolved feeling of indebtedness toward his mother was an underlying trope particularly vulnerable to being invoked by monastic authors in any situation characterized by anxiety surrounding women. The Buddha's decision to admit women into the monastic order was surely one such anxiety-provoking situation, due to the threat to male celibacy posed by the presence of women, as well as the disturbing sexual ambiguity characteristic of female renunciants. One troubling issue surrounding women thus called up the image of another, and the admittance of women into the Saṃgha became linked with the Buddha's unresolved debt toward Mahāprajāpatī. As the mother who survives long beyond the immediate context of birth-giving, Mahāprajāpatī, I contend, became a natural vehicle for such feelings of indebtedness, anxiety, and guilt.

If we return now to the larger comparison I am developing between Māyā and Mahāprajāpatī, it is clear from this discussion, I hope, that whereas Māyā is little more than a romantic fantasy and an impossible ideal, Mahāprajāpatī provides us with a much more realistic depiction of motherhood and of the mother's complex relationship to the son. Yet I hope also to have demonstrated how the two figures work together: Māyā, the idealized birth-giver, through her early death, spares her son both the guilt of abandoning his mother and the anxiety of being obligated to repay her, whereas Mahāprajāpatī, through her nurturance, care, and survival, allows the Buddhist tradition's renunciant sons an avenue of expression for guilt, anxiety, indebtedness, and other components of a complicated human relationship. In the next chapter, I will further substantiate this argument—and add another dimension to it—by looking at several contexts in which the two figures are directly compared.

5

"*Short-Lived*" *versus* "*Long-Standing*"

MĀYĀ AND MAHĀPRAJĀPATĪ COMPARED

AS WE HAVE seen, Māyā's status as the "good" mother who quickly exits the Buddha's life and thus leaves no lingering debt within the son becomes fully clear only when we contrast her with Mahāprajāpatī, the "problematic" mother who sticks around long enough to demand repayment for the debt her son has incurred. I believe this "sticking around" is an essential aspect of Mahāprajāpatī's character. In fact, I would describe Mahāprajāpatī as an overarching symbol of *displaced, leftover women*—women who become problematic once their men have departed on a spiritual quest, and women who do not conveniently die, as Māyā did, but instead continue to serve as living reminders of everything the son still owes to the mother, despite having renounced all familial ties.

Mahāprajāpatī's status as a "leftover" woman whose needs demand to be accommodated is, in fact, consistently developed throughout her entire life story. In an episode from the *Mahāvastu*,[1] we are told that when King Śuddhodhana decided to marry, he searched the entire country for an ideal wife. The ideal wife was Māyā, but she was the youngest of seven sisters and could not get married until her older sisters had done so. Thus, Śuddhodhana took all seven sisters (Mahāprajāpatī being the eldest), giving five of them to his brothers and keeping Māyā and Mahāprajāpatī for himself—Mahāprajāpatī thus becoming the representative of "leftover" women (or older spinster sisters) within Śuddhodhana's own house.[2] Subsequently, it was Māyā who first produced a son for Śuddhodhana (beating out Mahāprajāpatī by just a few days) and who predeceased her husband, as a good wife in India always should, whereas Mahāprajāpatī outlasted him to become an inauspicious widow—an "unattached" or "leftover" woman now needing the protection of her son. As Donald Lopez and Liz Wilson have rightly noted, in fact, Mahāprajāpatī's attempt to become a nun could be interpreted not as the act of a feminist trailblazer but instead in terms of the traditional, patriarchal Indian notion (derived from Manu) that a woman should always be dependent on her male kin—on her father before she is married, on her husband while she is married, and on her son once she has been widowed.[3] Thus, Mahāprajāpatī, having been widowed by the death of her husband Śuddhodhana, follows the traditional course of becoming dependent on her son—a dependency, moreover, that results in other women like her being allowed to invade the Saṃgha en masse. It is also pertinent to note that from this point on, Mahāprajāpatī becomes a corporate personality, for she is consistently associated with, and identified as the leader of, the large group of women who accompany her when she renounces the world. Her name itself, in fact, means "leader of a large assembly" and places her in stark contrast with the singular uniqueness characteristic of Māyā. Many of the women in Mahāprajāpatī's assembly, moreover, seem to have been women whose husbands had recently left them to be ordained as Buddhist monks—in other words, similarly "leftover" women.

Mahāprajāpatī's character as a "leftover" woman (and as a symbol of such women) thus remains consistent throughout her entire life: from the older spinster sister whose very existence complicates the ideal marriage between Śuddhodhana and Māyā, to the inauspicious widow who requires continuing protection once her husband has died, to the leader of an entire body of displaced women who are allowed to invade the Saṃgha based on Mahāprajāpatī's continuing hold over her son. In all of these ways, Mahāprajāpatī, by "sticking around," is the very opposite of the "short-lived" Māyā. Perhaps it is no surprise, then, that in the *Aṅguttara Nikāya*'s well-known lists of those monks and nuns who are the "foremost" in various different qualities, Mahāprajāpatī is described by the Buddha as the "foremost of those of long standing" (P. *aggaṃ rattaññūnaṃ*).[4] Although this designation is intended to be laudatory and refers most obviously to the fact that Mahāprajāpatī has more seniority than any other nun, we might also interpret it in a more negative light within the context of Māyā's short life span: It is the "short-lived" Māyā who appears as a chief queen, an auspicious wife, and the mother of the king's eldest son, and the "long-standing" Mahāprajāpatī who becomes an inauspicious widow, an unprotected mother, and, finally, a renunciant nun. It is the survival of the mother over time, in other words, that allows her to become a vehicle for anxiety and resentment.

The contrast I have drawn between Māyā and Mahāprajāpatī as "good" and "problematic" mothers—or as "short-lived" and "long-standing" mothers—is never made explicit, of course, but there are several contexts, scattered here and there, in which the two mothers are contrasted with each other in some intriguing and highly suggestive ways. In a *jātaka* found in the *Suvarṇabhāsottama Sūtra*,[5] for example, two of the characters are identified as the previous births of Māyā and Mahāprajāpatī, and these identifications are quite telling: A benevolent and compassionate queen whose breasts spontaneously lactate when she thinks that her son, the prince, might be in danger is identified as a previous birth of Māyā, whereas a starving tigress who has lost all mother-love for her cubs and is on the verge of devouring them, but then hungrily devours the human prince instead, thus causing his cruel and agonizing death, is identified as a previous birth of Mahāprajāpatī. The prince himself, of course, is a previous birth of the Buddha. In this remarkable juxtaposition of the previous lives of Māyā, Mahāprajāpatī, and the Buddha, we have Mahāprajāpatī devouring and consuming the Buddha at the precise moment that Māyā's breasts are lactating in a spontaneous effort to feed him. Thus, Māyā nourishes, whereas Mahāprajāpatī consumes and devours—an odd fantasy, of course, since it was actually Mahāprajāpatī who "breastfed the Blessed One after his mother had died."[6] And whereas the real Mahāprajāpatī selflessly forsook her own son Nanda in order to become a wet nurse to the foster baby Siddhārtha, Mahāprajāpatī-as-tigress does precisely the opposite, sparing her own offspring at the last minute and cruelly devouring the human prince instead. I would interpret this *jātaka* psychologically as a fantasy in which the son's crushing sense of debt toward his mother is dealt with by splitting the mother into "good" and "bad" aspects, demonizing the bad aspect as a cruel devourer, and falsely attributing all nourishment and care to the good aspect alone (who is conveniently dead now anyway).

A second intriguing contrast that can be drawn between Māyā and Mahāprajāpatī comes not from a single text, but from two separate yet well-established traditions involving the effect that the Buddha's relationship with each mother has on his teaching of the dharma. The debt the Buddha owes to Mahāprajāpatī results, as we have seen, in the existence of an order of nuns. And because of the creation of this order, the life of the dharma is shortened by half: What would have lasted for one thousand years, according to the Buddha's famous prediction in the Theravāda *Vinaya*, will now last for only five hundred, "just as a field full of rice will not endure for long if the sort of disease known as mildew befalls it."[7] The

Buddha's lingering debt toward Mahāprajāpatī thus causes the life of the dharma to be *cut in half*. The Buddha's relationship with Māyā, on the other hand, has a very different effect on his teaching of the dharma: It is a well-established tradition that the Buddha once spent an entire three-month, rainy-season retreat up in heaven, where Māyā had been reborn as a deity, preaching the dharma for her benefit. Though Buddhist traditions differ on the exact contents of this dharma,[8] the Theravāda tradition holds definitively that it was the *Abhidhamma Piṭaka* that the Buddha chose to preach, allowing human beings as well (through the offices of Sāriputta) to gain access to the wisdom of these teachings.[9] Thus, whereas the Buddha's tie to Mahāprajāpatī cuts the life of the dharma in half, his tie to Māyā results in the existence of the *Abhidhamma Piṭaka*—a "higher" and more concentrated form of the Buddhist dharma. (In Thailand, in fact, it is said that the Buddha believed that *only* the *Abhidhamma Piṭaka* was sufficient to honor his mother; neither the *Sutta Piṭaka* nor the *Vinaya Piṭaka* would do.)[10] Māyā, we might say, condenses and intensifies the "milk of the dharma," whereas Mahāprajāpatī seems only to curdle it. This contrast is quite similar, in fact, to the image found in the *jātaka* discussed above of a nourishing, lactating Māyā and a consuming, devouring Mahāprajāpatī.

It is clear, moreover, that while a lingering connection between mother and child is evident in both of these episodes, the emotional tone of this connection differs significantly from one to the other. Whereas the Buddha's tie to Mahāprajāpatī, as we have already seen, finds expression through the economic language of debt and repayment, his tie to Māyā does not seem to be subjected to such cold calculation, even when he is depicted as sojourning in heaven in order to preach the dharma for her benefit. In the *Dhammapada Commentary*,[11] the Buddha decides to undertake this task after coming to realize that this is an invariable rule for all buddhas. Even perfectly enlightened buddhas, then, cannot dissolve the tie to the mother; even buddhas—as a rule—remain dutiful sons who are responsible for ensuring their mothers' welfare. Nevertheless, this episode is always depicted in a wholly positive manner and free of the imagery of debt and repayment. In one Chinese version of the episode, in fact, Māyā lovingly breastfeeds the Buddha at the very same time as he lovingly teaches her the dharma.[12] Once again, the breast milk of the mother is exchanged for the dharma milk of the son—but this time without any anxious calculation of whose milk is superior. The lingering tie between mother and child is still recognized, in other words, but does not seem to become the object of any resentment.

A final context I might cite in which the contrast between Māyā and Mahāprajāpatī finds particularly odd expression is a passage from the *Udāna Commentary* in which the Theravāda commentator Dhammapāla conveys the opinion, held by some of his day, that the Buddha *would have instituted an order of nuns more willingly if it had been Māyā rather than Mahāprajāpatī who asked him to do so.*[13] According to this point of view, "even when Mahāpajāpatī Gotamī went to much trouble to beg the Blessed One for permission to go forth, she was [still] refused" (at least initially), whereas "if the Blessed One's biological mother Queen Mahāmāyā had lived, then . . . the Blessed One, out of veneration for his mother, would have very happily allowed women to go forth and receive ordination in his teaching; but because she was short-lived, this was accomplished [only] with great difficulty [by Mahāpajāpatī]."[14] Though Dhammapāla finds this view to be "baseless" (P. *akāraṇaṃ*) and says that the Buddha had to be cautious about allowing women's ordination—"whether [he did so] for his mother or for anyone else"[15]—the very fact that this opinion was current among some of Dhammapāla's acquaintances is worthy of note. It suggests a certain hostility toward Mahāprajāpatī and a resentment toward her demands, along with a corresponding idealization of Māyā as the venerated mother for whom the son would willingly have complied with any request—if only she had lived, of course. Here, as throughout the tradition, the "short-lived" Māyā and the "long-standing" Mahāprajāpatī are opposed to one another in a very particular way: A quick death, we might say, is the price paid by Māyā for her exalted status—whereas the survival of Mahāprajāpatī breeds only resentment.[16]

Māyā and Mahāprajāpatī in the Pali Jātakas

It is a well-known feature of Buddhist cosmology that the relationships the Buddha has with various characters within his previous lifetimes as a bodhisattva (as recounted in the *jātakas*) often run parallel to the relationships he later has within his final lifetime as a fully enlightened Buddha. Thus those who show enmity against the bodhisattva are often identified as previous births of the Buddha's evil cousin Devadatta, those who father the bodhisattva as previous births of the Buddha's father King Śuddhodhana, and those who marry the bodhisattva as previous births of the Buddha's wife Yaśodharā. In this way, the Buddha's relationships with those around him are seen to be long-standing in nature and are given a sense of karmic depth by being extended into the far distant past. From this perspective, the 547 *jātakas* gathered together in the Pali *Jātaka* collection might offer us yet another perspective on the contrast between Māyā and Mahāprajāpatī.

The first observation one might make in this regard is the general favoritism shown toward Māyā. As far as I can tell,[17] the mother of the bodhisattva is identified as a previous birth of Māyā in at least twelve different stories in the Pali collection, whereas Mahāprajāpatī appears in only two—suggesting a general preference for Māyā over Mahāprajāpatī. Moreover, although neither mother appears in a wholly consistent role throughout the collection, there are some suggestive differences between them that conform to the analysis I have presented above.

In chapter 3, I spoke of the erasure of Māyā, or the way in which the "good" mother—though highly idealized—is also made transparent or given an illusory quality. Correspondingly, it is striking to note that the Māyā of the Pali *jātakas* is often a figure whose motherhood of the bodhisattva is somehow backgrounded or diminished in favor of the connection between father and son. In the *Kaṭṭhahāri Jātaka* (No. 7),[18] for example, a lowly woman gives birth to a son, who is noble by nature because he has been fathered by a powerful king. The woman performs an Act of Truth that forces the king to recognize his paternity, and thus the son assumes his rightful succession to the kingship. The lowly mother plays an active and virtuous role, yet her only function in the story is to assert the essential link between father and son. This woman is a previous birth of Māyā. In the *Alīnacitta Jātaka* (No. 156),[19] an infant prince whose kingly father has died and whose kingdom is being attacked by an enemy king must rely on a sort of "substitute father"—a noble male elephant—to step in and save the day so that he can inherit his father's kingship. The mother of the infant prince, who proves to be powerless in this situation, is a previous birth of Māyā. Likewise, in the *Susīma Jātaka* (No. 163),[20] a young man possesses a hereditary right to the occupation of his father, but when his father dies, some evil brahmins attempt to steal this right away from him. Using his own wits and talents, he succeeds in preserving this right, while his mother merely stands by and cries. The helpless mother, once again, is a previous birth of Māyā. In all three stories, then, the link between father and son and the continuing rights and obligations that stem from this link are emphasized, while the mother's role is diminished. This is somewhat reminiscent of the illusory quality attributed to the "short-lived" Māyā, the desire to remove her quickly from the life of the son, and the urge to deny any inheritance from her. This theme is not consistent throughout all of the *jātakas* involving Māyā[21]—yet it is noticeable enough to be worthy of discussion.

A different emphasis is discernible in those stories involving the "long-standing" Mahāprajāpatī. In the *Cūlanandiya Jātaka* (No. 222),[22] a monkey who serves as the leader of a troop of eighty thousand monkeys is forced to renounce his powerful position in order to devote himself full-time to the care and feeding of his old, blind mother. Later, when a hunter threatens to shoot his mother, he offers up his own life in exchange for hers, yet the hunter cruelly kills both of them. This story emphasizes the adult son's obligation to his elderly mother and everything he has to sacrifice—even his life—on her behalf. It seems suitable, then, that the mother monkey is a previous birth of Mahāprajāpatī. The second story in which Mahāprajāpatī plays a role is the *Culladhammapāla Jātaka* (No. 358),[23] which I discussed briefly in chapter 1. Here an impetuous king orders the execution of his own infant son, whereupon his queen drops dead of a broken heart and the king himself is swallowed up into hell. These actions are brought about by the king's jealousy on seeing the affection between mother and son: "Even now," he thinks to himself, "this woman is full of pride on account of her son and thinks nothing of me. And as her son grows up, she will think, 'I have a man,' and will take no notice [of me]. I will have him killed immediately."[24] Here again, the king's words express anxiety about the future relationship between an elderly mother and her full-grown son, and how the lingering tie between them will make the mother "full of pride," able to make demands on her son. This "prideful" mother is a previous birth of Mahāprajāpatī.

Again, the roles played by Māyā and Mahāprajāpatī in the *jātakas* are not wholly consistent—and it would be foolish to expect them to be so. Nevertheless, the Pali *jātakas* as a whole, it seems to me, do offer some support to the contrast between the two mothers that I have outlined above. In the Buddha's previous lives—as in his last one—Māyā is the "good" mother who exits the scene without leaving any debt or obligation on her son, whereas Mahāprajāpatī, through her survival, is the focus of a lingering and anxiety-ridden tie.

Māyā: Mother Mired in Grief

The dour picture I have painted above of an ideal mother who dies and a problematic mother who sticks around has a crucially important flip side, however, that can be illuminated by considering each figure as a mother in grief. In various contexts, both Māyā and Mahāprajāpatī are depicted as grieving mothers—much like the mothers of the *Therīgāthā*—yet they differ from each other in what they do with their grief: Do they confront this grief, transcend it, and realize their spiritual potential? Or does their grief remain an impotent force? It is my contention that Māyā, as a consequence of her idealization, is forever reduced to the status of Mother, permanently "frozen" into the role of Birth-Giver, and is thereby unable to spiritually benefit from confronting and transcending her grief. Māyā's immediate loss of human status seems to limit her spiritual potential and turns her grief into an impotent force. As attractive as the idealized mother may be, therefore, the tradition also seems to recognize her profound limitations, finally choosing to depict her as a spiritually stunted creature. Mahāprajāpatī, on the other hand, is the paradigmatic example of the grieving mother transformed. Although the tradition never explicitly describes her confrontation with her grief, it makes clear to us, at the time of her death, that both grief and attachment have been wholly eradicated. Mahāprajāpatī thus constitutes the original model for the nuns of the *Therīgāthā* and the one who initiates the path they follow. By becoming a nun and eventually an arhat, Mahāprajāpatī proves herself to be more than just a mother. As such, she reflects the Buddhist tradition's recognition that only a woman who acts as an autonomous individual, and not just as the embodiment of perfect motherhood, is able to realize the ultimate goal. To be "long-standing" rather than "short-lived" in this context takes on a very different connotation.

I noted before that Māyā, because of her early death and removal to heaven, does not grieve when her son renounces the world and thus spares him the guilt that he would otherwise feel. Indeed, this is part of what makes Māyā the ideal mother and, according to the *Lalitavistara*, it is the very reason she must die. Māyā's failure to grieve on Siddhārtha's renunciation does not mean, however, that she is spared from maternal grief as a whole. There are two occasions on which Māyā (as a deity in heaven) is depicted as a mother in grief. The first occasion occurs during the bodhisattva's quest for buddhahood, as depicted by the *Lalitavistara*:[25] At one point during the period of time when the bodhisattva is engaging in his six years of severe asceticism, he is so overcome with fatigue and starvation that he collapses to the ground and appears to be dead. When the gods erroneously inform Māyā that her son has died, she descends to earth from heaven and begins to weep over his lifeless corpse, lamenting his unfulfilled destiny. In an echo, perhaps, of Kisā Gotamī, she refuses to accept this death and instead seeks to undo it: "Who can I resort to on behalf of my son? To whom can I call out in pain? Who will give me something to restore the breath of life in my only son?"[26] The bodhisattva, roused from his stupor by his mother's weeping, at first fails to recognize who she is: "Who are you who weeps so pitifully, with your hair disheveled and your beauty destroyed? Who are you who laments your son so excessively, as you writhe upon the ground?"[27] Māyā then identifies herself as his mother: "I carried you in my womb like a diamond for a full ten months. It's your mother, my boy, who is lamenting you with such great suffering."[28] Seeking to put an end to his mother's torment, the bodhisattva then consoles and reassures her:

> Do not fear, [O Mother] who longs for her son, your labor will bear fruit! The renunciation of a buddha is never in vain! I will accomplish what Asita foretold, and fulfill the prophecy of Dīpaṃkara. The earth may burst into hundreds of pieces; Mount Meru's jeweled peak may [fall into] the flooding seas; the sun, moon, stars, and celestial bodies may crash to the ground—but I will not die as a common man! So there is no reason for you to grieve. Very soon, indeed, will you see the awakening of a buddha![29]

On hearing these words, Māyā shivers with delight, showers him with flowers, circumambulates him three times, and retreats back to her heavenly abode.

There is no denying the lovely manner in which this scene gives expression to the continuing tie of love and concern between mother and son. Nevertheless, the differences between this episode and the scenes we encountered earlier from the *Therīgāthā*, in terms of the transformative power of maternal grief, are both stark and instructive. Unlike Kisā Gotamī, who needs to learn that her desire to restore her dead son to life is utterly futile, Māyā has no need for any such lesson: Her son is not really dead, and in fact springs back to life the minute he hears his mother's cries. Far from preaching to her about the inevitability and universality of death, moreover, he instead reassures her: "Your labor will bear fruit!" Her son has the ability to remain alive, in fact, until Mount Meru crumbles and the stars fall down from the sky—impermanence be damned—so what need is there for grief? Rather than transcending her maternal attachments, Māyā retreats back to heaven with her maternal desires fully satisfied. Grief, in this case, has clearly not had the power to transform.

In part, of course, this is fully understandable, since the bodhisattva has not in fact died. Perhaps it would be unreasonable to expect Māyā's grief to be transformative once she has found out that the grief itself is unwarranted because her son has not actually died. There is also a second occasion, however, on which Māyā is depicted as a mother in grief—and this time her son *has* actually died. Yet Māyā's grief on this occasion still seems powerless to transform. This second occasion occurs on the Buddha's death or parinirvana. In the *Mahāparinirvāṇa Sūtra* found in the Chinese *Dīrghāgama*,[30] Māyā is presented as one of the deities who descend from heaven to the Buddha's corpse to utter a verse of grief and lamentation. The verse she utters is somewhat puzzling, however, and does not tell us much: "From the garden of Lumbinī where the Buddha was born," she says, "his path spread to everywhere. [Now] he has returned to his place of birth in order to abandon his impermanent body forever."[31] Since, according to the Buddhist tradition, the Buddha's parinirvana took place in Kuśinagara rather than Lumbinī, André Bareau finds this verse somewhat confusing and speculates that "place of birth" here must refer to the entire region of North India that encapsulated both Kuśinagara and Lumbinī. In any case, although we do not get much sense from this verse of Māyā's grief or the manner in which she interprets it, it is interesting to note, at the very least, that she speaks of the Buddha's death in terms of his *birth*, as well as describing this death as the abandonment of an "impermanent body" only. We do not get a clear sense, in other words, of the mother's acceptance of the finality of the child's death, nor are any of the other deities who accompany Māyā on this occasion represented as transcending their grief. Māyā appears here only as a grieving mother, not as a grieving mother transformed.

A more intriguing depiction of Māyā's grief on the Buddha's parinirvana is available to us from the Chinese tradition. Although this tradition cannot be placed within India itself, I suggest that it at least represents a Chinese recognition of the basic logic of Māyā's character, as it was constructed in India, and thus might illuminate that character further. According to this tradition, when Māyā descended from heaven on the Buddha's parinirvana to grieve over his lifeless corpse, the Buddha temporarily came back to life and rose from his coffin to console his grieving mother.[32] The episode is related by the Chinese pilgrim Xuanzang in the following manner:

> When the Tathāgata had entered Nirvana and his remains had been laid in the coffin, Aniruddha ascended to the heaven to inform Lady

> Mahāmāyā, saying, "The great holy King of the Dharma has entered Nirvana." Upon hearing this news, Mahāmāyā was choked with sobs and fainted away. [When she had recovered her consciousness], she went with the heavenly beings to the Twin Trees, where she saw [the Buddha's] *saṃghāṭi* (double robe), alms bowl and pewter staff. She stroked these articles while weeping piteously until she fainted away, and when she regained her voice, she said, "Men and heavenly beings have come to the end of their blessedness, and the Eye of the World has disappeared. Now these things are without an owner!" By the saintly power of the Tathāgata, the coffin opened itself. The Buddha emitted a bright light and sat up . . . and he consoled his compassionate mother . . . saying, "Such is the law of all things. Please do not be overwhelmed by excessive grief." With a sorrowful mind, Ānanda asked the Buddha, "What shall I say if people in the future ask me about today's happening?" "You may say that after the Buddha's Nirvana, his compassionate mother came down from the heavenly palace to the Twin Trees. As a lesson to unfilial people, the Tathāgata sat up in the golden coffin and preached the Dharma [for his mother]. . . . "[33]

In some ways, this episode is quite similar to the episodes we looked at from the *Therīgāthā*, for in both cases, a mother's grief over the death of one particular son is confronted by the Buddha's universalizing message that "such is the law of all things." The difference, of course, is that here it is the *son himself* who springs back to life and rises from his coffin in order to impart this lesson to his mother—doing so, moreover, out of a sense of filial piety. The actions engaged in by the Buddha thus reinforce his connection to his mother and seem to contradict the depersonalizing import of his words. Because Xuanzang does not tell us anything about Māyā's response, the final outcome of the episode remains ambiguous: Does Māyā universalize her maternal grief and transmute it into a detached appreciation of suffering? Or is her grief merely assuaged by the temporary revivification of her beloved son?

In recounting this tradition, Xuanzang was most likely basing his remarks on two Chinese Buddhist texts that have been carefully studied by Hubert Durt:[34] the *Mo he mo ye jing* or *Mahāmāyā Sūtra* (T. 383) and the *Fo mu jing* or *Sūtra of the Mother of the Buddha* (T. 2919)—both of which, again, are most likely Chinese compositions. Although these two texts differ from each other in significant ways, both of them involve the theme of the Buddha rising from his coffin to console his mother Māyā. The evidence provided by these two texts in terms of the transformation of Māyā's grief, however, is again ambiguous and often contradictory. In the *Fo mu jing*, for example, the Buddha consoles his mother with a generalized statement of impermanence and avoids personalizing the situation in any way: "The world is suffering and emptiness, acts are transitory; this is the law of production and destruction. After the destruction of both production and destruction, the destruction which is calm brings happiness."[35] In the *Mo he mo ye jing*, on the other hand, he speaks in a quite personal manner about both mother and son, emphasizes the virtue of filial piety, and downplays the finality of his own death:

> Among all fields of merit, the Buddha is the superior field. Among all women, the treasure which is the jade woman is superior. Now I, who was born from my mother, surpass the incomparable. . . . This is why I rise from my coffin with my hands joined, happy to make praise, falling back on the gratitude born of consideration and showing my diverse sentiments of filial piety. Even if all Buddhas are extinguished, the treasures of the Dharma and Samgha subsist for a long time.[36]

Māyā's reaction to the Buddha's consoling words is also ambiguous. In the *Mo he mo ye jing*, she compares mother and son to a pair of birds who fly around separately during the day but are always reunited on the same tree at night, and then observes that because of the Buddha's parinirvana, these reunions will no longer occur, for all ties between them have been "eternally severed"[37]—a statement whose harshness and finality are somewhat reminiscent of the mothers of the *Therīgāthā* describing the arrow pulled out of their hearts. Yet Māyā continues, even after this point, to lovingly stroke the Buddha's possessions, beat herself on the head with grief, and lament her "unspeakable misfortune."[38] The *Fo mu jing* (T. 2919), on the other hand, tells us only that on the Buddha's words, Māyā flies up toward the sky, suddenly stops in midair, and cries out loud, with her tears falling to the ground.

In spite of such contradictory and ambiguous evidence, however, it is fairly clear that this episode as a whole is *not* concerned with demonstrating the opportunity presented by maternal grief to transcend maternal attachment once and for all. I would say, in fact, that its predominant concern is precisely the opposite: The depiction of Māyā as *mater dolorosa*, the mother grieving over the death of her son, consistently emphasizes the continuing tie of love between mother and son, the mother's continuing identification of herself as a mother, and her desire, even in the face of death, to be united with her son forever. And the central focus of the episode—regardless of which version—is the son's reversal of death itself in order to pay tribute to this eternal tie. In order to give voice to these emotional themes, however, the mother's autonomy, independence, and spiritual potential must be wholly sacrificed: She must be Mother and nothing other. Thus, the idealized mother is—in the final analysis—also a spiritually impotent figure.

Again, because the tradition of the Buddha rising from his coffin to console his mother comes only from Chinese sources, and nothing comparable can be found (as far as I know) in any definitively Indian source, it is difficult to conclude too much from it. Perhaps the Chinese were simply using this episode to hammer home one of their favorite themes—that of filial piety toward one's parents.[39] Nevertheless, I would argue that their invention of this episode—however novel it may have been—ultimately derived from the logic of Māyā herself, as a grieving mother who never succeeds in transcending or overcoming her grief. Even if we limit ourselves to Indian sources, it must surely be significant that Māyā's life as a deity in heaven represents the end-point of her narrative development, and no mention is ever made (as far as I know) of her eventually attaining nirvana. In the *Dhammapada Commentary*, she does attain the fruit of stream-entry as a result of the Buddha's preaching to her in heaven[40]—yet the tradition never gives us a definitive depiction of her attainment of nirvana. In this, as we will see, she stands in stark contrast to her sister Mahāprajāpatī.

Māyā: Child-Devourer?

If it can be argued that Māyā is a "good" mother who suffers an untimely death and a cruel frustration of her motherhood, who grieves and laments as a result, and who is not in a position to use this grief in the interests of spiritual growth, yet who still seems to be "alive" and able to interact with the world of the living, then a further and more intriguing possibility is also suggested. According to an ancient South Asian folk religious belief I have already mentioned, a woman who suffers an untimely death or whose motherhood is cruelly frustrated has the potential of coming back from the dead to haunt the living as a vengeful devourer of other people's children or an inflictor of epidemic diseases. The usual solution to this problem is to turn the frustrated mother into a minor mother goddess and institute a regular cult of worship on her behalf, entreating her either to stay away or to reverse whatever damage she has already inflicted. Such mother goddess figures, who make an appearance both in classical Sanskrit literature and contemporary anthropological fieldwork, are generally worshipped outdoors, away from the village. In many cases, their shrines are located in groves or thickets located at the crossroads of two major ancient trading routes.

Could Māyā herself, as a grieving and frustrated mother, ever have been perceived in such a way? As far as I know, Buddhist literature never depicts Māyā in such a fashion. But as D. D. Kosambi pointed out long ago,[41] and as Miranda Shaw has discussed more recently,[42] the site of the Buddha's birth, the Lumbinī grove, is today known by the local villagers as Rummin-dei or Rummin-devī. And at that site, a Gupta period image of the Buddha's mother Māyā is still worshipped as the local goddess Rummini, who presides over the safety of childbirth and the health of young children. Moreover, until fairly recently this goddess Rummini was worshipped with red vermilion and animal sacrifices—which perhaps suggests that her benevolence toward children had its flip side in angry and bloodthirsty vengeance, should she be ignored. Kosambi has further suggested that the ancient name Lumbinī is related to the modern name Rummini and that the word *rummini* itself means something like "harsh" or "dreadful." Kosambi thus speculates that perhaps the Lumbinī grove was a sacred site associated with an ambivalent mother goddess known as Rummini even in pre-Buddhist times (located, as it is, away from settled habitation and on the crossroads of two ancient trading routes), that Māyā went to this grove to give birth for the very reason of seeking this goddess's protection in childbirth, and that although this protection ultimately failed her, Māyā herself later became identified with the goddess. Alternatively, Kosambi also floats another intriguing possibility: Perhaps Rummini herself *is* Māyā. In other words, although the sacred site established at Lumbinī clearly commemorates the happy birth of the baby Buddha, perhaps its original intention was to appease the spirit of his unhappy mother, who died so soon after giving birth, and to prevent this ultimate "good" mother from flipping into one who was "bad." (The temple housing her image, in fact, is still known as the Māyādevī Vihāra.) If we remember, as well, that all three stories we looked at in chapter 1 involving vengeful and frustrated "bad" mothers shared the basic theme of two co-wives in competition with each other, then this might even shed a new and quite different light on the relationship between Māyā and Mahāprajāpatī.

All of this is highly speculative, of course, and forms no more than just a possible subtext underlying the mythology of Māyā. Nevertheless, even the possibility that Māyā is connected in some way to this cultic complex of ambivalent, child-devouring mother goddesses once again underscores the manner in which Māyā is *reduced to her motherhood*—and, as a consequence, lacks the spiritual potential of an autonomous and fully subjective individual.

Mahāprajāpatī: A Parinirvana Even Better Than the Buddha's

How does this compare to the depiction of the Buddha's other mother, Mahāprajāpatī? As we saw in chapter 4, Mahāprajāpatī is also depicted as a grieving mother, this time on her son's renunciation of the world. In a portrait quite similar to that drawn for the grieving mothers of the *Therīgāthā*, she is described on this occasion as weeping until her eyes are fused shut, wailing and lamenting, flailing her arms, and rolling on the ground, as well as being compared to a helpless and pitiable animal driven mad with grief over the loss of its young. Unlike the mothers of the *Therīgāthā*, however, Mahāprajāpatī is not depicted as directly confronting and transforming her grief. Most likely this is because her son had not actually died but had only renounced the world. In fact, even after his renunciation, Mahāprajāpatī would continue to be associated with her son throughout the remainder of her life, and because she predeceased him, she would never witness his death. It therefore makes sense that the tradition never depicts a particular, climactic moment when Mahāprajāpatī must finally confront her grief, as it does for the grieving mothers of the *Therīgāthā*.

Despite the absence of such a moment, however, it is interesting to note that the *Gotamī Apadāna*, the most elaborate biographical rendering of Mahāprajāpatī's story, takes pains to make it clear that on her death and final nirvana many years later (at the ripe old age of 120), Mahāprajāpatī had indeed overcome not only her initial grief, but also her particularistic, maternal attachment to her son. This is indicated in a number of ways. First, once Mahāprajāpatī announces her imminent death, various *other* parties, such as a group of goddesses, a group of laywomen, and the Buddha's attendant Ānanda, are themselves depicted as grieving and lamenting, and Mahāprajāpatī responds to this grief several times by pointing out its folly: "Enough of your weeping, Children, now's the time for you to laugh!"[43] In these scenes, Mahāprajāpatī is depicted as the *opposite* of the grieving mother—the one who snaps *others* out of *their* misguided grief. Rather than being compared by others to a helpless and pitiable animal, moreover, Mahāprajāpatī now compares herself to an animal in a wholly different manner: "The afflictions are burned away for me, all states of existence have ended. Free from all intoxicants, I dwell, like an elephant who has burst through its fetters."[44] Our former image of Mahāprajāpatī as a pitiful cow rendered senseless by the loss of its calf is thus replaced with the new image of a powerful elephant breaking loose from every fetter. This sense of freedom from all attachments pertains even to her love for her own son, for on taking leave of the Buddha for the very last time, Mahāprajāpatī makes a remarkable statement that clearly indicates her complete *lack of grief* at this separation: "Of what use is your physical form, in this world as it really is? Everything here is conditioned, ephemeral, and provides no [lasting] comfort."[45] Mahāprajāpatī thus makes it clear that the particularity of her own son has been wholly diffused into a generalized understanding of the conditioned nature of all things. As if to confirm her perfect detachment, the Buddha himself, after Mahāprajāpatī has died, makes several statements referring specifically to her transcendence beyond all grief, as well as the fact that others should not grieve over her:

> Oh, how wonderful for me—my mother has attained nirvana! She leaves nothing behind but a physical body—no grief or lamentation. She should not be grieved by anyone, she's crossed over the ocean of samsara. Her torment has been eradicated; she is cool and well gone out. . . . Her knowledge had reached perfection in literal and interpreted meanings, etymology, and verbal eloquence. Therefore, she should not be grieved![46]

The *Gotamī Apadāna* thus makes it clear to us that Mahāprajāpatī is no longer a mother in grief, that she has eradicated all attachments and thus the grief that comes in attachment's wake, and that even on her imminent death and permanent separation from her son, she is detached, peaceful, and calm. Though she speaks of the Buddha fondly and takes leave of him respectfully, there is no lingering sense of the mother's attachment to her son. In all of these ways, the depiction of Mahāprajāpatī forms a stark contrast with that of Māyā.

The very fact that we are reassured of Mahāprajāpatī's eradication of maternal attachment only on her death and not at some specific, transformative moment earlier in her lifetime is also, I believe, significant. Various sources give us evidence concerning Mahāprajāpatī's gradual progress toward arhatship. According to the *Dhammapada Commentary*, it was during the Buddha's first visit home to Kapilavastu that Mahāprajāpatī attained the fruit of stream-entry, after hearing the Buddha recite verse 169 of the *Dhammapada*[47]—the verse itself being rather bland: "One should practice the dhamma, which is good conduct, and not conduct that is bad. One who practices the dhamma lives happily, both in this world and in the next."[48] According to the *Therīgāthā Commentary*,[49] she first decided that she wanted to become a nun after hearing the Buddha preach the *Kalahavivāda Sutta* of the *Sutta Nipāta*,[50] which focuses on the fact that quarrels, disputes, pride, arrogance, selfishness, and suffering all arise from attachment, desire, and clinging. And according to the *Vinaya* and *Aṅguttara Nikāya Commentaries*, she attained arhatship after receiving a short exhortation from the Buddha on those states that lead to passion and those that lead to the absence of passion.[51]

None of these discourses pertain in any specific way to Mahāprajāpatī's motherhood or differ in any way from discourses that were instrumental in the spiritual lives of other famous monks and nuns. I would argue that this nondistinctiveness itself constitutes the best evidence we have for arguing that Mahāprajāpatī, for the majority of her lifetime, is treated not merely as the Buddha's mother or in terms of her maternal function but, rather, as a fully subjective and autonomous individual in her own right—comparable to any other such individual, including those who are male. In this sense, the depiction of Mahāprajāpatī moves beyond that of the grieving mothers of the *Therīgāthā*, who, in spite of *transcending* their motherhood, are still largely depicted *in terms of* their motherhood. The message conveyed through Mahāprajāpatī, by contrast, is that a woman's maternal status is finally irrelevant: *All women* (including *all mothers*) are fully autonomous individuals, and it is only when one acts as such an individual that one can take control over her own spiritual destiny and attain the highest goal of arhatship. Mahāprajāpatī's collective character as the "leader of a large assembly"—accompanied in death, as in life, by her five hundred followers—further supports her status as a stand-in for Womanhood as a whole. What is true of her spiritual development is equally true of theirs and, by extension, potentially true for all other women as well.

The *Gotamī Apadāna* is again helpful here, for it takes pains to demonstrate that despite her unique role as the Buddha's mother and her preeminence among the nuns, Mahāprajāpatī should be taken as a model for what every woman is capable of doing. At several points throughout the text, Mahāprajāpatī herself is "universalized," and the focus is intentionally shifted from *her* achievements to the spiritual capabilities of women as a whole. Thus, in verse 66, after reminding Ānanda how they worked together to obtain ordination for women, she observes with wonder: "Delicate young girls [only] seven years old have attained a state that was not experienced by the ancients nor by heretical teachers."[52] The Buddha himself also uses Mahāprajāpatī as an exemplar of womanhood as a whole, for he tells her that before she dies, she should put on a display of miracles in order to persuade "those fools who doubt that women can attain full insight into the dhamma."[53] She responds with a magnificent performance in which she multiplies herself, disappears and reappears, walks through walls, flies through the air, turns the earth and Mount Meru into a giant parasol twirled in her hands, conceals both sun and moon with one fingertip, and holds the water of the four great oceans in the palm of her hand. In her final miracle, significantly enough, she magically creates "an immeasurable assembly of nuns"[54] and then makes them vanish again—yet another reminder that Mahāprajāpatī, as the "leader of a large assembly," embodies the potential of *all women*. In this manner, the *Gotamī Apadāna* strikes a careful balance between the uniqueness and preeminence of Mahāprajāpatī and her embodiment of womanhood in general. What Mahāprajāpatī does *not* embody here, on the other hand, is Woman defined in terms of motherhood alone.

Jonathan Walters, in his study of the *Gotamī Apadāna*,[55] has pursued a similar argument, though from a different perspective, by emphasizing the parallelism this text establishes between Mahāprajāpatī and the Buddha. As Walters observes, Mahāprajāpatī is referred to throughout this text as Gotamī (in Pali) in order to emphasize her parallelism with the Buddha (known in Pali as Gotama); she is described as the founder of the nuns' order, just as the Buddha is the founder of the monks' order; she alone of all the monks and nuns is said to reach not only nirvana but also parinirvana, just like the Buddha; and the narrative of her parinirvana consciously mimics that of the Buddha (as found in the *Mahāparinibbāna Sutta*). By means of this parallelism, Walters argues, Mahāprajāpatī is able to serve as the paradigmatic model for the spiritual development of women, just as the Buddha serves as the paradigmatic model for the spiritual development of men:

> Gotamī is the Buddha for women . . . who represents the end of the Path traversed by women just as Buddha represents the end of that which is crossed by men. . . . [The *Gotamī Apadāna*] provided an independent ontological basis for the female Path, a female Buddha. Thus the arhatship of women is not dependent on Gotama, but on Gotamī: it was she who founded the nuns' order, it was her *parinibbāna* that cleared the way for nuns to reach the goal.[56]

In Walters's analysis, this move was made necessary by the strict gender segregation characteristic of the Theravāda tradition, which meant that the Buddha could not really serve as an appropriate model for women. Though Walters thus approaches the issue from a different perspective, he too concludes that Mahāprajāpatī is represented not merely as the Buddha's mother but, perhaps more important, as an embodiment and vindication of female spirituality.

Mahāprajāpatī's final triumph lies in her impressive parinirvana. The *Gotamī Apadāna* describes the manner in which she ascends through the four *dhyānas* and the four formless states, descends back to the first *dhyāna*, and then ascends back up to the fourth *dhyāna*, from which she "attained extinction, like the flame of a lamp with no fuel"[57]—an exact parallel to the description of the Buddha's parinirvana in the *Mahāparinibbāna Sutta*.[58] At the moment of her parinirvana, the earth quakes, lightning flashes, thunder roars, the deities cry out, and flowers fall from the sky. The Buddha's monks, as well as an impressive array of deities and supernatural beings, all gather together from far and wide to give Mahāprajāpatī (as well as her five hundred followers) an elaborate funeral. According to the *Gotamī Apadāna*, this parinirvana was so magnificent that it even outdid that of the Buddha: "[Even] the Buddha's parinirvana was nothing like that of Gotamī, which was even more wonderful than his!"[59]

If we consider the wider Hindu context in which these traditions were formed—a context in which female salvation was believed to occur largely *through* a woman's association with her father, husband, or son—then the distinctiveness of the Buddhist message conveyed by the *Gotamī Apadāna* and other traditions surrounding Mahāprajāpatī becomes apparent. The fact that this message of unqualified female spiritual autonomy was conveyed through the character of a 120-year-old widow and renunciant nun is both remarkable and, I believe, wholly intentional. By making Mahāprajāpatī a widow whose husband is absent from the scene, by having her live to the ripe old age of 120 among a community of renunciant women, and by lauding her as the "foremost of those of long standing," the tradition undercuts as much as possible any tendency to *reduce* Mahāprajāpatī to her function as a mother—even as it lauds her for mothering the most excellent being in the world. Merely by virtue of *surviving* long beyond the immediate context of her motherhood, Mahāprajāpatī reminds us that women are fully rounded individuals who surpass their maternal function and who might, if permitted, act beyond the context of motherhood. This recognition is cause for both celebration and fear; thus, in one context, Mahāprajāpatī's parinirvana might be described as even better than the Buddha's, while in another, she is depicted as a cruel and bloodthirsty tigress, or made into an object of resentment, hostility, and guilt. In short, Mahāprajāpatī both pays the price and reaps the benefits of exceeding her status as a mother.

I hope I have succeeded, in chapters 3 through 5, in demonstrating the usefulness of an analysis that considers the Buddha's mothers not in isolation, but in relation to each other. As I have tried to demonstrate, the "short-lived" Māyā, as a perfect embodiment of the Maternal Function, is highly idealized, but this idealization comes at the expense of her spiritual potential; the "long-standing" Mahāprajāpatī, as a representation of women's autonomy and full subjectivity, is treated with some ambivalence, but this ambivalence is a natural consequence of granting her her spiritual potential. In the final analysis, neither mother is either "good" or "bad." It is only when they are considered together that we are given access to a more complete and fully rounded exploration of the Buddha's complex tie to his mother—a tie both nurturing and devouring, sometimes furthering and sometimes hindering his dharma.

Although these relationships are attributed to the Buddha, moreover, they can be assumed to give expression to the thoughts and feelings of the monks who authored the texts—thoughts and feelings not only in relation to their own mothers, but perhaps also in relation to women in general and the roles such women played within the wider Buddhist community. The contrast I have drawn between Māyā and Mahāprajāpatī, it should be noted, is somewhat reminiscent of the contrast between the relationships

Buddhist monks typically maintained with laywomen and those they maintained with nuns. It is clear from Buddhist literature that laywomen were often idealized by monks as nurturing and adoring feeders, even though they were not spiritually advanced, whereas nuns—though often spiritually capable—were unable to offer monks anything in the way of nurture or material support, and often constituted a troublesome presence within the Saṃgha through their demands for equality and respect. We can also surmise that within monks' daily lives, laywomen must have been an occasional and temporary presence, reminiscent of the "short-lived" Māyā, whereas nuns, like the "long-standing" Mahāprajāpatī, were constantly nearby. As Nancy Falk pointed out long ago, "One cannot escape the impression that the community was more comfortable with its laywomen than with its nuns" and "preferred to see women at the hearth rather than on the road or within a monastery's walls."[60] From this perspective, too, it makes sense that Visākhā, who is celebrated in Buddhist sources as the foremost laywoman donor, is also depicted as a fertile, birth-giving mother, one who had ten sons and ten daughters, each of whom also had ten sons and ten daughters, and likewise in the following generation—yet "she always seemed to be about sixteen years old" (as recorded in the *Dhammapada Commentary*).[61] Thus, male monastic perceptions of laywomen and nuns, respectively, may constitute one possible explanation for the tradition's contrasting depictions of Māyā and Mahāprajāpatī. But in any case, it seems clear that these two figures should be considered together—and stand for far more than merely the Buddha's mothers.

6

"She Is the Mother and Begetter of the Conquerors"

PREGNANCY, GESTATION, AND ENLIGHTENMENT

HAVING CONSIDERED MOTHERHOOD as a general theme, prominent maternal emotions such as maternal love and maternal grief, and important mother figures such as Māyā and Mahāprajāpatī, I turn now to consider some of the biological processes that surround motherhood: pregnancy and gestation in the present chapter, and breastfeeding in the next. These processes, too, constitute powerful images and metaphors that are often subjected to the same rich development as motherhood itself. The depiction of these processes, moreover, often suggests and implies a particular kind of *mother* who is attached to them and who further contributes to and reinforces the larger Buddhist discourse on motherhood.

The present chapter focuses on the biological process of pregnancy that turns one into a mother in the first place. Metaphorically speaking, pregnancy, of course, is rich in possibilities: In particular, the gradual development of the embryo within the mother's womb seems to be a natural metaphor for an individual's spiritual progress over time, while its ultimate fulfillment in the birth of a brand new being out of the mother's body is an apt image of the dramatic transformation brought about by one's attainment of buddhahood. The process by which one attains enlightenment is thus likened to the phenomenon of pregnancy or gestation—pregnancy if one is envisioned as the mother, and gestation if one is envisioned as the developing child. In this pervasive imagery, one "conceives" the aspiration to enlightenment and finally "gives birth to" buddhahood; one is "reborn" as a buddha after developing within the "womb" of enlightenment; one is an "embryonic" buddha already possessing the potential to be "born" in the future; or enlightenment itself is carefully "gestated." In addition to such general usages, metaphors of pregnancy are also applied specifically to the Buddha Śākyamuni by being woven into narrative episodes from his life.

All of these usages involve the idea of gradual development over time (which is characteristic of both embryonic growth and spiritual cultivation), but they also, I contend, make effective use of the *time-bounded* nature of pregnancy. In other words, just as the old saying has it that one cannot be "a little bit pregnant," pregnancy is a process that is strictly bounded in time, with a definite beginning and a definite end. Metaphorically, then, pregnancy can be used to suggest a precise span of time, from the initiation of one's spiritual journey to its ultimate conclusion. Multiple metaphorical pregnancies can then be employed to posit alternative definitions of the process that leads one to buddhahood. I hope to demonstrate in the discussion that follows the several different ways in which metaphorical pregnancies define the Buddhist path—as well as the underlying assertion often made that actual, biological pregnancy is nothing more than a pale reflection of the ultimate pregnancy that results in buddhahood. Finally, we will also see in what follows that the mother suggested by such images of pregnancy has much in common with other mothers we have encountered.

Sujātā and the "Birth" of Buddhahood

The beginning (or "conception") of the Buddha Śākyamuni's own journey toward buddhahood, as recounted in his traditional life story, can be defined in a number of different ways. Taking a fairly long perspective, we might define the "beginning" of this journey as the moment when this being first embarked on the bodhisattva path, which is generally understood to have occurred in his previous life as the ascetic Sumedha, who makes a vow before the previous buddha Dīpaṃkara to one day attain buddhahood himself in the far distant future, and receives a prediction of his ultimate success. This is clearly the framework adopted, for example, by the *Buddhavaṃsa* and the *Nidānakathā*, both of which begin the Buddha's biography with the Sumedha/Dīpaṃkara story.[1] Alternatively, we could ignore the Buddha's previous lives altogether, and instead define his last rebirth as Prince Siddhārtha as the initiatory moment, as seems to be the choice made by the *Buddhacarita*.[2] Or, if we ignore his youth as a hedonistic and ignorant prince, the initiatory moment might be defined as the moment when he renounces the world and dramatically dispenses with all of the trappings of an ordinary, worldly life—as one finds, for example, in the *Ariyapariyesanā Sutta.*[3] It is not the case, of course, that any one of these "initiatory moments" is more valid than any another. Rather, the spiritual journey of the Buddha toward buddhahood is characterized by one dramatic initiatory moment after another, a series of "beginnings" that accelerate over time and finally culminate in the crowning achievement—the Buddha's attainment of buddhahood.

If we were to view this journey in the *shortest* possible timescale, then the ascetic Siddhārtha's acceptance of an offering of milk-rice from the woman Sujātā (or, in some versions, from the two maidens Nandā and Nandābālā) might be seen as the *last* possible moment of "beginning." It is this moment, after all, that brings to an end Siddhārtha's misguided six-year experiment with severe asceticism and establishes him on the correct path of the Middle Way. Moreover, it is directly after his encounter with Sujātā that Siddhārtha proceeds to the bodhi tree where he finally attains enlightenment, and it is her offering of milk-rice that physically sustains him for the next seven weeks, until he is ready to preach the dharma as a fully enlightened buddha. The acceptance of Sujātā's offering thus marks the proper "beginning" of the enlightenment sequence (Figure 6.1).

John Strong, drawing on various details, has interpreted the seven-week period of time from Sujātā's offering to the preaching of the First Sermon as a sort of *bardo*, or intermediate state between Siddhārtha's "death" as an ordinary being and his "rebirth" as a fully enlightened buddha.[4] We can equally interpret it, however, as a sort of *pregnancy*, with Sujātā as the "mother" who nourishes the embryonic buddha with milk until he can be "born" as a fully enlightened being. Thus, in the *Mahāvastu*, Sujātā is identified not just as any ordinary woman, but as one who served as the bodhisattva's *mother* in five hundred previous births and who still recognizes the bodhisattva as her own son.[5] In the *Abhiniṣkramaṇa Sūtra*, Sujātā's status as the bodhisattva's mother is expressed even more concretely through an earlier episode in which Siddhārtha approaches Sujātā's house to beg for alms, and she is so overcome by the sight of her (previous) son that her breasts begin to leak with milk.[6] There is also some invocation here of the grieving-mother motif, for in the *Mahāvastu* passage, on first encountering the bodhisattva, Sujātā tells him of the enormous grief she has suffered over his asceticism: "For the last six years, I have not slept comfortably in my bed, for I have been struck by the arrow of grief whenever I thought of your austerities."[7] Sujātā is thus represented as the bodhisattva's own grieving and breastfeeding mother. The *Nidānakathā*, on the other hand,

FIGURE 6.1 Sujātā offers milk-rice to the Buddha. Sujata Temple, near Bodh Gaya, Bihar, India. A sign at the temple reads: "This is The ancient place, Where Sujata of Village Senani (BAKROUR) had offered milk-rice to Siddhartha here Under Banyan tree." Photograph courtesy of Paulus Veltman and Anja Brunt, Amsterdam, The Netherlands.

takes a slightly different approach.[8] Here Sujātā is not identified as the bodhisattva's previous mother, but merely as a random local woman. She does, however, mistake the bodhisattva for a tree deity whom she had earlier worshipped in hope of obtaining a son, and she gives him the offering of alms in order to thank the deity for granting her wish. Thus the encounter, though slightly different, still involves an offering motivated by maternal love for a son. It is also pertinent to note, of course, that Sujātā, as a "mother," gives the bodhisattva not just any food offering but, more specifically, an offering of *milk-rice*. According to the *Nidānakathā* and other sources, this milk-rice has been elaborately prepared by circulating milk through an ever-decreasing number of cows, until its essence has been powerfully intensified. Since the cow in Indian thought is a preeminent symbol of maternal love, this intensified milk-rice offering might be seen as a concrete embodiment of Sujātā's motherly love for her "son."

In addition to these invocations of Sujātā as the mother, there are also invocations of Siddhārtha as the developing child. In the *Nidānakathā* account, Siddhārtha divides the milk-rice offering into forty-nine balls and eats them all at once. This is "the only food he ate for forty-nine days after becoming a buddha, as he sat for seven weeks at the seat of enlightenment"—a period of time during which "he did not eat any other food, he did not bathe, he did not wash his face, and he did not eliminate any waste."[9] These balls are referred to (in both Pali and Sanskrit) as *piṇḍa*, the term used not only for the almsfood given to Buddhist monks, but also for the rice balls offered to deceased ancestors in the Vedic funeral rites. These rice balls would be offered for a period of forty-nine days—just as the Buddha survives on the milk-rice for forty-nine days—which was the period of time believed to occur between the moment of death and the following rebirth. The purpose of the rice balls in the Vedic funeral rite was to sustain the deceased person through the dangers of the intermediate state and allow him to achieve a successful rebirth.[10] In light of these associations, it is clear that the Sujātā episode as a whole wishes to suggest that Sujātā is a mother who nourishes a developing embryo with milk, thus allowing him to survive the difficult passage from "death" as an ordinary being to "rebirth" as a fully enlightened buddha. During this dangerous, transitional time, Siddhārtha acts much like a fetus within the womb, not bathing, washing, or eliminating waste. The Buddha's attainment of buddhahood is thus subtly depicted as a process involving maternal nourishment and embryonic development and finally resulting in a successful "birth." Depicting it in this way effectively underscores the complete and dramatic transformation brought about by the attainment of buddhahood.

Interestingly enough, the definitive *end* of this process, I contend, is marked by another mother and another gift of food, for immediately after leaving the area surrounding the bodhi tree where he has spent the previous seven weeks, the Buddha encounters the merchants Trapuṣa and Bhallika, who give him another offering of alms—the first food he has consumed since ingesting the milk-rice. According to the *Aṅguttara Nikāya Commentary*,[11] moreover, these two merchant brothers have been instructed to make this gift by a local deity who had once been *their mother* in a previous existence. In a loose sense, then, we could see this second offering, too, as a maternal gift of nourishment, whose happy result is that Trapuṣa and Bhallika become the very first laypeople in the Buddhist community. The enlightenment sequence is thus nicely bracketed by two maternal gifts of nourishment, the first of which gives birth to the Buddha and the second of which initiates the wider Buddhist community. Depicting these newly established entities through invocations of pregnancy, maternal nourishment, and birth serves to emphasize their uniqueness and their unprecedented arrival—the fact that new things are *being born* into the world. Motherhood is drawn on for its strong association with the initiation of new life; it is *mothers* who bring about new things. Motherhood is valorized in the sense that both the attainment of buddhahood and the establishment of the wider Buddhist community are originally motivated by *maternal acts of love.* Behind every Great Man (or Great Community), these episodes seem to suggest, one will find the love and feeding of a mother.

At the same time, however, there is also a subtle difference between these two maternal gifts of food. In the case of the first gift, the mother gives food directly to her son, whereas in the case of the second gift, the mother orders her sons to give alms to the newly enlightened Buddha. Presumably, she does so because now that Buddhism has been established in the world as a powerful field of merit, the gift of alms, which produces abundant karmic returns, has in a sense *superseded* the maternal gift of ordinary food, which only produces physical nourishment. This mother, in other words, can do more to benefit her sons by telling them to offer alms to the newly enlightened Buddha than she could ever do by giving them regular food herself. The subtle message conveyed by both gifts, taken together, is that the role of Buddhism supersedes the role of the mother: Whereas the mother provides only physical nourishment, Buddhism provides spiritual nourishment in the form of karmic merit. Merit, in a sense, is a higher form of food that is available primarily through Buddhism.

This message is subtle, no doubt, and I may very well be reading too much into the slightest of narrative details. Nevertheless, such an interpretation would place this episode right in line with the other metaphorical pregnancies I examine below.

Yaśodharā, Rāhula, and the "Birth" of Buddhahood

A second metaphorical pregnancy that is used to represent the Buddha's journey to buddhahood involves a somewhat longer span of time, encompassing the entire six-year period between the bodhisattva's renunciation of the world and his attainment of enlightenment. This consists of the parallel drawn in several texts between the bodhisattva's ascetic quest and the pregnancy of his wife Yaśodharā with the couple's son Rāhula. Though many Buddha biographies maintain that Rāhula is *born* just prior to the bodhisattva's Great Renunciation, a significant number of them (including, for example, the *Mahāvastu*, the *Abhiniṣkramaṇa Sūtra*, and the Sanskrit *Mūlasarvāstivāda Vinaya*)[12] put forth a rather different story, according to which Rāhula is *conceived* on the night of the Great Renunciation, remains within the womb of Yaśodharā throughout Siddhārtha's entire six-year quest, and is born at the very moment when the Buddha attains enlightenment. In this way, an obvious parallel is drawn between the bodhisattva's quest for buddhahood and Yaśodharā's pregnancy with Rāhula: Yaśodharā conceives an embryo just as the bodhisattva is initiating his quest, and she gives birth to the child Rāhula just as he is "giving birth" to buddhahood.

John Strong has carefully analyzed this episode as it appears in perhaps its most elaborate form, that found in the *Saṃghabhedavastu* of the Sanskrit *Mūlasarvāstivāda Vinaya*.[13] Here Prince Siddhārtha, on the night of the Great Renunciation, thinks to himself: "There will be those who will say of me that Prince Śākyamuni was not a man [Skt. *apumān*], since he went forth without regard for Yaśodharā, Gopikā, Mṛgajā, and the rest of his sixty thousand wives. So let me now have sex with Yaśodharā."[14] As Strong points out, this presents us with a very different picture of the "renunciant" bodhisattva than we are familiar with from other versions of the story: "Instead of turning away in disgust from sexuality and abandoning the family life, the Bodhisattva here, in his last act as a prince, affirms the householder's state and fulfills his sexual duty by engendering a son."[15] This confluence between the conception of the son and the renunciation of the father does serve to reconcile the path of the householder and the path of the renunciant more effectively than it is reconciled in other versions of the story; more importantly, though, it also establishes a parallel between Siddhārtha's quest and Yaśodharā's pregnancy—a parallel that is carefully maintained throughout the remainder of the episode, not only in terms of general timeline, but also in terms of the actions undertaken by husband and wife.

Thus, when Yaśodharā learns of her husband's severe asceticism, she, too, engages in similar practices:

> Together with the harem, Queen Yaśodharā, upon hearing of her husband's condition, was overcome by grief for her husband. Dejected, her face wet with tears, her garlands and ornaments thrown aside, she [too] engaged in arduous practices. She [too] survived on one sesame seed, one grain of rice, one jujube fruit, one pulse pod, one bean; and she [too] slept on a bed of grass.[16]

And just as such severe ascetic practices only hinder Siddhārtha's spiritual progress, they have the same deleterious effect on Yaśodharā's pregnancy: "The embryo within her deteriorated."[17] When King Śuddhodhana sees that her pregnancy is in danger, he prevents his daughter-in-law from hearing anything further about her husband's asceticism; as a result, Yaśodharā resumes eating in moderation, and the fetus within her womb begins to grow again. Apparently, this occurs only after the fetus has been deteriorating within her womb for six long years, for while Yaśodharā may not know it, her decision to resume eating coincides with Siddhārtha's decision, after six years of starving himself, to once again accept solid food. The *Mūlasarvāstivāda Vinaya* consciously emphasizes the parallelism between husband and wife:

> *On the very day* when the bodhisattva departed [from home], on that day Yaśodharā became pregnant. And when the bodhisattva engaged in arduous practices, *at the same time* Queen Yaśodharā began engaging in arduous practices, and the embryo within her deteriorated. And when the Blessed One, realizing that arduous practices were fruitless, resumed inhaling and exhaling comfortably, eating proper food such as porridge and gruel, rubbing his limbs with butter and oil, and bathing his body in warm water, *at the same time* the queen, too, resumed inhaling and exhaling comfortably, eating proper food . . . [etc.]. . . . And the embryo again began to thrive, and she became visibly pregnant [emphasis added].[18]

The fetus itself, then, is clearly a symbol of Siddhārtha's spiritual quest: When subjected to severe asceticism, it withers away, and when properly nourished with food, it prospers.

The parallelism between Siddhārtha's quest and Yaśodharā's pregnancy now continues in the reactions of those around them. Just as Siddhārtha's five ascetic companions leave him in disgust as soon as they see that he has begun eating solid food, so also the Śākyas begin to scorn Yaśodharā and accuse her of infidelity as soon as she becomes visibly pregnant—for how could she become pregnant six years after her husband has left home? Once left in isolation, however, both Siddhārtha and Yaśodharā finally see their respective quests come to fruition, for Yaśodharā gives birth to Rāhula at the very moment that the Buddha is attaining enlightenment: "And at the moment when the Blessed One attained the highest wisdom, a son was born to Yaśodharā."[19] Finally, just as the Buddha later rejoins his five ascetic companions and succeeds in convincing them that he has reached full enlightenment, so also Yaśodharā proves her wifely fidelity to the Śākyas by placing the baby Rāhula on a stone in the middle of a pond and performing an Act of Truth: "If this child has been fathered by the bodhisattva, may he float in this pool, along with the stone; if he hasn't, may he sink . . . and let him [also] come from the other shore to this shore."[20] As Strong notes,[21] this again makes the infant Rāhula symbolic of the Buddha's spiritual status, for the Buddha is one who has "gone to the other shore" of nirvana, yet returned to this shore of samsara in order to preach the dharma to others. Similarly, in the version of this story found in the *Za bao zang jing* (T. 203),[22] a collection of tales extant only in Chinese, the Śākyas go so far as to throw Yaśodharā into a fire, whereupon she performs an Act of Truth that instantly turns the fire into a cool pond, on which Yaśodharā is safely seated on a lotus. This again is reminiscent of the Buddha, who is frequently compared to a fire that has been extinguished, and to a lotus that is rooted in the muck of samsara but successfully rises above it. In all of these ways, the bodhisattva's ascetic quest and its culmination in buddhahood are likened to the pregnancy of his wife and its culmination in the birth of a son.

Strong's interpretation of this account strongly emphasizes the parallelism established between husband and wife, who together might be seen as embarking on "a family quest."[23] According to him, this shared quest is one that ultimately reconciles, rather than opposes, the life of the householder and the life of the renunciant. "Indeed," he notes,

> in achieving the goal of renunciation—enlightenment—the Buddha also achieves the goal of lay life—fatherhood. But conversely, and just as importantly, in achieving the goal of motherhood, Yaśodharā makes possible the goal of renunciation. This story, then, could serve as a soteriological model not just for monks and nuns at the time of their "wandering forth" but also for laypersons (both female and male) who, willy-nilly, choose the family life. It implies a parallelism and balance between at least two Buddhist paths, both of which lead to enlightenment: a *śramaṇic* one involving ordination and a stay-at-home one for householders.[24]

Serinity Young, in her discussion of this episode, also emphasizes the parallelism and balance between husband and wife, this time in terms of their contrasting forms of fertility:

> Surely here is an eloquent image of the powerful productivity of an auspicious female, as Yaśodharā's prolonged pregnancy resonates with the power of the Buddha's withheld male fertility; eventually, he gives birth to enlightenment and she to a son. In the [*Mūlasarvāstivāda Vinaya*], her pregnancy, the evidence of her powerful female fertility, does not simply parallel the Buddha's asceticism, it actively sustains him in his efforts.[25]

While I do not wholly disagree with these statements, I do believe that "parallelism and balance" are only part of the picture. There is also, of course, a powerful sense of *hierarchy* that elevates the male path of asceticism far above the female path of pregnancy. This hierarchy is apparent when we consider the degree of *agency* exhibited by husband and wife: Whereas Siddhārtha is always depicted as an autonomous individual who makes his own decisions—whether to renounce the world, engage in severe asceticism, or accept solid food—Yaśodharā's pregnancy is marked throughout by features of passivity. For example, whereas Siddhārtha actively undertakes his Great Renunciation, Yaśodharā does not *choose* to become pregnant; her conception of Rāhula is wholly passive—the result of Siddhārtha's own decision to prove his manhood by making love to his wife. Likewise, whereas Siddhārtha himself decides to engage in severe asceticism for six long years, Yaśodharā's six-year pregnancy is explained more passively, either in terms of a mere imitation of her husband's actions, or as the negative karmic result of sinful deeds done in a previous life: A *jātaka* is told, in fact, in which a lazy daughter deceives her mother into carrying a twice-as-heavy load of milk on her head for a distance of six leagues, while the daughter hides in the bushes; thus, the daughter is reborn as Yaśodharā, who must bear a child within her womb for six years. (An additional *jātaka* also explains why Rāhula had to suffer such a long gestation.) And finally, whereas Siddhārtha chooses to accept solid food because he has realized the fruitlessness of severe ascetic practices and the correctness of the Middle Way, Yaśodharā accepts solid food merely because she is being deceived by King Śuddhodhana and no longer hears about what her husband is doing. The two decisions may coincide in time, but one is active and informed by wisdom, whereas the other is passive and driven by ignorance. Even the dramatic Act of Truth by means of which Yaśodharā proves her marital fidelity and absolves herself of blame relies for its effectiveness on her *husband's* actions in fathering Rāhula. Throughout the account, Yaśodharā may appear to be undertaking her own decisions, but in truth they are merely reflections of the more powerful forces emanating from her husband.

What this account suggests to me, then, is not so much a parallelism between the ascetic quest of the father and the reproductive quest of the mother as the idea that it is the *father alone* who ultimately fulfills both quests. In truth, it is Siddhārtha's actions alone that establish and direct the two parallel tracks that ultimately result in both buddhahood and the birth of a son—almost as if once Siddhārtha has deposited his seed within the womb of Yaśodharā and left to embark on the quest for buddhahood, the seed itself, still driven by the will of the father, then embarks on its own, parallel quest to develop and be born. Yaśodharā as the mother, on the other hand, shares something of the transparency that we saw to be characteristic of Māyā, acting only as a vessel or a medium for the more powerful will of her husband. It is intriguing to note, for example, that whereas Yaśodharā, on the night of Rāhula's conception, has an inauspicious dream in which she sees "her own maternal lineage broken,"[26] Siddhārtha has an auspicious dream tinged with hints of male power and sexual virility, in which he sees himself

> using the great earth as an enormous couch, with Sumeru, the King of Mountains, as an all-pervading pillow, with his left arm resting in the eastern great ocean, his right arm resting in the western great ocean, his two feet resting in the southern great ocean, and a blade of grass rising up out of his navel, standing upright until it reached the sky.[27]

In my view, then, this episode could be read as conveying a double message—on the one hand, that the father's quest for buddhahood is the *real* "pregnancy" of which the mother's biological pregnancy is only a weak reflection, and, on the other hand, that even the latter pregnancy is finally attributable to the father alone. Both messages obviously undercut and devalue the mother, even as they make effective use of the imagery surrounding pregnancy, gestation, and birth. This interpretation, I believe, does not invalidate the "parallelism and balance" that Strong has emphasized but, rather, exists in conjunction with it. I would argue that although there is a certain degree of "parallelism and balance" expressed here between the path of the householder and the path of the renunciant, the same cannot be said for the mother and the father, for it is the father alone who has full agency in the fulfillment of both paths.

The passivity and exclusion of Yaśodharā as the mother and the co-optation of her fertility to assert the link between father and son now continue as we follow the episode through to its conclusion. According to the *Mūlasarvāstivāda Vinaya*, six years later, when the Buddha returns home to Kapilavastu, Yaśodharā asks herself: "How can I seduce the Blessed One?"[28] She gives the six-year-old boy Rāhula an aphrodisiac sweetmeat to give to his father, hoping in this way to seduce the Buddha back to the household life. Her plan backfires, however, when the Buddha, rather than eating the sweetmeat, feeds it to Rāhula, whereupon the son falls in love (as it were) with his father, follows him around persistently, and is quickly ordained into the Saṃgha himself. Thus, the sweetmeat intended by Yaśodharā to reassert the tie between mother and father has instead tied together father and son, and the mother, in the process, has been excluded.

Once again, there is a double message conveyed here: On the one hand, Rāhula's status as the spiritual "son" of his father is seen to take precedence over his status as the mere biological son of his mother. But on the other hand, the father's *biological* paternity is also forcefully expressed, for the Buddha uses this occasion to provide another infallible proof of it: When Rāhula first approaches him, he magically creates 499 replicas of himself, yet Rāhula knows immediately which of the 500 identical figures before him is his biological father. Why include such a scene involving the son's definitive identification of his father? Though the Buddha is presented as doing this on behalf of Yaśodharā—for he thinks to himself, "an untrue rumor about Yaśodharā has appeared; it must be disproven"[29]—I cannot help but think that it really has more to do with *himself* and the assertion of his own biological fatherhood. Such a scene must surely be responding to the male anxiety caused by the uncertainties surrounding biological paternity. Just as we saw before, then, the imperative of this episode seems to be to credit the father alone with *both* the literal pregnancy that leads to the son's birth *and* the metaphorical pregnancy that leads to the son's rebirth within the dharma.

Yaśodharā, in this episode, is not completely neglected, for according to the *Mūlasarvāstivāda Vinaya*'s telling, on the very next day, being "exceedingly overtaken by desire and passion,"[30] she tries again to seduce the Buddha back to the household life, and on failing, "deprived of her husband's love and overcome by despair, she climbed to the roof of the palace and threw herself off."[31] The Buddha, however—because "blessed buddhas are [always] alert"[32]—saves her life and preaches the dharma to her, whereupon she attains the fruit of stream-entry, joins the Saṃgha as a nun, and eventually becomes an arhat. Much as we saw in the *Therīgāthā*, then, Yaśodharā's grief over losing both husband and son is not necessarily a spiritual dead end; it is also an opportunity for her to transcend all attachments whatsoever and attain the highest goal. Ultimately, the text concludes, all people—including all mothers—are potential "children" of the Buddha. Still, this does not erase the manner in which this episode finally attributes both male and female forms of generativity to the will of the father alone. The pregnancy of the mother and the birth of the child provide a wonderfully concrete image of the bodhisattva's gradual development into a buddha—yet ultimately it is the father alone who gets credit for both the image and the real thing.

The Bodhisattva as a Pregnant Woman

Just as the Buddha Śākyamuni's own journey toward buddhahood was sometimes envisioned in terms of one or another metaphorical pregnancy, in Mahāyāna literature the same came to be true of bodhisattvas in general, who were occasionally envisioned as pregnant women "giving birth" to buddhahood. Here the "aspiration to enlightenment" (Skt. *bodhicitta*) that initiates the bodhisattva career might be seen as the moment of conception, the bodhisattva career itself as a long and often-difficult pregnancy, the ten stages through which the bodhisattva passes as the ten lunar months of gestation, and the final attainment of buddhahood as the climactic moment of birth. The gradual and time-bounded nature of pregnancy thus mimics that of the bodhisattva path.

Several passages from the *Aṣṭasāhasrikā Prajñāpāramitā Sūtra* and its versified summary, the *Ratnaguṇasaṃcayagāthā*, can be used to illustrate this kind of comparison. These passages focus in particular on the advanced bodhisattva whose attainment of buddhahood is imminent—just as a woman in an advanced state of pregnancy is on the verge of giving birth. Thus according to the *Ratnaguṇasaṃcayagāthā*:

> Just as when a pregnant woman struggles in pain,
> one should know that the time has come for her to give birth,
> so also, the bodhisattva who, upon hearing the wisdom of the Conquerors,
> regards it with pleasure and delight,
> will soon attain enlightenment.[33]

The comparison here seems somewhat forced, relying merely on a shared sense of *urgency* or *imminence* between the two situations: Just as a woman in labor is agitated and eager to get the baby out, so also an advanced bodhisattva who pursues wisdom with zest and enthusiasm is eager to give birth to buddhahood. Despite this shared sense of urgency, however, we again see a familiar dichotomy between the passivity of the woman and the agency of the man, as well as the physicality of the woman and the spirituality of the man: The laboring woman is subject to physical forces beyond her conscious control, whereas the male bodhisattva actively pursues and cultivates the wisdom that leads to enlightenment.

A corresponding passage from the *Aṣṭasāhasrikā Prajñāpāramitā* seems equally preoccupied with difference rather than similarity. Here the same sense of urgency again pervades both halves of the comparison—yet they otherwise seem to stand in stark conflict, for the laboring woman's pain and suffering run counter to the bodhisattva's joy and delight:

> Blessed One, suppose there were a pregnant woman with a heavy womb. Her body leans over and is completely exhausted, and she has trouble walking around. She eats little food, has little sleep or rest, doesn't speak much, and has little strength. She's in a lot of pain and often cries, and she can no longer engage in sex. She realizes that she is experiencing such pain in her body as a result of indulging in, practicing, cultivating, and observing insufficient mental attention in the past. When these signs appear in her, Blessed One, then one should know that this woman will surely give birth very soon.
>
> In just the same way, Blessed One, when this profound Perfection of Wisdom approaches a bodhisattva mahāsattva so that he can see it, praise it, honor it, and hear it, and if his heart delights upon hearing this Perfection of Wisdom, and he arises with a desire for it, then one should know that this bodhisattva mahāsattva will surely obtain a prediction to unexcelled, perfect enlightenment very soon![34]

Once again, the comparison here seems more like a contrast: On one side we have a vaguely sinful woman (described as "indulging in . . . insufficient mental attention in the past") who experiences the pain and suffering of labor, which will inevitably result in the samsaric phenomenon of birth, while on the other side we have the advanced bodhisattva who is joyfully devoted to the pursuit of wisdom, which will inevitably result in his complete enlightenment. The two situations may share a sense of urgency, imminence, or inevitability, but otherwise they are polar opposites.

Why do these comparisons between the bodhisattva and a pregnant woman fail to work? The awkwardness of such comparisons, as well as their relative infrequency, derive, I believe, from certain tendencies we have encountered before in the Buddhist discourse on motherhood—the tendency to favor the *son's* perspective, rather than the mother's, when considering the mother/son pair, as well as the tendency to contrast an ignorant, suffering mother and her liberated, Buddhist son. In light of these propensities, it was *gestation* rather than pregnancy that perhaps struck Buddhist authors as a more natural metaphor for the spiritual path leading one to buddhahood. Certainly, the male fetus's steady, forward advancement through the phases of embryonic development—gradually gaining in strength until it could burst through and see the light of day—must have been a more appealing image for male authors to envision than the corresponding image of the aches, pains, and increasing immobility characteristic of a woman's advancing pregnancy. Thus we might expect that metaphorical pregnancies in which the male hero is likened to the *fetus* rather than the pregnant woman—or the *son* rather than the mother—would be more resonant for Indian Buddhist authors.

The Perfection of Wisdom as the "Mother" of All Buddhas

One example of such a son-centered discourse is the extended metaphor found in the *Prajñāpāramitā Sūtras* that celebrates the "Perfection of Wisdom" (Skt. *prajñāpāramitā*) as the "mother" of all buddhas, for it is she who "gives birth" to them.[35] As Yuichi Kajiyama and Jacob Kinnard have both noted, the general purpose of this metaphor is to advance the "cult of the book" rhetoric characteristic of the *Prajñāpāramitā Sūtras* as a whole, that is, the Mahāyāna rhetoric that attempts to shift Buddhist devotees away from the worship of the Buddha's bodily relics (and the *stūpas* that contain them) and toward the worship of *prajñāpāramitā*—both the Perfection of Wisdom itself and the physical Mahāyāna sūtras in which it is put forth.[36] Since *prajñāpāramitā* is the ultimate *source* of all fully enlightened buddhas—so the argument goes—it is more meritorious to worship *prajñāpāramitā* directly than to worship the bodies of the beings who issue forth from it. Thus, we are told repeatedly throughout these sūtras that it is far more meritorious to worship even a single verse of the *Prajñāpāramitā Sūtras* than it is to worship an entire universe full of *stūpas* containing buddha relics, since the former is the ultimate source of the latter.[37]

It is in emphasizing the status of *prajñāpāramitā* as the *source* of all buddhas that the maternal metaphor becomes particularly valuable. Just as the mother is the ultimate source of her sons, according to the *Ratnaguṇasaṃcayagāthā*, so is *prajñāpāramitā* the ultimate source of all buddhas:

> The World Protectors of the past,
> and those who exist now in the ten directions,
> have [all] been born [from her],
> and the future ones will be as well.
> She is the begetter and mother of the Conquerors.
> She shows [them] the world,
> and reveals [to them] the thoughts and deeds of other beings.[38]

Moreover, just as sons are devoted to their mother, so also buddhas and bodhisattvas should be devoted to *prajñāpāramitā*:

> Just as when a mother with many sons gets sick,
> they all become sad and take care of her,
> So also, buddhas in world-systems throughout the ten directions
> honor this Perfection of Wisdom as their mother.[39]

The metaphor is interesting in that it exalts the Perfection of Wisdom as the *mother*, while at the same time encouraging its audience to identify themselves not with the mother, but with the mother's *sons*, that is, the buddhas who issue forth from her womb. The metaphor clearly adopts the position of the son, encouraging its audience not to *be* the mother but rather to *treat* the mother in a particular way. By envisioning this mother as ill, moreover, the metaphor again invokes the familiar contrast between the suffering mother and the rescuing son.

This dynamic becomes particularly clear when we look at the extended passage from the *Aṣṭasāhasrikā Prajñāpāramitā* that corresponds to the verse of the *Ratnaguṇasaṃcayagāthā* cited above. While paying some attention to the crucial role of the mother in mothering her sons, this passage is more concerned with describing the mother's enormous suffering and encouraging the son's compassionate and devoted response:

> Suppose there were a woman, Subhūti, who had many sons. . . . If that mother became sick, then all of them would exert themselves [to make her better]. [They would ask themselves:] "How can our

> mother's life not be cut short? How can our mother live for a long time? How can our mother's body not perish? How can our mother have a long life? How can our mother's name not be lost? How can our mother's body be free from painful, uncomfortable, and unpleasant feelings? For she gave birth to us. With great difficulty, she gave us life and showed us this world." Thinking this, those sons would support, protect, and care for their mother very well, with every happiness and kindness, wishing that she be free from any painful feelings or sensations whatsoever. . . . Thus would those sons honor, care for, cherish, and protect their mother with every happiness and kindness, thinking: "She is our mother and our begetter. With great difficulty, she gave us life and showed us this world."
>
> And in just the same way, Subhūti, do the Tathāgata Arhat Samyaksambuddhas honor this Perfection of Wisdom. . . . [They ask themselves:] "How can this Perfection of Wisdom endure for a long time? How can this Perfection of Wisdom's name not be lost? How can the evil Māra and his hosts pose no obstacle to those who speak of, copy, and learn this Perfection of Wisdom?" In this way, Subhūti, do Tathāgata Arhat Samyaksambuddhas care for, cherish, and protect this Perfection of Wisdom. And why is that? Because she is the mother and the begetter of Tathāgata Arhat Samyaksambuddhas. She is the one who reveals omniscience [to them] and shows [them] this world. From her, Subhūti, have the Tathāgata Arhat Samyaksambuddhas come forth. . . . In this way, Subhūti, is the Perfection of Wisdom the mother of Tathāgata Arhat Samyaksambuddhas. . . .[40]

The mother here is exalted as one who *previously* brought forth her children, instructed them, and showed them the nature of the world, yet she is also imagined as one who has *now* fallen sick and been afflicted by suffering. This characterization of a mother whose situation has deteriorated over time makes little logical sense when applied to the Perfection of Wisdom—but it does fit in nicely with the familiar trope of the suffering mother and the obligated son. Those who hear the passage are asked to imagine themselves as dutiful and debt-ridden sons who are wholly devoted to alleviating the pain of their suffering mothers, just as buddhas and bodhisattvas are wholly devoted to cherishing, cultivating, and protecting the Perfection of Wisdom. This is a metaphor, then, that superficially exalts the mother as the source of the son, but in actuality exalts the son for his undying devotion to his mother. The mother is simultaneously exalted and turned into an object of need and pity.

For all of these reasons, I must agree with Kinnard's assessment that "this is just a metaphor"[41]—in other words, that previous scholars such as Edward Conze and Joanna Macy have misinterpreted this rhetoric when they have seen in it an exaltation of fertile Motherhood or even the reemergence within the early Mahāyāna of an ancient "Cult of the Mother Goddess."[42] As Kinnard has noted, these interpretations "simply are not warranted by what the texts themselves actually say."[43] Moreover, Kinnard asserts that even in the later Pāla period, when Prajñāpāramitā came to be envisioned as an actual female deity, the artists who sculpted her physical form (basing themselves on the *Prajñāpāramitā Sūtras*) "did not take the mother language literally, but *figuratively*, representing her iconographically as she is described textually, as the true source of the *dharma*."[44] Thus, whereas Conze had emphasized the fact that Pāla-period images of the goddess Prajñāpāramitā are "bare to the waist," with "full breasts [that] are conspicuous,"[45] Kinnard maintains that such features are iconographically insignificant and that such images are more properly seen as being dominated by symbols indicative of wisdom, such as a book or the *dharmacakrapravartana mūdra*[46] (Figure 6.2). Prajñāpāramitā may be *compared to* a mother, in other words, but her maternal characteristics are not foregrounded.

At the same time, however, by strongly emphasizing the fact that *prajñāpāramitā*'s motherhood is "just a metaphor" meant to indicate its status as the *source* of all buddhas, Kinnard does, in my opinion, ignore the substantial *emotional* work that this particular metaphor might have performed. For, as we have seen above, this metaphor (as it appears in the *Aṣṭasāhasrikā*) does not end with the basic idea of the mother as a "source." Instead, it goes on to invoke all of the tender emotions that a grown-up son might still harbor toward his *actual mother*—noting, for example, that such a son would remember everything the mother had done for him, how she "gave [him] life and showed [him] this world," and that he would therefore strongly desire to "support, protect, and care for [his] mother very well, with every happiness and kindness, wishing that she be free from any painful feelings or sensations whatsoever." The mother's status as the source of the son seems less important here than her status as the object of the son's lingering emotions and affections. Thus, while there may not be any ancient "Mother Goddess" here, it does appear that actual

FIGURE 6.2 The goddess Prajñāpāramitā. Nālandā, 9th c. CE. Nālandā Site Museum, Bihar, India. Photograph by John C. Huntington, courtesy of the Huntington Photographic Archive at The Ohio State University.

mothers are *not* wholly absent from this scene. Instead, the renunciant son's emotions toward the actual mother are purposefully stoked, only to be redirected toward the Perfection of Wisdom that makes one a buddha. I would describe this as a process of *displacement*, in which all of the lingering emotions the renunciant son still feels toward his mother are given elaborate and affectionate expression, but only after being rendered "safe" through their displacement onto another, suitably Buddhist object. The son's love for his mother is encouraged, harnessed, and then redirected away from the mother herself and toward the furtherance of Buddhist aims. From this point of view, perhaps one could surmise that neither the full breasts nor the symbols of wisdom on an image of the goddess Prajñāpāramitā are more significant than the other; instead, they are intended to work together: The full breasts perhaps invoke within the male observer a nostalgic longing for his days as a baby at the mother's breast, while the symbols of wisdom then suggest to him the proper object toward which that longing should be directed. The son's feelings for his mother are highly valued and lovingly expressed—only to be subverted in the end by the claim that Prajñāpāramitā is the *true* "mother" toward whom these feelings are owed.

Finally, another question may be worth asking: If wisdom is characterized as a "mother," then who is the corresponding "father"? In *Prajñāpāramitā* literature, it is generally means (Skt. *upāya*) or compassion (Skt. *karuṇā*) that is characterized as the "father," such that buddhas are born from the combination of wisdom (as mother) and compassion/means (as father). While this again might seem to suggest a sense of "balance" between mother and father, this is not the interpretation that came to be offered in the Tibetan exegetical tradition. As José Ignacio Cabezón has pointed out,[47] Tsong kha pa's *Lam rim chen mo*, for example, explains that whereas wisdom is *common* to *śrāvakas, pratyekabuddhas,* and bodhisattvas, compassion and means are *unique* to bodhisattvas alone. Thus, it is the quality of the *father* that determines one's "Mahāyāna ethnicity": "If the father, method, is particularly prominent . . . then the child will be a Buddha. If, on the other hand, the father is relatively impoverished in these qualities, the result will be the lesser enlightenments of the Hīnayāna (the states of śrāvaka and pratyekabuddhahood)"[48]—just as (in both India and Tibet) the ethnicity of a child was determined by the ethnicity of the father, not by that of the mother. Tsong kha pa, in fact, states that compassion, the "uncommon cause," is like the "seed" that determines what kind of plant will result, whereas wisdom, the "common cause," is like the "water and fertilizer and so on" that are common to all kinds of plants.[49] As Cabezón notes, this does not exactly constitute an exaltation of motherhood:

> If we take into account all of the aspects of the symbol, we cannot overlook that at the root of the metaphor is an implicit assumption demeaning to the status of women, namely that a woman's ethnic heritage is of no consequence in determining the ethnic heritage of her children, that the man's ethnic background is the sole determinant of the child's ethnicity. Just as man is "more important" in determining the ethnicity of the child, so too is father-love in the spiritual realm. When mother-wisdom is the progenitress of a variety of spiritually accomplished beings . . . is not her position inferior to that of father-love's who is unique in determining the Mahāyānic ethnicity of the child?[50]

The characterization of Wisdom (or the Perfection of Wisdom) as a "mother" who "gives birth to all buddhas" is thus neither simple nor straightforward. It exalts the mother, yet also asks the audience to identify with the mother's sons. It venerates the mother for everything she did in the past, yet also imagines her in the present as being sick and afflicted by suffering, thereby foregrounding the devoted response of the son. It gives loving expression to the son's lingering emotions and affections toward the mother—yet also co-opts and redirects these emotions away from the mother herself. Finally, it recognizes the mother as the source of the son, yet also subordinates her to the father, who alone determines the child's identity. In light of all this, it is clear that the use of "positive" maternal imagery in this context cannot be interpreted simplistically as a mere exaltation of motherhood. As Cabezón aptly puts it, "Much more dangerous than Greeks bearing gifts is the patriarchy bearing female symbols."[51]

"Like an Impoverished Woman Who Bears a Son of Noble Degree": Tathāgata-Garbha

One final metaphorical pregnancy will again illustrate the essentially son-centered nature of such metaphors, even when ample attention is paid to the mother. This is the Mahāyāna notion of *tathāgata-garbha*, which can be literally translated as "Tathāgata-womb" (in the sense of "having a Tathāgata within the womb") or "Tathāgata-embryo" (in the sense of "having a Tathāgata as embryo")—an unsystematic line of thought that first finds expression in the *Tathāgatagarbha Sūtra* (composed in perhaps the middle of the third century CE) and is subsequently developed and highly philosophized in a number of Mahāyāna texts (including the *Ratnagotravibhāga*, the *Śrīmālādevīsiṃhanāda Sūtra*, the *Mahāyāna Mahāparinirvāṇa Sūtra*, and the *Laṅkāvatāra Sūtra*), but never becomes a full-fledged philosophical "school" in the manner of either Mādhyamaka or Yogācāra.[52] In brief, *tathāgata-garbha* refers to the basic idea that all beings already possess within themselves all of the qualities of a fully enlightened buddha, but these qualities are obscured and covered up by adventitious defilements (such as passion, hatred, and delusion); once these defilements are eradicated, however, the buddhahood inherent within every being will reveal itself in all its glory. Thus we should not be discouraged by the distance between ourselves and buddhahood, even if we are not yet bodhisattvas—in fact, even if we are the most immoral or lowly creatures—for in truth *we are already buddhas* and only need to rid ourselves of the defilements to see our indwelling buddhahood revealed. *Tathāgata-garbha* is thus a highly optimistic line of thought which maintains that *all beings* are constitutionally capable of attaining buddhahood. It stands in opposition to an alternative idea, also found in some Mahāyāna literature, that there were some beings—the so-called *icchantika*—for whom buddhahood was constitutionally impossible.

The connection between *tathāgata-garbha* and the imagery of pregnancy lies in the meaning of the Sanskrit term *garbha*. The primary meaning of *garbha* is "womb," but by extension, it also refers to the "embryo" contained within the womb.[53] This double meaning of the term *garbha* as both "container" and "contained" corresponds nicely to the two aspects of the *tathāgata-garbha* idea: If one interprets *garbha* as "womb," one is emphasizing the idea that the qualities of a buddha are obscured, covered up by, or contained within a covering of adventitious defilements (the womb). If one interprets *garbha* as "embryo," on the other hand, one is emphasizing the idea that despite this covering, the qualities of a buddha are *already there* and are destined to eventually be free of the womb, thus resulting in one's "birth" as a buddha. The double meaning of *garbha* as both "womb" and "embryo" thus allows the *tathāgata-garbha* concept to encompass both the idea that we are already buddhas and the idea that we currently exist in a state of delusion. The coexistence of delusion and enlightenment is here envisioned through the image of an embryo hidden within the womb.[54]

It is also the case, however, that the term *garbha* has multiple meanings, many of which have no explicit connection to the phenomenon of pregnancy. In addition to the primary meaning of "womb," the term *garbha* can also refer to "the inside, middle, [or] interior of anything," the "calyx (as of a lotus)," or "any interior chamber," and, again by extension, whatever "essence" lies within that interior chamber.[55] Thus, the Chinese, drawing on the "container" aspect of *garbha*, translated it with the term *zang*, meaning "storehouse," "container," or "hidden place," whereas the Tibetans, drawing on the "contained" aspect of *garbha*, translated it with the term *snying po*, meaning "essence," "seed," or "heart." It is noteworthy that neither the Tibetans nor the Chinese used a term with the more explicit meaning of either "womb" or "embryo."[56] While taking note of the primary meaning of *garbha* as "womb/embryo," then, we should be careful not to overemphasize the degree to which *tathāgata-garbha* necessarily invokes the idea of pregnancy. This is especially true given that the concept of *tathāgata-garbha* was soon subjected to substantial philosophical development, being equated with *ālaya-vijñāna*, *dharma-kāya*, and other such highly philosophical categories, and wandering further and further away from the poetic images and metaphors used in its original context, the *Tathāgatagarbha Sūtra*. For this reason, my discussion of *tathāgatagarbha* will ignore the substantial philosophical development to which the concept was later subjected and consciously limit itself to the *only passage I am aware of in which the imagery of pregnancy is actually invoked*—that is, the eighth simile of the *Tathāgatagarbha Sūtra*.

The *Tathāgatagarbha Sūtra*, as William H. Grosnick has noted, is not a doctrinal or philosophical text but, instead, a highly poetic and inspirational text that was most likely "promulgated primarily to inspire beings with the confidence to seek buddhahood, and to persuade them that despite their poverty, suffering, and bondage to passion, they still have the capacity to attain the ultimate goal of Mahāyāna Buddhism, the perfect enlightenment of the Tathāgata."[57] The bulk of the text consists of a series of nine similes, each of which portrays "something extremely precious, valuable, or noble . . . contained within something abhorrent and vile"[58]—for example, a beautiful buddha image hidden within the calyx of a rotten and withered flower, pure honey hidden inside a tree and surrounded by a swarm of stinging bees, or a statue of pure gold wrapped up in dirty, worn-out rags. In each case, ordinary people see only the vile, external object and are unaware of the precious item hidden within—yet the Buddha, with his all-seeing eye, understands that the valuable object is there, and if one can only remove the wilted flower petals, stinging bees, or worn-out rags, one may lay claim to the treasure that lies within. In just the same way—so the analogy goes—all beings, no matter how lowly, should be confident that they possess within themselves, underneath a covering of mental afflictions, a core of fully enlightened buddhahood.

Among these nine similes, it is the eighth simile alone that draws on the meaning of *garbha* as both "womb" and "embryo."[59] The simile asks its audience to imagine "a woman who is impoverished, vile, ugly, and hated by others" yet "bears a noble son in her womb." The son "will become a universal monarch, replete with seven treasures and all virtues," who will one day "possess as king the four quarters of the earth." But his mother "is incapable of knowing this and conceives only thoughts of inferiority," constantly thinking of him "as a base-born, impoverished child." In just the same way, "all sentient beings are carried around by the wheel of saṃsāra. . . . Within their bodies is the tathāgatagarbha, but they do not realize it." The Buddha, however, sees through their mental afflictions to the perfectly enlightened buddhas that lie within, and this is why he constantly preaches the dharma to sentient beings, telling them, "Good sons, do not consider yourselves inferior or base. You all personally possess the buddha nature. . . . If you exert yourselves . . . you will attain the path of very highest realization. . . ." The ignoble mother who does not realize that she bears a noble son in her womb is thus compared to the ordinary, deluded being who does not realize that his intrinsic nature is one of buddhahood.

Given the details involved in this simile—which is, again, the *only* passage I am aware of that explicitly describes *tathāgata-garbha* in terms of a woman's pregnancy—it is difficult for me to agree with those scholars who have seen *tathāgata-garbha* as a concept that valorizes either pregnancy or motherhood. Clearly, it is the *embryo* who is valorized here as an image of indwelling buddhahood, while the mother (and her womb) represent the state of delusion—or the covering of mental defilements whose rejection and eradication alone can allow one's buddhahood to shine through. The son-centered nature of the simile is clear in the sharp (and by now familiar) contrast drawn between an "impoverished, vile, ugly, and hated" mother and her "noble" and virtuous son. The imagery of pregnancy may be utilized, but only to suggest that the embryo must break free from the vile womb of his mother in order to be free. Also hinted at here is another notion we have encountered before—the suggestion that it is the *father alone* who determines the child's true identity. Presumably, the son within the simile has been fathered by a noble king, and thus he is destined to be a Universal Emperor (Skt. *cakravartin*), completely unaffected by the low-born status of his mother. The mother, however, being ignorant of this, continues to mistake him for a "base-born" child. Not only does this contain a hint of the mother's possible promiscuity (for why doesn't she know who has fathered her child?); it also places the Buddha in the position of contradicting the mother, correcting the mother's erroneous point of view, and persuading the son not to believe what his mother says. Addressing his audience as "good sons," the Buddha conveys the underlying message of the simile, which is that every being has been fathered by the Buddha—despite what their mothers may have told them. They must reject their descent from the womb of the mother and recognize their true identities as the children of their fathers. The mother here stands for the entire realm of ordinary, samsaric becoming, whereas the father offers the son a patrimony of permanent escape from its clutches. I am much in agreement here with Alan Cole's interpretation of the simile, when he observes:

> Purity is generated [in the simile] by the joint action of excluding the polluting mother and appropriating her reproductive functions so that the son appears to be born already defined by his paternal connections—all of which escape the mother's input and knowledge. In fact, it is just in escaping her input—her ugliness and lowliness—that he can in fact become the opposite: the king.[60]

In light of this, I cannot agree with Rita Gross's opinion that the concept of *tathāgata-garbha* provides "a remarkably strong basis for feminist interpretations and criticisms of Buddhism."[61] This is so, according to Gross, because through the concept of *tathāgata-garbha*, "the biological processes of gestation and pregnancy are valorized as the most apt metaphor for the existence and effects of indwelling inherent Buddhahood"—and "it is self-contradictory to valorize these processes symbolically but at the same time to diminish and denigrate those among human beings who are most intimately involved with them."[62] What Gross ignores is that this metaphor consistently views the process of pregnancy not from the perspective of the mother but from that of the son. This is not an image in which a mother successfully gives birth to the buddha that lies within but, rather, an image in which a son successfully escapes from the womb of delusion that envelops him. In order for the *tathāgata-garbha* concept to work as an image that valorizes pregnancy, the mother's and son's perspectives would have to be fused together rather than bifurcated. In fact, if one reads the simile carefully, one can see that there is a strange lack of congruence between the simile and what it represents, for in the simile, the mother and son are opposed to each other, such that the son must escape from and deny his mother, whereas in the real situation that the simile represents, the being that is deluded and the buddha that lies within him are—ultimately—the same person.

In line with Gross's interest in "reconstructing" and "revalorizing" (rather than merely analyzing) Buddhist concepts from a feminist perspective, I would suggest that contemporary Buddhist feminists might reconceive the simile in a manner that does not deny and eradicate the mother. Perhaps a mother who only *thinks* that she is "impoverished, vile, ugly, and hated," but who comes to realize *her own* noble status through successfully and actively giving birth to a noble son (or perhaps a noble daughter), would allow for a simile that invokes the imagery of pregnancy in a more positive way. But this is clearly *not* the manner in which *tathāgata-garbha* functions within the *Tathāgatagarbha Sūtra*. Instead, the concept of *tathāgata-garbha* makes use of the metaphor of pregnancy only to draw a contrast, once again, between a suffering mother and a noble, liberated son, and to encourage the "son" within each one of us to deny our descent from the mother's womb.

Mothers, Fathers, and Sons

If we consider these five "metaphorical pregnancies" together, then perhaps we can draw some general conclusions about Buddhism's use of pregnancy as a metaphor for the attainment of enlightenment. First, pregnancy is attractive as a metaphor for several different reasons: its nature as a definite, time-bounded phenomenon, with a specific beginning and a specific end; its suggestion of a state that may be *hidden* or *concealed*, involving a "container" and something that is "contained"; the fact that it is *difficult* and *arduous* and necessarily involves much "labor"; its suggestion of gradual growth, development, and increasing maturity over time; and, at the same time, its culmination in a dramatic and joyful moment suggestive of complete transformation and permanent *escape*. All of these features make pregnancy an attractive image for religious potential, spiritual development, and the final attainment of buddhahood.

Nevertheless, we have also seen that in using this metaphor, the Buddhist tradition, in line with other aspects of its discourse on motherhood, has a strong tendency to view this process not from the perspective of the *mother* but, rather, from the perspective of the *embryo*—or, more specifically, from the perspective of the *son*, for the embryo is inevitably envisioned as being male. Thus, it is *gestation* rather than pregnancy that strikes Buddhist authors as the more appealing image in envisioning the attainment of enlightenment. And in addition to adopting the perspective of the son, the use of this metaphor has a further tendency to slide into the familiar Buddhist opposition between a *suffering mother* and a *noble, heroic son*—even in those instances in which the suffering of the mother doesn't quite make sense in terms of the overall metaphor. One of the advantages of depicting the mother in a state of suffering, however, is to encourage within the son a remembrance of the love he has for his mother and all of the sacrifices she performed on his behalf and, thus, strong feelings of *debt, gratitude,* and *obligation* on his part to save the mother from her suffering. In this way, the son's emotions toward his mother can be harnessed and redirected toward whatever Buddhist entity the mother now stands for within the metaphor—a process I have referred to as *displacement*. The son's positive emotions toward his mother are harnessed for the promotion of Buddhist aims, even as the literal mother herself is devalued.

The depiction of the mother as one who is ill, ignoble, or suffering also leaves the door open for the entrance of the *father*, who is the implicit third player in such metaphors of pregnancy. In conjunction with the devaluation of the mother, we sometimes find the suggestion that it is the *father alone* who gives the son his true identity. Thus, in some instances, the son's status as the spiritual descendant of his father is seen to take precedence over his status as the mere biological descendant of his mother; in other instances, the further suggestion may be made that the father alone is responsible for *both* one's biological birth from the womb of the mother *and* one's spiritual rebirth within the Buddhist dharma. In this sense, the mother may be doubly negated, even as her reproductive abilities are appropriated.

The conclusions I have reached here concerning the co-optation of maternal reproduction to assert the link between spiritual fathers and their spiritual sons can be related to a growing body of scholarship that has reached similar conclusions. Serinity Young, for example, has discussed the importance of male-only lineages in certain Buddhist traditions, such as the guru/disciple lineages characteristic of Tantric Buddhism and the *tulku* lineages found in Tibet. She notes:

> Both types of male-only lineages take reproduction out of the physical realm and place it in the spiritual; the first [i.e., Tantric guru/disciple lineages] by displacing reproduction onto the transmission of knowledge from male to male (master to disciple), and the second [i.e., Tibetan *tulku* lineages] by emphasizing the male ability to continually reincarnate in the same monastic office, if not as exactly the same person. . . . [Both types] are co-opting procreative sexuality; and their product, that which they reproduce, is male-only lineages. . . . [In short,] Male-only lineages allow Buddhism to reproduce itself through the trivialization of women's reproductive abilities, the exaggeration of female pollution, and the portrayal of women as sexual threats to celibate males.[63]

Young also cites the work of Robert Paul, who describes the Tibetan *tulku* or reincarnate lama as "living proof of . . . the possibility of asexual reproduction," which he calls "the eternal dream of the male sex. . . ." The *tulku*,

Paul asserts, "comes as close as humanly possible to being self-generating, immortal, and asexual. . . ."[64] June Campbell, speaking again of the Tibetan *tulku* tradition, notes that "the implication that a lama was actually 'self-born' by virtue of his miraculous powers, and could control the means and manner of his own rebirth, established a belief in the male lineage of succession as one which simply *made use* of the female, rather than *depended* on her"—which "reduced the value of the female in the system, and attributed to the patriarchal system an ability for a symbolic male motherhood."[65] And finally, Alan Cole's discussion of Buddhism and the family again emphasizes the father-son chains of authority that structure the Buddhist monastery and that work to exclude the mother—although in this case the emphasis is on the way in which Buddhist patriarchal lineages mirror, reinforce, and perfect those that have already been established in the home:

> The monastic space was regularly organized as something like a patriarchal family that employed the language of fathers and sons to structure discipline, identity, and authority. . . . It may even be worth hypothesizing that the monastic version of the patriarchal family functioned as a perfected version of the at-home patriarchal family in a way that simultaneously confirmed the monastic family as "natural" and familiar even as it proved the deepest claims of patriarchy—that life and abundance could be harnessed and managed without the direct assistance of women.[66]

If we move beyond the immediate context of Buddhism, moreover, to ask about the larger, cross-cultural structures on which such notions might be founded, then the anthropologist Nancy Jay's work on the link between sacrifice and patrilineal descent systems becomes especially pertinent. In brief, Jay has argued that patrilineal descent systems, or those systems in which authority and property pass down unilineally through the male line (from father to son), encounter a fundamental problem in their dependence on the reproductive functions of women: The patrilineal family *needs* external women to reproduce itself, but must also *deny* such women any membership in the patriline—a problem made worse by the fact that descent from the mother is clear and obvious, whereas descent from the father is inherently uncertain. According to Jay, this is where sacrifice comes into the picture: "When the crucial intergenerational link is between father and son, for which birth by itself cannot provide sure evidence . . . [then] what is needed . . . is an act as definite and available to the senses as is birth"[67]—and that act, Jay argues, is the ritual of sacrifice. Thus, those men who sacrifice together—in a bloody ritual that mimics the blood of childbirth—belong, by definition, to the same patriline. Sacrifice, then, is interpreted by Jay as a sort of "man's childbearing";[68] while it mimics women's birth-giving and often draws on its imagery, "sacrifice can expiate, get rid of, the consequences of having been born of woman . . . and at the same time integrate the pure and eternal patrilineage. . . . In this sense, sacrifice is doubly a remedy for having been born of woman."[69] Sacrifice, Jay concludes, is "birth done better, under deliberate purposeful control, and on a more exalted level than ordinary mothers do it."[70]

Jay extends her argument, moreover, beyond patrilineal family systems to consider other, nonfamilial forms of male-to-male succession, including those that no longer rely directly on childbearing women, yet still use sacrifice to assert male, intergenerational continuity over time—such as the Roman Catholic priesthood and its sacrificial use of the Eucharist.[71] It is here that we might draw a connection to Buddhism. Buddhism, too, is a patriarchal and patrilineal tradition in which wisdom, power, property, and authority have been passed down through a male lineage over time, from metaphorical "fathers" to their metaphorical "sons," and to the relative exclusion of women. And although Buddhism is not an explicitly sacrificial religion, it *is* one of the renunciatory and ascetic traditions of India that have often been interpreted as "internalizations" of Vedic sacrifice:[72] The renunciant is one who internalizes the sacrificial fire within his own body as *tapas*, or the "heat" of his ascetic austerities, and who performs the sacrifice within himself by means of his renunciation and detachment. If we follow this line of argument through to its conclusion, then perhaps it is no surprise to encounter within Buddhist texts narrative tropes and metaphors in which the mother's reproductive functions are co-opted to assert the link between spiritual fathers and their spiritual sons—a link forged not through the ritual of sacrifice, but through Buddhist "sacrificial" values such as renunciation, selflessness, and detachment. Although the connection is somewhat roundabout, Jay's thesis does allow us to better understand the linkage between images of pregnancy and birth-giving, the denial and exclusion of women, and the concern with male-to-male lines of succession invested with power and authority. The application of Jay's argument to the case of Buddhism also fits well with Cole's description of the patriarchy of the Buddhist monastery as a higher-order and perfected version of the patriarchy that exists at home.

The conclusions of these scholars regarding the exclusion of the mother and the co-optation of her reproductive function are thus in general agreement with my own. What my analysis perhaps adds to this discussion, I hope, is a greater understanding of the poetic and narrative *use* of the mother, and not merely an assertion of her exclusion. Throughout my discussion, I have tried to emphasize not only the co-optation of the mother's fertility, but also her equally powerful emotional appeal and the manner in which Buddhist authors clearly recognized the value of this appeal and thus redirected it toward Buddhist aims. Ultimately, I believe, the mother's womb and reproductive abilities were *not* isolated by Buddhist authors from the memory of her tender, loving care, or from the son's reciprocal desire to express his affection and gratitude—these, too, were tied up with her reproductive functions and were similarly drawn on and appropriated. It is striking to note, in fact, that despite these metaphors' general assertion of the precedence and superiority of the father, it is the *mother* who is painted in warmer, flesh-and-blood tones—as Sujātā, as Yaśodharā, as the sick and suffering mother of the *prajñāpāramitā* metaphor, and even as the poor and ignoble mother envisioned by the *Tathāgatagarbha Sūtra*. The mother's reproductive functions may be appropriated, but the process is somewhat messy, and the rest of the mother's personality tends to tag along as well.[73]

Moreover, just as the mother in these metaphorical pregnancies is a more holistic figure than she may at first appear, so also, it seems, is the father. Here, too, I hope to have added some nuance to the continuing discussion. Whereas Young, for example, asserts that Buddhism spiritualizes the father/son relationship but does so "at the expense of male fertility,"[74] and that "true masculinity is thus defined as an eternal spirituality detached from the material world,"[75] my discussion of Yaśodharā's pregnancy with Rāhula has instead demonstrated that—at least in some instances—the claim is made that the father alone is responsible not only for one's spiritual rebirth within the dharma, but even for one's biological birth from the womb of the mother. Male fertility, in other words, is *not* necessarily sacrificed, and "spiritual" fathers such as the Buddha himself continue, on occasion, to show concern with biological paternity. In this sense, my view of the implicit father within these metaphors has much in common with John Powers's recent study of Buddhist images of masculinity. In contrast to the highly asexual and androgynous Buddha of contemporary Western popular culture, Powers argues,

> in Indian Buddhist literature . . . a very different version of the Buddha and his monastic followers appears: the Buddha is described as the paragon of masculinity, the "ultimate man" (*puruṣottama*), and is referred to by a range of epithets that extol his manly qualities, his extraordinarily beautiful body, his superhuman virility and physical strength, his skill in martial arts, and the effect he has on women who see him. Many Buddhist monks are depicted as young, handsome, and virile, and the greatest challenge to their religious devotion is lustful women propositioning them for sex.[76]

In a similar manner, the implicit father within these metaphorical pregnancies is sometimes envisioned as a virile man who both impregnates the mother with his seed and gives his son a higher and truer identity.

In short, just as we learn in adulthood to see our parents in a more complex manner than we did when we were children, so, too, texts written by the grown "sons" of the Buddhist tradition may very well deny and exclude the mother and elevate and spiritualize the father—yet both figures turn out to be more complicated than such a simple hierarchy would suggest.

7

"Just as a Mother's Milk Flows from Her Breasts"

BREASTFEEDING AND COMPASSIONATE DEEDS

JUST AS PREGNANCY and gestation constitute rich, natural metaphors for the attainment of buddhahood, so the act of breastfeeding might seem to be a natural metaphor for the Buddha's teaching of the dharma. The chronological sequence in which these phenomena occur makes the metaphor a particularly apt one: In the same way that a mother first gives birth to her baby and then lovingly gives the baby her milk, so too the Buddha is described as first attaining enlightenment and then compassionately showering down the dharma on all sentient beings. The effortless and generous manner in which the Buddha teaches the dharma did, in fact, lead to an image of the dharma being "showered down." In a famous parable from the *Lotus Sūtra*,[1] for example, the Buddha is compared to a great rain cloud, and the point is made that just as a rain cloud showers down rain effortlessly, equally, and impartially on all plants, yet each plant responds to the rain in its own unique manner, so the Buddha "showers down" (Skt. *vāri pramuñcet*)[2] the dharma equally on all beings, yet each being responds to it differently. The automatic and wholly natural manner in which a rain cloud showers down rain is similar to the instinctual manner in which a mother's body produces milk in response to the cries of her child. One might surmise, then, that the trope of breastfeeding would frequently be found in contexts associated with the Buddha's teaching of the dharma.

In fact, however, the comparison with breastfeeding never seems to have taken hold in Indian Buddhism. I am aware of it in one place only, a verse already cited from the *Gotamī Apadāna* of the Theravāda *Apadāna* collection, in which Mahāpajāpatī compares her literal breastfeeding of the baby Buddha with the Buddha's metaphorical "breastfeeding" of her with the "milk of the dharma":

I might be your mother, but you are my father, Hero . . .
Gotama, I've been born from you!
Well-Gone One, I may have nourished your physical
body,
but my faultless dharma-body was nourished by you.
For I fed you the milk that quenches thirst for just a
moment—
but you fed me the dharma-milk that is perpetually tranquil.[3]

This comparison suggests, as I noted before, that the Buddha constitutes the *true* mother, next to whom all ordinary mothers pale in comparison. Likewise, his teaching of the dharma constitutes the *true* breastfeeding next to which an ordinary mother's breastfeeding is little more than an animal's instinct. Mahāpajāpatī's physical nourishment of the baby Buddha may have been necessary, but ultimately it cannot hold a candle to the Buddha's spiritual nourishment of Mahāpajāpatī.

It is interesting to note, however, that Mahāpajāpatī refers to the Buddha in this verse not as her *mother* (true or otherwise) but, rather, as her *father*. Perhaps this provides us with a clue as to why the breastfeeding comparison failed to take hold or be developed any further: The tradition was so accustomed to envisioning the Buddha as a *father* that the explicit comparison to a mother may have seemed unnatural or somehow unseemly. After all, we have already seen that even when pregnancy and gestation are freely drawn on as metaphors for the attainment of buddhahood, there is a strong tendency to identify oneself with the *embryo* who is born rather than with the mother who gives birth. The identification with the mother, though found occasionally, strikes us as awkward and hesitant. One of the disadvantages of breastfeeding as a metaphor, perhaps, is that this flexibility of identification—with either the mother or the child—is absent: The metaphor works only if the Buddha is compared to the mother. And this comparison—with just a single exception—simply did not take root in India.[4]

The Buddha as a Breastfeeding Mother in Medieval Theravāda

What did not occur in ancient India, however, does seem to have taken place in the later Theravāda tradition of medieval and modern Sri Lanka. As Richard Gombrich noted more than thirty years ago,[5] the comparison between the Buddha and the mother is a fairly common feature of Sinhalese Buddhism. This comparison goes both ways: The mother is compared to the Buddha (for example, in the Sinhalese saying *ammā gedara Budun*, "the mother is the Buddha of the home"), and the Buddha is compared to the mother (for example, in the epithet *amā mâṇiyô*, "the immortal mother").[6] Gombrich traces this comparison back to the *Butsaraṇa* of Vidyācakravarti, an important Sinhalese Buddhist text composed in the thirteenth century.[7] Not only does this text draw an elaborate and multifaceted comparison between the Buddha and the mother; in addition, many aspects of this comparison deal specifically with the act of breastfeeding. Thus the Buddha is said to have performed many difficult deeds for living beings throughout the course of his bodhisattva career—"like a mother who eats medicinal food to cure a suckling baby who is ill." The Buddha is happy for living beings when he teaches them the dharma—"like the mother who ponders that when her child gets milk from her breast it benefits." The Buddha ignores his own suffering in order to help others—"like a wet-nurse in charge of a prince, who saves her breast-milk for the prince though her own child cry." And finally, living beings, in return, receive the dharma from him with happiness—"like a child which gazing on its mother's face and laughing with happiness drinks milk."

The breastfeeding comparison appears in several other medieval Sinhalese Buddhist texts as well and goes on to receive its most elaborate treatment in an eighteenth-century Sinhalese text called the *Mātṛ Upamāva* (or *Mother Simile*), which was the most popular of several texts used within the context of a type of all-night preaching session known as the "twin-seat sermon" (a ritual that is now obsolescent). This text explains at great length why "the Buddha is like a mother . . . the Dharma is like milk . . . [and] the Sangha is like milk-drinking children."[8] Many of its passages are highly emotional in nature and paint a sensual and erotic portrait of the mother suckling her child. The text notes, for example, that

> when a mother holds her babies and carries them on her hip, because they do not know their mother's quality they hit their mother with hand and foot and scold and abuse her, but the mother does not get at all angry but kisses and comforts [them] . . . [and] gives them delicious sweet milk to drink and thus consoles them.[9]

The mother's breast milk is celebrated for its "clear colours and wholesome sweet tastes,"[10] and the text goes on to note that

> any babies who grow by drinking their mother's milk and are attached to its flavour, do not like to stay separated from their mother, but constantly run to their mother, calling her by name and . . . embrac[ing] her; and when they go to sleep at night [they] do not leave their mother but lie just where their mother is lying.[11]

This intimate and intensely physical connection between the nursing mother and her suckling child is then compared, in various ways, to the Buddha's compassionate teaching of the dharma to his monks and nuns within the Saṃgha. The Buddha is thus depicted as the ultimate breast-feeding mother.

I have already discussed a rhetorical strategy that I am referring to as *displacement*—a process by which all of the lingering emotions the son still feels toward his mother are given elaborate and affectionate expression, but only after being redirected or displaced onto another, suitably Buddhist object. In this manner, the son's love for his mother can be harnessed for the promotion of Buddhist aims, becoming an effective emotional "hook" that guarantees one's devotion to Buddhism. It is clear that this is the strategy being employed by the Buddha/mother comparisons of the *Butsaraṇa*, the *Mātṛ Upamāva*, and other medieval and modern Sinhalese texts. We can further illuminate this strategy, however, by looking at the specific, historical context in which this comparison first arises: What is it that motivates the medieval Sinhalese Buddhist tradition to counteract the strong association between the Buddha and the father—at least enough to allow the mother comparison to flourish?

Charles Hallisey has noted that medieval Sri Lanka (after 1000 CE) witnessed a surge of popular Buddhist literature written in vernacular Sinhalese and aimed equally at monastics and laity, whose aim was to tie Sinhalese Buddhist society together into a single, coherent community (consisting of monastics, lay people, rulers, and so forth) in the wake of strong pressures for vertical integration coming from the Hindu imperial formations of South India.[12] One strategy pursued in this attempt was the use of a particular type of devotional rhetoric that would persuade people of all types to approach Buddhism with a strong sense of *personal self-involvement*—in other words, a strong sense of *mamāyana* (in Sinhalese), the feeling that something is "mine" (P. *mama*), that it belongs to me or relates to me or pertains specifically to myself. For example, one of the major strategies employed in this rhetoric of *mamāyana* was the combination of honorific and possessive forms in referring to the Buddha (as "our Buddha," "my Buddha," etc.). "It is precisely this combination," Hallisey observes,

> that . . . sets the Buddha apart from other objects of honor. Kings, monks, relics, and a few sacred books . . . may all receive [honorific treatment] . . . but they are never called "our monks," "our relics," "our great bodhi tree." But the Buddha, even as the Bodhisattva, is routinely called "our Buddha," "our Muni," etc. . . . Such usages suggest that it is the combination of superior status—as indicated by honorific language—and relational involvement—as indicated by first person possessives—which creates the peculiar force of this [devotional rhetoric].[13]

By means of this rhetoric, Hallisey argues, such texts encourage their audience to reconfigure their relationship to the Buddha, learning to see the Buddha not as "a great, but distant figure from the past" but, rather, in terms of "each individual's direct and personal dependence on this same figure."[14] Regardless of his or her station in society, each person is thus persuaded to be personally devoted to the Buddhist tradition and in return to have strong feelings of gratitude, obligation, and indebtedness. In this way, Sinhalese Buddhist society could be vertically integrated into a single unified and highly committed whole and thus adapt to its competitive religious environment.

The Buddha/mother comparison found in medieval Sinhalese Buddhist texts, according to Hallisey, is another prominent feature of this *mamāyana* rhetoric.[15] It is easy to see how the Buddha/mother comparison might work in a similar way as the combination of honorific and possessive forms: Just as honorifics and possessives work together to instill within their audience a feeling of both deference/respect and personal relationship in regard to the Buddha, so too the Buddha/mother comparison may be employed likewise, since the Buddha is an object of respect, esteem, and deference, while the mother is the focus of one's most intimate childhood memories. We can restate the same ideas in terms of the strategy of *displacement:* Possessive forms trigger one's personal emotions, while honorific forms designate the object toward which those emotions should be *displaced*—and the two halves of the mother/Buddha comparison work in a similar way.

Consideration of the particular historical context in which this *mamāyana* rhetoric first arose can also help us to understand both the risks and the possible payoffs involved in making use of the strategy of displacement. On the one hand, we might say, the Buddhist tradition needs to assert its patriarchal power, authority, and legitimacy through male-to-male lineages, exclusions of women, and images of the Buddha as a father. On the other hand, the Buddhist tradition also needs to motivate one's emotional commitment to this very image of Buddhism by manipulating one's feelings for the mother. These feelings are somewhat dangerous, however, in the sense that they could—if not directed properly—undercut and detract from the very commitment they seek to encourage. Images and memories of the mother may become so potent, in other words, that the Buddhist object onto which the resulting feelings are displaced is ultimately weakened rather than elevated. Perhaps we might surmise that during periods characterized by instability, stress, or competition from other political and religious entities, a tradition becomes more willing to take such risks—and reap their benefits.

The historian Barbara Watson Andaya, in seeking to explain the broad success enjoyed by Sri Lankan Theravāda Buddhism in its penetration of mainland Southeast Asia (Cambodia, Thailand, Laos, and Myanmar) during the twelfth and thirteenth centuries CE, offers an explanation that seems to run along these lines.[16] Instead of focusing on the influential role played by Southeast Asian rulers, as many previous historians have done, Andaya (somewhat like Hallisey) focuses on the wide appeal Theravāda Buddhism enjoyed at this time throughout the whole of Southeast Asian society—including among women. How can we explain this wide and broad appeal? Andaya offers the "considered speculation rather than assertion"[17] that the success of Theravāda Buddhism within the populace—at least in part, and especially among women—was a result of medieval Theravāda's greater willingness to promote positive images of motherhood that would counteract the highly patriarchal nature of traditional Theravāda, while still encouraging one's devotion to Buddhism. In this way, the Theravāda tradition would be more in accord with the traditionally high status enjoyed by women in Southeast Asia, and thus more appealing to both men and women. The comparison drawn between the Buddha and the mother in many medieval Sinhalese texts is cited by Andaya as one prominent example of this promotion of the mother, but several others are offered as well: Throughout much of Southeast Asia, for example, novitiate ordination was explicitly tied to the debt a son owes to his mother and the repayment of this debt through the merit the mother accrues by giving her son to the Saṃgha. The mother thus plays an important and highly valued role in the ritual context of novitiate ordination. Thus, in Thailand, novitiate ordination is preceded by chants that proclaim the boy's debt to his mother, praise her selflessness in enduring the pain of childbirth, and describe his ordination as *kha nom*, the "price of milk." In Burma, a boy's *shin-byu* or novice ordination is believed to be the religious act that produces the greatest amount of merit, yet it is also believed that "a novice's debt to his mother remains so great that the *shin-byu* can repay her for the milk he drank from only one of her breasts."[18] The imagery of childbirth is also invoked: In some Cambodian contexts, for example, the novice's entry into the monastery is conceived as a return to the womb of the mother Māyā, which will enable the novice to be spiritually reborn; similarly, the monk's waist belt may be equated with an umbilical cord, his cloak with a caul, and his robe with a placenta.[19] These phenomena might all be described in terms of the project of displacement, with the wide success of Southeast Asian Theravāda resulting, at least in part, from its successful linkage between feelings for the mother and commitment to Buddhism.

There is also evidence, however, that the strategy of displacement, in some instances, can reverse its course and operate in the *opposite* direction: Rather than encouraging a link between Buddhism and the mother in order to promote one's devotion to Buddhism (and ultimately undercut one's obligation to the mother), the exact opposite can occur—the process may be subverted so that the mother and her contributions are revalorized, often at the expense of Buddhism. I would cite, as one possible example of this type of "reversal," the celebration of the Tawadeintha (i.e., Tāvatiṃsa) festival in Burma, as described by Sir James George Scott (under the pseudonym Shway Yoe) back in 1882.[20] This festival, which Scott describes as "probably the most joyous and striking of the Burmese religious ceremonies,"[21] commemorates, and sometimes elaborately reenacts, the Buddha's ascent into heaven to preach the dharma to his mother Māyā (now reborn in heaven as a deity) and his descent back to earth in the city of Sāṅkāśya. But whereas the Theravāda textual tradition claims definitively that the Buddha used this occasion to preach the *Abhidhamma Piṭaka*, the Burmese monks who reenact these events for the festival present the contents of his sermon quite differently. Here the subject of the sermon is filial piety, and the Buddha himself (as voiced by one of the monks) is made to say (according to Scott's report):

> I, the great Sramana, the mightiest of all beings, the teacher of ne'ban [nirvana] and the Law; I, the all-powerful, who by my preaching can lead my mother into the path of salvation and the final deliverance; I, who know all things and have beat down the passions under my feet; even I, with all this can but repay the debt due to one of the breasts that suckled me. What then can man offer in love and gratitude to the mother who nourished him at her breast?[22]

The sentiment expressed here is, of course, an exact *reversal* of what we earlier saw in the *Gotamī Apadāna*: Whereas the *Gotamī Apadāna* devalues the mother's literal breastfeeding of the son in comparison to the son's salvational "breastfeeding" of his mother, the Tawadeintha festival asserts categorically that even leading one's mother to salvation can never constitute adequate repayment for the physical nourishment one received at her breast.[23] Thus, it is the *Buddha* who is indebted to his *mother*, rather than the other way around. Here, in a localized, vernacular, Burmese ritual context, displacement seems to move in the opposite direction as it does in the Pali canonical text.

This example not only illustrates the inherently risky and slippery nature of such projects of displacement; it also leads me to posit a more general hypothesis: *In general*, I would surmise, the further removed a particular context is from the level of the elite, the orthodox, and the canonical, the more likely it is to promote motherhood itself—as an actuality and not merely as a symbol. This is perhaps simply a result of the fact that the presence and influence of actual mothers would become stronger as one gets further away from cultural artifacts based in the most elite spaces within the monastery. Thus just as we saw in chapter 2 that the traditions surrounding the popular goddess Hārītī were more accommodating of mother-love than the traditions surrounding the nuns of the canonical *Therīgāthā*, so we now see that the relationship between the Buddha and his mother in a Burmese ritual context is the very opposite of what it was in the Pali *Gotamī Apadāna*. The further one gets from the ivory tower of elite, monastic, patriarchal Buddhism, it seems, the greater is the pull exerted by the mother.

Breastfeeding and the Bodhisattva's Bodily Self-Sacrifice

I speculated above that one of the reasons the comparison between breastfeeding and the Buddha's teaching of the dharma did not take root in Indian Buddhism (as opposed to medieval Theravāda) was that the Indian

Buddhist tradition was too accustomed to envisioning the Buddha as a *father* rather than as a mother. We should also remember, however, that to gender something as masculine (or as a "father") is implicitly to contrast it with—and suggest its superiority to—that which is gendered as feminine (or as a "mother"). As many feminist theorists have noted, the attributes of "masculine" and "feminine" cannot be seen in isolation; instead, they must be seen as parts of an ideological gender system by means of which "masculine" and "feminine" are opposed to each other and made to appear as mutually exclusive categories standing in a hierarchical relationship of dominance and subordination.[24] This should lead us to ask: If the Buddha is seen as the "father," then who is the corresponding "mother"? And if the Buddha's teaching of the dharma is conceived as the gift of the father, then what is the corresponding gift of the mother? And is *this* gift ever envisioned in terms of breastfeeding?

The figure of the bodhisattva—as a future buddha or "buddha-to-be"—is, by definition, inferior and subordinate to the fully enlightened Buddha. Therefore, if the Buddha is conceived as a father, perhaps it would be natural for the bodhisattva to be conceived as a mother. Moreover, just as the Buddha is distinguished by his compassionate "gift of the dharma" (Skt. *dharma-dāna*), so the bodhisattva, in Indian Buddhist tradition, is distinguished by his compassionate "gift of the body" (Skt. *deha-dāna*), or the many deeds of bodily self-sacrifice (Skt. *ātma-parityāga*) he performs on behalf of sentient beings throughout the course of his long career. Although this propensity to sacrifice life and limb on behalf of others—whether to feed hungry beings, serve as medicine for those who are ill, or merely to satisfy a supplicant's request—seems to be characteristic of bodhisattvas in general,[25] it is most characteristic of the Buddha Śākyamuni himself, during his previous lives as a bodhisattva, as recounted in the many Buddhist *jātakas* that feature such deeds. Stories involving the bodhisattva's many deeds of bodily self-sacrifice, which are often set forth as preeminent examples of the bodhisattva's *dāna-pāramitā* (Skt.) or "perfection of generosity," constitute an important subgenre of Indian Buddhist literature that I have elsewhere subjected to lengthy treatment.[26]

I have also demonstrated elsewhere[27] that both a parallel and a hierarchy are consistently drawn between the bodhisattva's gift of his body in the past—when there was no Buddhism in the world—and the Buddha's gift of the dharma in the present, which gives rise to the presence of Buddhism. Many stories dealing with the bodhisattva's bodily self-sacrifice suggest, in various ways, that whereas the bodhisattva gives away a *physical body*, the Buddha gives away a *spiritual body*, which is the "body of dharma" (Skt. *dharma-kāya*), that is, the body of his teachings. The bodhisattva enacts a physical salvation, while the Buddha enacts a spiritual salvation.[28] The two gifts are thus parallel, yet they also stand in a hierarchical relationship that clearly makes the Buddha superior: Whereas the bodhisattva gives away his physical body to appease the base sufferings of hunger, thirst, and illness, the Buddha gives away his "dharma-body" to eradicate permanently the great suffering of samsara. One is life-saving food; the other is soul-saving nectar. This contrast is very similar, in fact, to that drawn by Mahāpajāpatī in the *Gotamī Apadāna*, in which her gift of breast milk "that quenches thirst for just a moment" is contrasted with the Buddha's gift of "dharma-milk that is perpetually tranquil."

Perhaps it is no surprise, then, that in Indian sources it is the bodhisattva's paradigmatic deed of bodily self-sacrifice, rather than the Buddha's teaching of the dharma, that is sometimes envisioned in terms of a mother's breastfeeding. This serves simultaneously to praise and celebrate the bodhisattva for his motherly love and compassion and to suggest that the limited and primarily physical salvation offered by the bodhisattva is subordinate to the *true* salvation offered by the fully enlightened Buddha. The bodhisattva's gift of his body is subtly cast as "physical" and "female" in nature, whereas the Buddha's gift of the dharma is "spiritual" and "male." Just as we have seen in so many other contexts, then, motherhood, in this usage, is at once valued and undercut.

One example of this type of imagery may be found in several versions of the story of Kṣāntivādin, a prominent *jātaka* tale involving the Buddha's previous life as an ascetic named Kṣāntivādin ("Preacher of Forbearance"), who calmly tolerates the mutilation inflicted on him by an angry king, feeling no anger or hatred whatsoever. Although this tale—as the name Kṣāntivādin suggests—is generally depicted as an illustration of the bodhisattva's *kṣānti-pāramitā*, or "perfection of forbearance," rather than his *dāna-pāramitā*, or "perfection of generosity," it can be loosely aligned with stories involving the bodhisattva's gift of his body, since it, too, features an act of bodily sacrifice. While the version of this story found in the Theravāda *Jātaka Commentary* explicitly states that Kṣāntivādin's body flows with *blood* as each of his limbs is successively hacked off, and the version found in Ārya Śūra's *Jātakamālā* does not mention any specific substance,[29] two other versions of the story effect an interesting change: In chapter 13 of the *Lalitavistara*, as the gods are recounting for Prince Siddhārtha's benefit many of the exploits he performed in his previous lives, they recount his birth as Kṣāntivādin as follows: "Formerly, when you were a king's son and an excellent seer, an evil king cut off your limbs in anger. You suffered death, yet your mind was undisturbed, and milk (BHS *payu*) gushed forth from your hands and feet."[30] Though there is no explicit mention here of either mothers or breastfeeding, the mention of *milk* clearly serves to liken Kṣāntivādin's bodily sacrifice to a mother's breastfeeding. This comparison becomes explicit in the *Mahāvastu*'s retelling of the tale, for here it is said:

> The king cut off the seer's finger with the blade of his sword, and from the seer's finger, milk flowed, *just as a mother's milk flows from her breasts out of love for her son* [emphasis added]. And in just the same way, he whose mind was benevolent toward beings had all five fingers from each of his hands cut off, one by one, and in each case, milk gushed forth.[31]

Milk continues to flow as Kṣāntivādin suffers, in quick succession, the cutting off of his hands, feet, ears, and nose. In effect, Kṣāntivādin himself becomes like a giant, milk-spewing breast, the milk serving as a physical embodiment of the love, compassion, and forbearance he feels toward the angry king.

Similar invocations of the breastfeeding mother may be found in the famous story of the tigress, in which the bodhisattva is a man who sacrifices his own body to feed a starving tigress.[32] This starving tigress also happens to be a new mother: She has just given birth to a litter of cubs, but is so exhausted and crazed with hunger that she intends to devour her newborn cubs instead of feeding them. The bodhisattva saves both the mother and her cubs by offering his own body as food and thus appeasing the mother's devouring hunger. This juxtaposition between a "bad mother," who refuses to feed her offspring and wishes only to devour them, and the bodhisattva, who offers up his own body to save the cubs' lives, clearly suggests that the bodhisattva is the "true" mother, the "real" mother, the "good" mother who freely gives her body away. The very structure of the story suggests a comparison between the bodhisattva's gift of his body in the form of food and the mother's gift of her body in the form of breast milk.

In one version of the tigress story, the imagery of breastfeeding becomes explicit. In the version found in the *Suvarṇabhāsottama Sūtra*, the bodhisattva is a prince named Mahāsattva who goes out into the forest with his two brothers, encounters the starving tigress, evades his brothers, and then sacrifices his body to the tigress—falling down before her, cutting his throat open with a bamboo stick, and allowing the tigress to drink his blood and then devour him. Just as this momentous deed is occurring, Prince Mahāsattva's *own mother*, the queen, has an inauspicious dream in which her teeth are torn out and her breasts are cut off. On waking, she says to her husband, the king: "Not long ago, milk was released from both of the nipples on my breasts. My body is afflicted as if it were being split apart by needles, and my heart is bursting open."[33] The pricking of the queen's body by needles, the flow of milk from her breasts, and the splitting open of her heart seem to constitute an exact reflection of Prince Mahāsattva's deed of cutting his throat with a bamboo stick, flowing with blood, and then being devoured—suggesting an identity between Prince Mahāsattva and his mother. By means of these associations, the bodhisattva's compassionate deed of self-sacrifice is once again likened to the mother's act of breastfeeding: Both mothers and bodhisattvas are compassionate—and both mothers and bodhisattvas display their compassion in a concretely physical manner by *giving their bodies away*.

Finally, perhaps the clearest example of this comparison is offered by the story of Rūpāvatī, which exists in several Sanskrit versions[34] and which I have elsewhere analyzed at some length.[35] Here the Buddha Śākyamuni, in a previous life as a woman named Rūpāvatī, cuts off her own breasts and feeds them to a starving young woman who has just given birth to keep the woman from devouring her own newborn infant. Once again, the story juxtaposes a "bad mother" who refuses to feed her child, and instead intends to devour him, with the bodhisattva as a "good mother" who willingly offers her own body to save the child's life—thus suggesting that the bodhisattva is the child's *true* mother. The *Divyāvadāna*'s version of the story, in fact, goes out of its way to suggest that Rūpāvatī, and not the starving woman, constitutes the child's "true mother": Rūpāvatī and the child physically resemble one another, for both are described in exactly the same terms, as "pleasing, attractive, and beautiful, endowed with an excellent, bright complexion"[36]—a description that sharply contrasts with the appearance of the starving woman herself. Indeed, at the end of the story, Rūpāvatī is identified as a previous life of the Buddha, whereas the child is identified as a previous life of the Buddha's son Rāhula—once again suggesting that Rūpāvatī is the boy's "true" mother. In this story, then, the bodhisattva who gives away his body is, at the same time, a kind of "mother" who has intense compassion for a newborn child. Moreover, she is a mother who very literally *breastfeeds*, by cutting off her own breasts and allowing them to be eaten. The bodhisattva's gift of his body in the form of food and the mother's gift of her body in the form of breast-milk are once again made parallel—or, in this case, virtually collapsed into one.

At the same time, of course, if we consider exactly *how* Rūpāvatī "breastfeeds" the child, we can see that this comparison with the mother—yet again—is ultimately just a foil for the contrast. For Rūpāvatī does not breastfeed in the passive way that ordinary mothers do, by emitting milk from her breasts. Instead, she "breastfeeds" in a much more active and heroic manner, by slicing her breasts off and feeding them to the other woman. Within a Buddhist context, the contrast between these two modes of breastfeeding could not be more stark: Whereas ordinary breastfeeding involves breast milk leaking and oozing out of the breasts, and thus calls to mind the way in which women's bodies are generally depicted in Buddhist literature as a mottled array of open orifices continuously oozing all manner of vile substances,[37] Rūpāvatī's more heroic "breastfeeding" is a dramatic instance of the bodhisattva's bodily self-sacrifice out of compassion for others. Ultimately, then, the story seems to suggest that even the best mother's breastfeeding is nothing more than a pale reflection of the *true* breastfeeding—which is the bodhisattva's heroic self-sacrifice.

Finally, we should also take note of the conclusion of Rūpāvatī's story and the way in which it points still further, toward an implicit contrast between the bodhisattva and the Buddha. At the end of the story, when the deity Śakra, disguised as a brahmin, asks Rūpāvatī about the motivation behind her gift, Rūpāvatī performs an Act of Truth that transforms her breastfeeding body forever. In Haribhaṭṭa's version of the story, she states:

> I wish only for the state of a Victor
> in order to bring peace to the three worlds.
> O Brahmin, by means of this truth of mine,
> let my sex become male immediately,
> for manhood is an abode of virtue in this world.[38]

As wonderful as this bodhisattva's self-sacrifice may be, then, its true utility lies in its power to transform its agent into a *man*—and ultimately into a *buddha*, since permanently becoming male and being forever free from rebirth as a female was commonly understood as a necessary prerequisite to the attainment of buddhahood. Thus, the final message conveyed by the story is that the *truest* breastfeeding is that which gets rid of the breasts altogether and allows its agent to transform herself into a man and, finally, a buddha. The bodhisattva may be the "true mother," but the *truest* mother is really the *father*—or the Buddha himself. The Buddha will eschew such "physical" and "female" gifts as the gift of breast milk and the gift of the body in favor of the ultimate gift—the gift of the dharma. And this is the gift of a father.

The complexity of the gender symbolism employed within these tales finds a striking parallel in medieval Christian art and devotion, as interpreted by Caroline Walker Bynum.[39] The distinction I have drawn between the bodhisattva as "female" and the fully enlightened Buddha as "male" can be loosely compared to the tendency in medieval Christian literature to see Christ's *divinity* as *male* and his *humanity* as *female*. As Bynum has amply demonstrated, the subtle depiction of Christ's physical body as "female" was thus a way of emphasizing his humanity, his embodied nature, his human suffering, and his fleshliness—as opposed to his nature as God, which was implicitly coded as "male." Perhaps it is no surprise, then, that—much as we saw in the case of Kṣāntivādin—many medieval theologians saw the wound in Christ's side as a lactating breast and repeatedly drew parallels between Christ's bleeding on the cross and Mary's breastfeeding of the baby Jesus. The connotations of the breastfeeding theme are different, of course, in these two cases, yet both rely on a complex system of gender symbols that opposes "female" to "male."

I hope these examples have served to demonstrate the way in which maternal breastfeeding imagery is used in Indian Buddhist texts both to celebrate the bodhisattva's great compassion and to suggest that his salvational powers are still inferior to those of the fully enlightened Buddha. Many feminist theorists have written of the way in which women tend to be intimately associated with the physical and natural realm. Women often become emblematic of physicality itself, in contrast with the spirituality that tends to be associated with men. "Women," as Elizabeth Grosz has noted, "function as *the* body for men," thereby denying men's corporeality and allowing men to inhabit a pure, disembodied, and transcendent place of authority.[40] Therefore, if one wishes to draw a hierarchical distinction between the physical salvation offered by the bodhisattva and the spiritual salvation offered by the fully enlightened Buddha, women and feminine imagery constitute one important symbolic resource for doing so. The bodhisattva's physical salvation of beings through dramatic deeds of bodily sacrifice is indeed celebrated and praised, yet because this salvation is subtly likened to the physical ministrations of a breastfeeding mother (without being equated to them, of course), it is effectively subordinated to the spiritual salvation offered by the fully enlightened Buddha.

It also seems, however, that in certain contexts the benefits of allowing such maternal imagery to "migrate upward," so that it is applied to the Buddha himself, may outweigh any negative consequences. In the world of medieval Theravāda, for example, perhaps it was the necessity of adapting to a new cultural context in which women had higher status than they had in early India, as well as the desirability of attracting a broad spectrum of women as committed adherents, that led to the application of maternal breastfeeding imagery directly to the Buddha himself and his gift of the dharma—even though this had traditionally been depicted as an inheritance from the *father* (such as we see in the famous story of Rāhula asking the Buddha for his inheritance and being ordained into the Saṃgha). Moreover, in local and less elite contexts that are perhaps closer to the presence and influence of actual mothers (e.g., the Burmese Tawadeintha festival), the acceptance of positive maternal imagery may become so great that the Buddha is finally subordinated to the mother herself. Here, at last, the mother's gift of her breast milk is, indeed, the *true* breastfeeding, and it results in a debt that even the Buddha's teaching of the dharma is powerless to repay.

8

"What Here Is the Merit, May That Be for My Parents"

MOTHERHOOD ON THE GROUND

IN CONTRAST WITH earlier generations, contemporary scholarship in Buddhist Studies has increasingly sought to relocate premodern Indian Buddhism back "on the ground"—in other words, to recognize Buddhist texts as elite and normative statements rather than accurate representations of "what Indian Buddhists actually practiced and believed,"[1] and thus to move beyond the idealized world of the text by drawing on other kinds of sources (such as inscriptions and art history) that may more accurately reflect the lived experiences of actual Buddhists in India. Gregory Schopen, whose scholarship has been particularly influential in this regard, sees the overwhelming bias toward textual evidence—and its underlying assumption that texts constitute the only source of "real" religion—as a basic element of our Western intellectual heritage, one that ultimately derives from the Protestant Reformation's emphasis on the legitimacy of the Word alone.[2] In an astonishingly prolific body of scholarship stretching over the last three decades,[3] he has made effective use of inscriptions, archeology, and art history (in addition to texts) to paint a picture of Indian Buddhist monasticism that differs significantly from the idealized portrait familiar to us from an earlier generation of scholars. In his work, the Indian Buddhist monastic emerges not as an asocial and homeless renunciant who spends most of his or her time meditating and striving for nirvana but, instead, as somebody much like us—one who is fully embroiled in the world and deeply involved with the surrounding community; one who owns personal wealth and property and engages in complicated financial transactions; one who has little concern with meditation or the goal of nirvana, but is instead deeply committed to cultic practices (such as the worship of images and relics); and—most important for our purposes—one who continues to worry about his or her parents or children and to be intimately connected to family. Since I have invoked, on more than one occasion, the simple observation that Indian Buddhist monks were not only Buddhist monks, but also the sons of their mothers, it seems fitting for me to pursue at least a cursory examination of such familial ties—although here I will largely limit myself to citing the careful work done by others.

Thus, while the previous chapters have focused on the discourse of motherhood as it is developed in Buddhist texts, this final chapter will attempt to extend this focus to look at the relationship between motherhood and Indian Buddhism as it actually existed "on the ground." In considering this question, I will be particularly concerned to elucidate the relationship between two seemingly contradictory phenomena: On the one hand, Buddhist texts routinely depict the Buddhist renunciant as one who has renounced and severed all familial ties—a depiction that seems central and fundamental to the Buddhist tradition as a whole. On the other hand, such a picture is everywhere belied by abundant historical evidence showing that Buddhist monks and nuns both continued to be concerned with the welfare of their own parents and had a sometimes-ambiguous status vis-à-vis their own parenthood. How do these two contradictory phenomena relate to one other? Were they experienced by Buddhist monastics as a true conflict between theory and practice, or are there other ways of understanding their relationship? Does this "conflict" in fact boil down to a difference in genre and the kinds of sentiments expressed through different forms of media? And, finally, how might this relationship be related to the overall discourse on motherhood discussed in the earlier chapters? Toward the end of the chapter, I attempt to further elucidate the on-the-ground relationship between motherhood and Buddhism by moving beyond the realm of premodern India and offering some suggestive hints taken from more contemporary Buddhist contexts.

Monks and Their Families

Buddhist texts routinely describe the Buddhist monastic as one who "goes forth from the home into the homeless life" (P. *agārasmā anagāriyaṃ pabbajjati*). This resonant phrase is not meant to be taken literally, as the physical act of leaving one's home and entering into a permanent state of homeless wandering; in fact, we know that most Buddhist monks abandoned such homeless wandering fairly early in the history of Buddhist monasticism. Instead, "going forth from the home into the homeless life" is a shorthand formula for the ideological and social act of renouncing the world, joining the Saṃgha, and being ordained as a Buddhist monk or nun. It suggests a dramatic transformation in one's status, lifestyle, and mental attitude, by means of which one rejects and renounces the worldly life of the householder in favor of a life of renunciation and asceticism within the Buddha's dharma.

If we remember that the Buddha himself is the original model for "going forth from the home into the homeless life," then it is clear that this act—ideally speaking, at least—*does* involve the rejection of one's family and the severance of ordinary family ties. In his biography, the Buddha himself, on "going forth," dramatically leaves behind his wife, son, and parents, and forever renounces the worldly roles of husband, father, and son. On attaining enlightenment, he makes it clear to his father that he is no longer a "son" within his father's royal lineage of kings; now he is a "son" within the lineage of the buddhas: "Your Majesty," he says in the *Nidānakathā*, "this lineage of kings is indeed your lineage (P. *vaṃso*), but mine is the lineage of the buddhas, from Dīpaṅkara to Kondañña, and all the way down to Kassapa."[4] Similarly, though he continues to be referred to as the "father" of Rāhula, he is equally depicted as the "father" of all monks and nuns within the Saṃgha. Though he continues to recognize his former relationship with his family—for example, by returning to Kapilavastu in order to convert them—it is clear that he is relating to them *as a buddha* rather than as a member of the family. In the *Nidānakathā*, in fact, the Buddha performs a miracle during this visit whose specific purpose is to counteract his family's mistaken assumption that "Prince Siddhattha is [still] junior to us, he is our younger brother, our nephew, our son, our grandson."[5] When the Buddha refers to the Śākyas as his "kinsmen," therefore, I take this to mean that he is acknowledging the worldly, familial relationship he once had with them, not that he continues to function within this role.

Early Buddhist discourses such as the famous *Rhinoceros Horn Discourse* (P. *Khaggavisāṇa Sutta*) of the *Sutta Nipāta*[6] likewise make it clear that the life of the ideal Buddhist renunciant necessarily involves a rejection of familial ties. According to this text, "one should not desire a son";[7] in fact, one should "abandon son and wife, and father and mother,"[8] and free oneself completely from "the affection one has for sons and wives,"[9] just as one would free oneself from an entangling tree. In all ways, one should "remove the signs of a householder" and "cut the householder's ties"[10]—like "a king abandoning the kingdom he has conquered"[11] or "a fish breaking out of a net."[12] Although this discourse is particularly extreme in its recommendation of solitude—repeatedly encouraging the Buddhist renunciant to "wander alone, like the [single] horn of the rhinoceros"[13]—and should not be taken as representative of Buddhist literature in general, it is by no means unusual in its recommendation to sever familial ties. We have already seen before that the ideal Buddhist monk is sometimes described as one who does not acknowledge any relationship with his own mother;[14] likewise, on her attainment of parinirvana, even Mahāprajāpatī has no use for the continuing presence of her son, the Buddha.[15]

How does this idealized picture of the Buddhist renunciant as one who has severed all familial ties correspond to the evidence on the ground? Epigraphy constitutes one important resource here, since the Buddhist donative inscriptions scattered throughout the Indian subcontinent represent the interests of a much wider spectrum of Indian Buddhists than most Buddhist texts do, and also have a more practical and quotidian nature. As Shayne Clarke has observed, if we look at such inscriptions, we can see, first of all, that many monks and nuns continued to identify themselves in terms of their familial relationships, even after they had renounced the world—describing themselves as "brother of X," "son of X," "mother of X," and so forth. Likewise, many laypeople continued to identify themselves in terms of their familial relationships with monastics, even after those monastics had renounced the world.[16] While these references to family members could be interpreted as mere acknowledgments of former relationships that had since been renounced, the very fact that they were mentioned at all suggests that they continued to be an important aspect of their authors' self-identities. Some inscriptions, moreover, record gifts that were given to the Saṃgha by monks and nuns *together with their family members* (who might also be monks or nuns)—for example, a gift given by the "female disciple Budharakhitā, and by her granddaughter Cūla-Budharakhitā"; a gift given by "the Elder . . . Reverend Budhi, and his sister the *bhikṣuṇī* Budhā"; and a gift given by "the *bhikṣuṇī* Budharakhitā . . . with her daughters" (all taken from Sāñcī).[17] Such inscriptions go beyond mere self-identification to suggest that these monastics continued to have some kind of ongoing relationship with members of their families. It thus becomes clear that these monks and nuns had *not* necessarily severed all familial ties, nor did their family members consider those ties to have ended.

Inscriptions also provide us with evidence that family members—especially parents—continued to be objects of emotional affection, care, and concern for their monastic relatives. In an extensive review of Buddhist donative inscriptions (including Kharoṣṭhī inscriptions from Northwest India, and inscriptions from Mathurā, Bodh-Gayā, Nāgārjunikoṇḍa, Sārnāth, and Ajaṇṭā), Gregory Schopen has established conclusively that "concern for the 'well-being' of both deceased and living parents was a major preoccupation of Buddhist donors in India; that one of the most frequently stated reasons for undertaking acts of religious giving was to benefit the donors' parents, both living and dead; and that this concern was both very old and very widespread in India."[18] In other words, whenever gifts of any kind were made to the Buddhist Saṃgha, the donor was able to compassionately transfer the merit resulting from the gift to whomever he or she wished. This transfer would frequently be recorded in an inscription, and in many cases the donor's own parents were the intended beneficiaries. (Though some inscriptions refer to the mother alone, it is much more common to find mention of both parents.) Thus, gifts to the Saṃgha were said to be undertaken "for the benefit of [my] mother and father," "as an act of *pūjā* for my parents," "as an act of *pūjā* for [my] deceased parents," and so forth.[19] Or a common donative formula (with numerous variations) was used in which the donor declared: "What here is the merit, may that be for my parents." Especially interesting are those gifts that were given for the benefit of "[my] mother and father and all living beings" or "for the benefit of my parents at first"—phrases that suggest a sort of tension between the donor's particularistic devotion toward his own parents and his universal devotion toward the welfare of all.

Though Schopen's survey of donative inscriptions includes both lay and monastic donors, it is important to note that this expression of special concern for one's own parents and desire to benefit them specifically appears to have been equally prevalent in both groups. "In fact," Schopen notes,

> if we take the total number of inscriptions in our sample, it would appear that not only was the concern for their parents . . . a major preoccupation among our monk-donors, *but it was perhaps a special concern of this group:* in more than 60 percent of all of the Indian inscriptions in our sample in which acts were undertaken to benefit the donors' parents, the donors were monks, and the percentage . . . is considerably higher . . . at Mathurā, Ajaṇṭā, and Sārnāth.[20]

This includes not just ordinary monks, but also highly learned ones who describe themselves with titles such as "one who knows the *Tripiṭaka*," "a preacher of the Dharma," and "one who is versed in the canonical doctrine as a whole."[21]

The inscriptional evidence thus suggests that Buddhist monks from across India and from every time period were highly concerned with the welfare of their living and deceased parents—perhaps even *more* concerned than were the Buddhist laity—including the elite and educated monks who produced, passed down, and preached from the very canonical texts cited above, in which the ideal renunciant is presented as one who has severed all familial ties. Rather than seeing this as a contradiction, however, perhaps we should see it as an inevitable consequence. In fact, Schopen himself, in another context, has speculated along just these lines: Since the renunciation of worldly life, he notes, was clearly "a move fraught with difficulty" that "generated strong familial reactions," perhaps it is only to be expected that "it created a disproportionately strong sense of anxiety in regard to their 'abandoned' parents on the part of individual monks and nuns"[22]—an anxiety that is reflected in the inscriptions. This speculation accords well with some of my own comments on the discourse of motherhood as found in the texts: Just as the renunciant son's anxiety over his lingering ties to his mother may have resulted in the ambivalent and contradictory images of motherhood we find in the texts, so also it may have resulted, in the inscriptions, in reassurances to himself that he was, indeed, taking care of his parents. Bernard Faure, speaking of mothers in particular, likewise asserts that it is precisely because monks "abandoned" their mothers that the monastic discourse on motherhood is pervaded by "feelings of nostalgia and survivor's guilt"[23]—the same survivor's guilt that is reflected in a different way within the merit transfers of the inscriptions. This is not a question, then, of an earlier and more pristine ideal found only in the texts that later proves to be "corrupted" when we look at the inscriptions; rather, it is a question of imperfect human beings who express both their ideals and their anxieties in a variety of different ways and through a variety of different media.

In addition to identifying themselves through their familial relationships and expressing special concern for the welfare of their family members, there is also evidence that Buddhist monks and nuns in India continued to associate with—and may have spent significant time with—members of their own families, as well as continuing to bear the burden of ordinary familial obligations. Here we can do no better than to summarize the conclusions of Shayne Clarke's work on Indian Buddhism and the family.[24] Methodologically, Clarke focuses less on the distinction between texts and inscriptions, and more on the distinction between different types of texts. In particular, Clarke maintains that the vision of the renunciant as one who has severed all familial ties is found solely in the sūtras—texts that present the "public face" of Buddhism and are especially concerned to put forth an exemplary ideal. A more accurate depiction of Buddhist monasticism as it existed on the ground must be sought, therefore, in the *Vinayas* (or texts on monastic discipline), which Clarke describes as "strictly 'in-house' texts, for monastic eyes and ears only," or "internal documents" that "transmit an 'in-house' vision of what monks and nuns should and were thought to do."[25] Though he occasionally overstates his case, Clarke's thorough study of monks' and nuns' relationships with their families, as depicted in all of the extant *Vinayas*, clearly demonstrates that there was little or no expectation that most Buddhist monastics would *really* sever all familial ties.[26]

In the area of alms-gathering, for example, Clarke demonstrates that it was considered unexceptional for monks to go to their own families' homes for alms and sit down together with them at a meal, perhaps even on a daily basis; that it was allowable for monks to accept certain kinds of food from their own families that they would not be permitted to accept from other people; and that when food was scarce, a nun was permitted to eat with her own family every day, even if she had to travel there alone (which was otherwise forbidden). In fact, going beyond such occasional meals or short visits, it was permissible for monks and nuns to stay overnight with their own families, and it is even possible that some monks and nuns never really "went forth" from their homes at all. Clarke cites the famous story of Sudinna, who is ordained as a monk yet continues to live at home and to "interact with his relations just as he had formerly as a layman."[27] Though Sudinna's behavior is not encouraged—he is, in fact, the monk whose eventual transgression with his wife leads the Buddha to promulgate the very first *pārājika* offence in the *prātimokṣa*, forbidding monks from having sexual intercourse—neither is his living at home outright prohibited. Clarke thus concludes that "Buddhist renunciation, the going-forth from home into homelessness, seems not to perforce require any physical separation from the home, much less the forsaking of kinship or social bonds."[28] Alternatively, members of a family might enter the Saṃgha together and continue within the monastery the same familial relationships—and physical proximity—they had formerly enjoyed at home. This seems to be the case in one story (found in several *Vinayas*) cited by Clarke,[29] in which a widower and his two young children enter the Saṃgha together and accompany each other on their alms-rounds. Though this does lead the Buddha to promulgate a rule concerning the minimum age at which such children might be ordained, there is no criticism of the family's behavior itself—either the father's desire to bring his children with him to the monastery and supervise their alms-gathering, or the children's desire to remain in close physical proximity to their father. Much the same is true of husbands and wives: The *Vinaya* seems to regard it as unexceptional for a monk to visit his former wife—though it *is* wary of the prohibited behavior that might ensue—or for husbands and wives who enter the Saṃgha together to continue to have some kind of relationship (albeit one that is not sexual).[30]

The obligations attached to such family relationships may also have remained in force, at least within the minds of individual monks and nuns. Thus, in another story cited by Clarke,[31] two monks are both castigated by their former wives for not fulfilling their obligations as fathers by arranging the marriages of their adult children. The two monks agree to solve this problem by having one monk's son marry the other monk's daughter. Although they are reprimanded by the Buddha for violating the rule that prohibits monks from acting as go-betweens in sexual or marital liaisons, they are *not* criticized for feeling the burden of the obligation itself. (Presumably, if fulfilling the obligation *without* violating a rule of the *Vinaya* had been possible, they would not have been criticized at all.) Familial relationships, in fact, are even explicitly recognized, to some extent, within monastic law itself. Citing a story from the *Mūlasarvāstivāda Vinaya*, Schopen has demonstrated that monks retained their right to inherit family property even after renouncing the world (and even in light of the standard assumption that monks have renounced all private property).[32]

It thus appears that a significant number of Buddhist monks and nuns in India—even after "going forth from the home into the homeless life"—continued to identify themselves in terms of their familial relationships, continued to express concern for the welfare and benefit of their family members (both living and dead), continued to associate with their families (either inside or outside the monastery), may have lived with their families on a temporary or permanent basis, continued to feel and perhaps fulfill traditional family obligations, and continued to function, in some contexts, as legal members of their families. This is a far cry indeed from the picture of the Buddhist renunciant as one who has severed all familial ties and no longer engages in familial roles. Inscriptional and textual evidence both suggest that renouncing the world and "going forth from the home into the homeless life" may have been more rhetorical than literal in nature and that rejection of one's family was not necessarily considered a strong marker of such renunciation—in spite of its importance ideologically and within the paradigmatic life story of the Buddha.

In itself, of course, this is perhaps not very surprising. Ideologically speaking, the "world-renouncer" is one who turns his back on family, community, culture, and society—but in reality, such "world-renouncers," if they existed, would not have left many traces of their existence, let alone a fully developed religion, a long literary tradition, or a large body of artistic and archeological remains. The Buddhist monastic's continuing entanglements with his family is thus of a piece with his continuing existence as a social and cultural being. Thus, while I agree with Clarke concerning the general differences between sūtra and *Vinaya*, I also think that he misconstrues the situation when he characterizes the sūtras as depicting "the religious life as envisioned by a handful of ascetic athletes and spiritual supermen," and the *Vinayas* as reflecting "the lived religion of men and women attempting, struggling, to come to terms with what it meant for them to be—to live life as—a Buddhist."[33] I do not believe that visions of the renunciant as an austere, family-rejecting ascetic were all composed by "ascetic athletes," while visions of the renunciant entangled within the family were composed by those who were somehow "struggling." Instead, I see these two groups as being the same body of conflicted people.[34] All literature is produced by imperfect human beings who struggle to express their hopes, aspirations, disappointments, and despair by giving voice to both their ideals and the realities that undercut them. Ideals and the anxieties surrounding them, far from contradicting each other, should be seen as naturally coexisting.

Motherhood and the Monastery

While the discussion above pertains to familial relationships in general, I turn now to the special case of nuns who are also mothers. To what extent are these two roles compatible? Earlier, we saw that most of the idealized nun-mothers of the *Therīgāthā* became exemplary nuns by eradicating their own motherhood—learning to see their deceased children with indifference and viewing their former relationships with their children as nothing more than strangers meeting along a road. The sole exceptions to this pattern were Vaḍḍhamātā and Vāsiṭṭhī, both of whom somehow managed to combine within themselves the ideal nun's eradication of all attachment and craving *and* the mother's special concern for her own particular children. The texts themselves are thus characterized by varying degrees of accommodation between being a nun and being a mother.

How does this compare to what we see on the ground? Here again I rely on the careful work of Clarke, who has addressed this question in terms of both *Vinaya* texts and inscriptions.[35] With regard to the latter, Clarke observes that inscriptions in which nuns identify themselves as "mother of X" demonstrate that nuns might continue to identify themselves as mothers, even after renouncing the world. Likewise, inscriptions in which nuns make donations together with their children seem to suggest some kind of ongoing relationship. Aside from this minimal information, however, inscriptions do not tell us much. *Vinaya* texts, on the other hand, offer us a wealth of intriguing evidence of nuns engaging in the actual practice of mothering within the confines of the monastery and reveal, as Clarke puts it, "a surprising accommodation of motherhood in Buddhist monasticism."[36] Below I give a brief review of the evidence gathered by Clarke.

In the *Dharmaguptaka Vinaya* (T. 1428), for example, although the ordination of a pregnant or nursing woman is discouraged, it is by no means prohibited. In fact, such a woman, once ordained, is expected to take care of her baby while pursuing the life of the nun. The Buddha states: "If [the child is] still unable to live on its own, I authorize [the nun] to nurse and nurture [her baby], in accordance with motherhood, until she has weaned [the child] and stopped [breastfeeding]."[37] It is clear, moreover, that the baby should actually live with its mother, for despite the rule forbidding nuns from staying together with males, the Buddha allows such a nun to sleep with the child, even if it is a boy. The same is true in both the *Mahīśāsaka Vinaya* (T. 1421) and the Theravāda *Vinaya*, but here the Buddha also allows another nun to be assigned as the mother's attendant, both women being permitted to hold and sleep together with the child. The nun's mothering of her child is thus not only permitted, but to a surprising degree accommodated, by the Saṃgha. As Clarke has observed, these *Vinayas* suggest "that Indian Buddhist convents saw—and were legislated so that they might provide for—not only nuns giving birth and breast-feeding, but actually raising their children [within the monastery]. . . . [N]unneries could in a very real sense have become, at least in part, nurseries with monastic mothers looking after teething toddlers."[38]

It is interesting to note, however, that in the *Mahīśāsaka Vinaya*, when a nun-mother and her attendant both "adorn" and "coo at" the child, the Buddha reprimands them, saying, "That should not be done."[39] This suggests that while the *Vinaya* redactors wanted such nuns to fulfill the basic obligations of a mother—perhaps to avoid the social censure of the surrounding public—they also took some care to discourage the mother (or any other nun) from becoming too emotionally attached to the child. The same may also be implied by the Buddha's further instructions (immediately after the statement above): "If he [is old enough to] leave your bosom, you should give him to a *bhikṣu*, and make him go forth into the religious life. If you do not wish to have him go forth into the religious life, you should give him to relatives, and have him brought up." Thus, once weaning had occurred and the physical aspects of mothering were completed, the male child was to be separated from his mother. Female children, however, are not mentioned; presumably, if the child were a daughter who was to become a nun, she could remain in the monastery with her mother.

The *Sarvāstivāda Vinaya* (T. 1435) appears to be somewhat stricter in these matters and to take even greater care that the nun's mothering of her child be restricted in various ways—although, again, these concerns seem to be stronger in the case of a child who is male. Here there is no assigning of any attendant, and it is the mother alone who is allowed to touch and sleep with the child; provision is made, in fact, for such a nun to be assigned a solitary cell to limit the child's contact with other nuns. Once a male child is weaned, however, the mother must stop this behavior, on threat of committing an offense: "If [the child] is able to be separated from the mother, and the mother touches him, [she incurs] a *duṣkṛta* [i.e., a very minor offense of wrongdoing]. . . . If [the mother] spends night[s] together [with the baby boy] once he is weanable, the mother incurs a *duṣkṛta*."[40] Female children again are not mentioned. Also interesting here is the fact that although these rules are established for the specific case of the pregnant nun Guptā, the *Sarvāstivāda Vinaya* notes that they should also apply to "further nuns like this"—a tantalizing suggestion that pregnant and mothering nuns may have been more common than we might suppose.[41]

Strictest of all in these matters is the *Mahāsāṅghika Vinaya* (T. 1425), which states outright that a pregnant woman should not be ordained until after she has given birth. If the baby is a girl, she may be ordained immediately (with the baby presumably coming to the monastery with her); but if the baby is a boy, she should wait until the child has been weaned, unless her relatives agree to raise him from the start. No special accommodations are provided to the mother, however, in the form of an attendant, separate living quarters, or permission to sleep with her child. This *Vinaya* therefore seems to discourage the presence of such children within the nunnery—although, again, it leaves open that possibility when such children are female.

Finally, most interesting of all, from my perspective, is the *Mūlasarvāstivāda Vinaya*, in both its Tibetan and Chinese translations. Here, when the pregnant nun Guptā gives birth to a son and doesn't touch him because of the rule forbidding nuns from any contact with males, her own relatives criticize her behavior: "The World-Honoured One is very compassionate," they say in the Chinese version (T. 1451). "How could he not allow one to touch one's own son? If the mother does not touch him, how could he survive?"[42] This criticism not only cites Guptā's responsibilities as a mother, but also draws an implicit connection between maternal care and the compassion of the Buddha, seeing them as fully complementary rather than in contradiction. The other nuns are said to praise this advice, and when they report it to the Buddha, he allows such touching to occur. In the Chinese version, he says, "One's own child one should touch. There is no fault in nurturing him and taking him in one's arms," while in the Tibetan version, he says, "Henceforth, with authorisation he should be touched. He should be fed. He should be nurtured. He should be brought up."[43] The link between maternal care and the Buddha's compassion thus moves gradually from laypeople to nuns, and finally to the Buddha himself, who promulgates the resultant ruling in what seems like more emotional and affectionate language than is found in other *Vinayas*. Though I do not want to read too much into the passage, it seems to me that this *Vinaya* is perhaps on the verge of suggesting that nuns should nurture their children not merely as a practical matter, or for the sake of appearances, but also because maternal love is fully harmonious with the compassion of the Buddha himself. It seems to introduce this quasi argument cautiously, however, making it originate in the mouths of Guptā's relatives and only gradually placing it in the mouth of the Buddha.

In any case, taking the *Vinaya* evidence as a whole, I must agree with Clarke's conclusion that "Buddhist monasticism was much more open to monastic motherhood than might otherwise have been suspected" and seems to have made a significant attempt "to accommodate pregnant and newly-delivered mothers into the religious life."[44] Perhaps it might be useful, however, to draw out some of the underlying and limiting principles that govern this accommodation. First, it is clear that the accommodation of motherhood applied only to women who had become pregnant *before* being ordained as nuns. Those who became pregnant *after* ordination were guilty of committing a *pārājika* offense and liable to immediate expulsion from the Saṃgha (as Clarke has demonstrated in the case of the nun Mettiyā, discussed in several *Vinayas*).[45] Second, the consistent emphasis on maternal care coming to an end at the time of weaning suggests that the Saṃgha's primary concern was to make sure that mothers did not abandon their obligation to physically nourish and care for young children, even after renouncing the world. The rules allowing the mother to sleep with her child, giving her a solitary cell, or providing her with an attendant likewise seem to be geared toward meeting the demands of early childcare and breastfeeding. There is little suggestion, on the other hand, that the Saṃgha had any interest in encouraging an emotional attachment between mother and child. In fact, the *Mahīśāsaka Vinaya*'s reprimand of the two nuns who "adorn" and "coo at" the child suggests precisely the opposite—as does the complete lack in Buddhist literature of any scenes of tender affection between nuns and their young children. As impractical as it might be to command mothers to breastfeed and care for their children while also discouraging them from becoming too emotionally attached, this, it seems to me, might be a natural consequence of the attempt to reconcile the image of the Buddhist renunciant as one who has detached herself from such familial ties with the Saṃgha's desire to avoid the criticism it would likely receive from the surrounding public for allowing mothers to abandon their helpless infants. I do not see an outright contradiction, then, between the image of the nun as one who has renounced her motherhood, and the presence of nuns who actively mother their children within the monastery walls. Instead, what I see is the tradition as a whole constantly struggling to negotiate a complicated mixture of factors—religious ideals and aspirations, the Saṃgha's economic dependence on the surrounding public, natural human frailties and weaknesses, and the pull of love exerted by children themselves.

There is a second general observation to be made here as well. The consistent distinction drawn between male and female children, with rules of contact being significantly stricter in the case of male children, may suggest that ultimately the Saṃgha was more concerned with maintaining the separation of the sexes as much as possible than it was with any other issues surrounding contact between nun-mothers and their children. The fact that daughters are not mentioned in many contexts in which restrictions are placed on contact with sons leaves open the possibility that a nun-mother might very well give birth to a daughter, breastfeed and raise her, and continue to live with her for the rest of her life—all within the monastery walls. If the nun's renunciation of motherhood—rather than her commitment to celibacy—were the primary concern, then more attention would have been paid to limiting the contact between mothers and daughters. The greater attention paid to sons perhaps indicates that the community at large was more insistent on the celibacy of its monastics than on their renunciation of family.

Continuing Family Ties in Contemporary Buddhist Monastic Lives

The evidence presented above clearly suggests the continuing familial entanglements that likely characterized the lives of most Buddhist monastics in India. What was true of premodern India, moreover, has no doubt been equally true of Buddhism wherever and whenever it has existed. Historical and anthropological accounts of Buddhism present abundant evidence for such familial ties, even though such evidence is usually presented in an offhand manner and is rarely the main focus of attention—which makes it difficult to gather and summarize. For this reason, individual biographies of contemporary Buddhist monks and nuns are especially useful for gaining some sense of how thoroughly such family ties might shape the lives of individual Buddhist monastics.

In Hanna Havnevik's brief biography of the contemporary Tibetan Buddhist nun Yeshe Drolma[46]—to cite just a single example—we learn that before becoming a nun herself, Yeshe Drolma went on pilgrimage for over a year in the company of her own sister, who was already a nun, along with another nun and that nun's mother. Once she herself was ordained, her brother built her a hermitage, which was funded by her immediate family; she spent the next several decades in isolation at this hermitage, yet her family sent a horse for her every summer so that she could return home for an extended visit. During the winters, she often accompanied her nephew, who was also a monastic, to another monastery. At one point, she went on a pilgrimage with a highly esteemed male lama—who, she casually mentions, had both his mother and his nephew living with him at his hermitage. She later goes on another extended pilgrimage, again in the company of her close relatives. From beginning to end, then, Yeshe Drolma's monastic life is thoroughly shaped by her familial ties to parents, siblings, and other family members—as are the monastic lives of those around her, including an esteemed male lama.

Similarly, in Sid Brown's account of the life of a contemporary Thai Buddhist nun called Māechī Wābī,[47] we learn that Māechī Wābī spends several years helping to care for her monastic teacher's elderly father and mentally retarded sister; that Māechī Wābī later has an unpleasant altercation with the *mother* of another teacher (who is staying in the teacher's hermitage when the altercation occurs); that this leads to a full-blown spiritual crisis, during which Māechī Wābī seeks shelter at the temple of her own father, a Buddhist monk, even though this temple has no appropriate accommodations for nuns; that she recovers with the help of her brother, who is himself a novice in her father's temple; and that she later returns back home for a time to help her mother recuperate after a car accident. Again, Māechī Wābī's entire monastic life is colored by her own familial ties, as well as those of her various teachers. These ties, moreover, have varying effects on her spiritual vocation: While caring for her mother is experienced by her as a significant hindrance, the time spent with her brother and father succeeds in bringing her out of a paralyzing spiritual crisis. And while one teacher's mother causes her significant spiritual pain, another teacher's father and sister become objects of care that constitutes an integral part of her spiritual training. Within the context of an individual life, then, family ties are not always experienced as a hindrance to one's monastic career.

Though I have focused here on the biographies of two contemporary nuns, the same kinds of familial entanglements may be found in a great number of such monastic biographies, regardless of their region of origin, historical period, and whether they pertain to monks or nuns. A similar situation appears to prevail, moreover, in the case of those nuns who are also mothers and often continue to function as mothers. The well-known Thai Buddhist nun (and advocate for full *bhikkhunī* ordination) Chatsumarn Kabilsingh, for example, explains that her own mother became a nun when she was only ten years old, transformed their house into a nunnery, and had other nuns come to live with them—all while continuing to function as a mother.[48] Hiroko Kawanami likewise speaks of a Burmese nun who brings her daughter to the nunnery with her when she renounces the world. Later on, like any mother who wants her child to get ahead, she gets her daughter admitted to a prestigious nunnery school, accompanies her daughter to the school, continues to raise her there, and studies the Buddhist scriptures at nighttime, while her daughter is sleeping. Eventually, mother and daughter establish their own nunnery school together.[49]

Speaking more generally (and less anecdotally) of Buddhist nuns in Sri Lanka, Tessa Bartholomeusz notes:

> In my primary research site, and in the majority of the other lay nunneries I visited, the female renunciants continue to play an active role in the lives of their own families. . . . [Each of those nuns who were mothers] was visited almost daily by her children. Sometimes the children came bringing alms and had a formal "religious" visit. At other times, however, they came seeking maternal affection.[50]

In a footnote, she further elaborates: "In fact, the lay nuns who are mothers whom I interviewed all maintained a very motherly relationship with their sons and daughters; these children are very prevalent in the lay nunneries . . . [and] continue to regard the renunciants as their mothers."[51] While this is perhaps only to be expected of nuns in Sri Lanka, Thailand, or Burma—since it is well-documented that Buddhist nuns who lack the full *bhikkhunī* ordination and have a relatively low status within their cultures generally maintain much closer ties to their families than do the corresponding monks (due largely to economic necessity)[52]—the same situation can be found even in a place like Taiwan, where Buddhist nuns are fully ordained and enjoy significant power and autonomy. Speaking of one Taiwanese Buddhist nunnery, Hillary Crane notes:

> At Zhi Guang, many of the nuns bring their families with them. Of the eighteen female nuns who are still minors, the mothers of twelve of them are also nuns. Of the other six, all but one have an older immediate family member who is also a monastic. One nun . . . brought a daughter who did not want to become a nun. The daughter lives on the temple grounds, but not as a monastic. She still relies on her mother to be a mother to her at times, and this relationship is perceived by others at the temple, and by the nun/mother herself, as a hindrance. One nun . . . brought her entire family to become monastics (including her four children, her siblings, her mother and some of her aunts), except for her husband. . . . Despite being a nun, she often has to fulfil the role of mother to her children.[53]

This passage is particularly interesting, since it demonstrates that—on the ground—there is not necessarily any contradiction between the matter-of-fact acceptance of such children at the nunnery and the recognition, nevertheless, that the resulting maternal obligations might constitute a significant "hindrance" to the nun's monastic career.

Though the evidence I have presented is obviously anecdotal and scattered, and can never be more than suggestive for the case of premodern India, I believe it is useful for understanding that the monastic ideal of renouncing one's family and the realities that often undercut this ideal—once we place them on the ground—are *not* two entities standing in opposition to one another but, rather, are thoroughly interwoven within the complicated tapestry of any individual monastic life. It is perhaps because premodern India lacks any genre of literature that would be comparable to contemporary ethnographic biographies of individual Buddhist monastics that we *miss* this complicated tapestry and are instead confronted by fragments suggestive of *contradiction*. Thus, as Clarke has pointed out, the sūtras (at least some of them) tend to emphasize the ideal of renunciation, while the *Vinayas* (as well as inscriptions) more often reflect the reality of continuing family ties. No surviving genre, however, seems to reflect the actual manner in which these elements may have been thoroughly intertwined within any individual life.

As a rough analogy, consider the following: What if a Martian were to land on earth from outer space and, attempting to understand as much as possible about *me* and *my life*, had access to only two sources of information: (1) personal e-mail messages written by me and addressed to my spouse, my children, and my close personal friends, and (2) the Dartmouth Faculty Handbook? Not only would such a Martian possibly perceive a strong sense of *contradiction* between these two sources, but in addition, he would completely miss many other facets of my experience, as well as the sense of an integrated whole—a tapestry, as it were—in which all of these threads were woven together. A sense of this complicated tapestry perhaps *could* be recovered, however, if such a Martian also had access to various stories and images I had imaginatively composed concerning wives, mothers, and Dartmouth professors. And the same holds true, perhaps, of the Buddhist discourse on motherhood itself: The ambivalent depictions we find in Buddhist literature of good mothers and bad mothers, dead mothers and living mothers, mothers who help and mothers who hinder one's spread of the dharma may be one way in which the Indian Buddhist tradition conveys its sense of the complicated mixture of ideals, aspirations, anxieties, and weaknesses that constitute an actual monastic life.

Mothering as Spiritual Cultivation

The preceding speculations lead me, finally, to another possibility as well. If women's ideological renunciation of family life and their continued mothering of their own and others' children were, in fact, more complexly intertwined than may be evident from the surviving literature, then an additional possibility also rears its head: Were there some Buddhist nuns in India—not to mention Buddhist laywomen—who saw *mothering itself* as a legitimate mode of Buddhist practice?

Viewing mothering itself as a form of spiritual cultivation fully compatible with Buddhist values and reframable in Buddhist terms is one strategy for reconciling Buddhism and motherhood that seems relatively absent from the Indian Buddhist discourse I have discussed so far. Rather than viewing motherhood as *opposed* to Buddhist values (as we have seen), or merely *accommodating* motherhood by metaphorically aligning it with this or that Buddhist concept (as we have also seen), this is a strategy that would actively foreground the act of mothering itself as a legitimate form of Buddhist praxis. Rita Gross has observed that traditional Buddhism's failure to do so is especially noteworthy when we consider that many other everyday, mundane activities have indeed been revalorized in such a way—for example, gardening or working in the fields in the Chan/Zen tradition, or engaging in sexual intercourse in some strands of the Tantric tradition.[54] In a similar manner, Kim Gutschow has noted that when famous Tantric *siddhas* (such as Tilopa) assume the lowly occupations of fishmongering or wine-selling, "these serve to teach a hidden message about selflesslessness and saintliness" or demonstrate "the equivalence of conventional and absolute reality"—yet when contemporary Himalayan Buddhist nuns immerse themselves in housework and childcare, their actions are never framed in such an exalted way. "Household drudgery," she notes, "rarely appears as a means for gaining ultimate realization."[55]

It seems fairly obvious that the failure to envision the practice of mothering as a form of spiritual cultivation stems from the simple fact that mothering is performed by *women*, and women, on the whole, have lacked a significant voice in traditional Buddhism. One would expect, then, that as women gain more of a voice within modern Buddhist contexts and greater power to envision alternative forms of Buddhist practice (as well as having such forms be publicly recognized), the possibility of viewing mothering in terms of spiritual cultivation would increase—and this has indeed been the case. Here I will summarize a few brief examples as a mere sampling of what is no doubt a growing trend in the development of modern Buddhism.

In a perceptive discussion of modern Thai Buddhist nuns (or *māechī*), Sid Brown asserts that the extensive domestic entanglements characteristic of many *māechīs'* lives—although no doubt resulting from the *māechīs'* low social status and continuing economic dependence on their families—seem to have led them to a particular vision of spiritual cultivation that is not necessarily shared by Thai monks: "[I]t appears that *māechī* are making a new role for themselves, combining the qualities of the ascetic role that are so admired of men in Thailand with those of the mother/nurturer role so admired of Thai women."[56] As a consequence, many *māechī* have become "contemplative-activists" who engage in a variety of social campaigns that often focus on bettering the lives of mothers and their children. In Brown's view, they are "renunciants who nurture"[57]—and these two qualities are not contradictory but, rather, dependent on one another. It is precisely because they have renounced the particularistic attachments of marriage and children that they are able to cultivate toward the wider community a certain "love without possessiveness, attention without bias, involvement without panic."[58] Yet they have been motivated to do so not so much by the normative ideal of the compassionate buddha or bodhisattva as by their own continuing engagement in family life and the care of children. In this way, they fuse the male mode of renunciation with the female mode of mothering/nurturing. In a sensitive invocation of the *Vessantara Jātaka*, Brown further describes the stance of the *māechī* as bringing together the best qualities of Vessantara and of his wife Maddī—with Vessantara's "stalwart rule-abiding nature" being softened and leavened by Maddī's "nurturing, empathy, perceptiveness, and attention to particulars."[59] In her estimation, moreover, this stance is "a new kind of spirituality, a woman's spirituality"[60] that is not held in common with Thai monks.

While the revalorization of maternal qualities characteristic of Thai *māechī* no doubt gives greater meaning to the domestic labor so often required of them, it also lacks any wider and more public recognition or power within Thai Buddhist society at large. The same cannot be said, however, for an organization like the Ciji Gongdehui (Buddhist Compassion Relief Foundation) of Taiwan. Beginning in 1966 with just a single nun, her five disciples, and thirty laywomen, Ciji today is "the largest civic organization in Taiwan, claiming 4 million members worldwide in 1994, and nearly 20 percent of Taiwan's population. It gives away well over US

$20 million in charity each year, runs a state-of-the-art hospital, and has branches in fourteen countries."[61] Nevertheless, according to Julia Huang's and Robert Weller's analysis, Ciji has attained this enormous success by pursuing much the same strategy as Brown describes for the *māechī* of Thailand: encouraging women to universalize their maternal instincts, see them in terms of Buddhist compassion, and then apply them to society at large—thus forging a new identity as "mother to the world." One member of the organization put it this way:

> I realized that I used to love too narrowly. I had only two children, whom I was killing with my possessive love. And I was never happy with this aching love. But now I have so many children. I see everyone I help as my own child. I have learned that we have to make our mother love into a world love. And we will live a practical life every day! We will be happy every day![62]

Here, Huang and Weller state, "the universalizing values of Buddhist salvation [are] finally at peace with the particularistic values of filial piety and motherhood."[63] Also in line with the practice of motherhood is the fact that Ciji emphasizes practical, concrete actions within the world rather than abstract philosophy: "For Ciji, only action counts in the last analysis. Core texts, in so far as they can be said to exist, tend to be stories about real behavior."[64] Ciji thus valorizes the particularistic, context-dependent, and situational ethics so characteristic of mothering.

The two examples I have discussed so far both involve an extension of the concept of "mothering," such that one "mothers" society at large. The strategy of revalorizing motherhood in terms of Buddhist practice may also be pursued, however, in a more literal sense—or, in other words, with regard to the mothering of one's own children. Dipa Ma Barua, a twentieth-century Theravāda Buddhist meditation teacher from East Bengal who was a pupil of the famous Burmese meditation master Mahasi Sayadaw, as well as being influential among the earliest American proponents of *vipassana*, provides a good example of this approach.[65] After she married at a very young age yet failed to get pregnant for many years, her husband reportedly said to her: "Why don't you just make every person your own? Adopt each person you meet and treat them as if they were your only child."[66] Though Dipa Ma did follow this advice—addressing every person she met in her later years as "son" or "daughter"—this does not mean that she would neglect the spiritual usefulness of mothering one's own children.

We can see, in fact, the constant intertwining of motherhood and Buddhism throughout Dipa Ma's life, which helps to make sense of the manner in which she later reconciled them. After years of infertility, she eventually gave birth to three children (as well as raising her own younger brother), but when two of her children died in infancy, along with her beloved husband, it was her paralyzing grief over these familial losses that first drove her to devote her life to meditation. She gave everything away, left her surviving daughter in the care of a neighbor, and went to study meditation at a retreat center in Rangoon. Though she intended to stay there forever, however, the pull of motherhood (in the form of her daughter's distress) soon brought Dipa Ma home, and she remained with her daughter for the rest of her life, often bringing the young girl to the meditation center with her. After living in Burma for many years, she eventually moved back to Calcutta to give her daughter more opportunities, and it was there that she became a well-known meditation teacher. These experiences clearly influenced the form that Dipa Ma's teachings would take: Her very first student was a harried Calcutta housewife and mother of six young children whom Dipa Ma taught to be "steadfastly mindful every time she held and nursed her infant son,"[67] thus integrating her practice of meditation with her practice of mothering. Throughout her life, she repeatedly emphasized the importance of bringing meditation into every aspect of one's mundane, daily existence. To the American *vipassana* teacher Jack Kornfield, she instructed: "Live your life, do the dishes, do the laundry, take your kid to kindergarten, raise your children or your grandchildren, take care of the community in which you live, and make all of that your path."[68] But it was the qualities of *mothering*—rather than parenting in general—that she emphasized among her female students, telling them: "You can go more quickly and deeper in the practice than men because your minds are softer. . . . Women's tendency to be more emotional is *not* a hindrance to practice."[69] Kate Wheeler, another American who sought out Dipa Ma's instruction, describes her careful consideration of the nature of mothering as follows:

> Dipa Ma countered the common argument that children are a distraction by saying that, on the contrary, children build up mental strength and focus and are excellent practice for a meditator. A mother cannot wallow in ordinary, self-centered thoughts, according to Dipa Ma. A mother has to put her attention fully outside of herself, focusing here, there, and there, in very quick succession.

> The attention has to be not merely focused, but also soft and loving, aware of its own quality.[70]

Mothering here is clearly not just a metaphor, but a literal practice directed at one's own children—a practice, moreover, that is seen as being *especially* suited to the fulfillment of Buddhist aims.

Perhaps it is not surprising that in the modern American context, too, with its strong emphases on individualism, the authenticity of individual experience, and the equality of women, the type of thinking enunciated by Dipa Ma has led to a burgeoning genre of contemporary "baby-as-zen-object" Buddhist literature[71]—earnest books with titles like *Buddha Mom: The Path of Mindful Mothering*, or *Momma Zen: Walking the Crooked Path of Motherhood*.[72] In an informal survey of American Buddhist women who have come to frame their mothering in terms of Buddhist practice, Kate Wheeler notes that "for Buddhist women who are sincere and deep practitioners, motherhood nearly invariably seems to inspire a restatement of orthodox doctrine."[73] The American Buddhist mothers surveyed by her often "rephrased texts and doctrine in order to equate the conditions of motherhood to the rules of discipline for celibates" and "defiantly compared their daily praxis, usually favorably, with that of an ordained monk or a person on retreat."[74] Thus, the mother's lack of sleep can be compared to the short sleeping hours of the monk, and catering to the constant needs of children can be compared to being bound by the monastic rules of discipline. A crying baby might be likened to an unreasonably demanding Zen master—or, perhaps, to an especially inscrutable *koan*. And, as any mother knows, caring for children on a daily basis seems to offer ample opportunities for realizing the basic Buddhist truths of impermanence, suffering, and conditionality. As Wheeler notes, "these philosophizing women are committing a rather subversive act, rephrasing some of the most precious tenets of the religion in terms that would be seen as antithetical to what was intended"—yet the women themselves see these rephrasings "as a deep expression of truth."[75]

The question this discussion raises for me is this: Is it possible that figures like Vaḍḍhamātā or Vāsiṭṭhī (whom I earlier described as the "spiritual mothers" of the *Therīgāthā*, or those who somehow seemed to combine arhatship with mother-love), and even figures like the demoness Hārītī, are literary representations of the same type of "subversive" thought? Are they seen only fuzzily because they are seen from the outside—conveyed through a male perspective rather than through the autobiographical voices of women themselves? Can we read *through* such accounts to imagine the complicated women on the ground they might represent—women who may indeed have viewed their mothering in such terms?

Maternal Grief Revisited

Just as mothering itself can be interpreted as a legitimate mode of Buddhist practice, so also the death of children and resulting maternal grief might be entwined with Buddhist doctrine in a manner quite different from what we saw in the *Therīgāthā*. As a final example of the complexity of the relationship between motherhood and Buddhism as it exists on the ground, I conclude this chapter with an evocative account of a modern Buddhist mother in grief. The account is entitled "Remembering My Child" and was written in 1949 by a Soto Zen Buddhist laywoman named Nakayama Momoyo, whose only son was killed during World War II.[76] The account is interesting because of the way this mother's musings both conform to and depart from the standard Buddhist discourse on motherhood, mothers and sons, and the transcendence of maternal grief.

In line with the Buddhist idealization of devoted motherhood, Nakayama first depicts herself as a long-suffering woman whose very identity depends on her status as a mother, a woman whose existence derives its meaning only from her devotion to her son: "I had put my whole heart into raising my son; his growing up had filled me with delight. This great objective of my beloved son's adulthood, had been the one and only shining light in my life; whatever pain, whatever sorrow I experienced were nothing. My life had been full to bursting, like an always full moon."[77] Also familiar to us by now is the exaggerated opposition she draws between a *sinful mother* and a *noble son*: "I never stopped reflecting, 'Can this child have developed in my womb? Can he have been born and raised by a mother with such deep sins as I? There must have been some mistake for me to come to be his mother.'"[78] Predictably enough, when her beloved son dies, she is plunged into grief and paints a picture of herself that strongly resembles the grief-crazed mothers of the *Therīgāthā*: "I was pushed from a world of light into a world of gloom. I lost all desire to live. . . . A soulless puppet, I mourned day in and day out, wretched with the loss of my son. . . . People criticized me as a foolish mother, a prisoner of my emotions."[79] Also in common with the *Therīgāthā*, this descent into madness is halted only when she encounters a saintly Buddhist teacher—the Soto Zen nun Nagasawa Sozen Roshi—and realizes that she possesses an "exalted experience surpassing that of the world's mothers."[80] Much like Paṭācārā or Kisā Gotamī, moreover, she then succeeds, under her teacher's guidance, in completely eradicating her "clinging" to her beloved, dead son.[81]

Yet despite these many strong echoes of the mothers of the *Therīgāthā*, there are also several statements that suggest that the resolution of Nakayama's maternal grief is more complicated than the cut-and-dried *eradication of motherhood* we saw in their case. When she tries, yet repeatedly fails, to achieve any success in her struggle with the koan *Mu*, for example, it is the *suffering of her son* and her desire to achieve *his* release—rather than the more familiar trope of a son's desire to save his suffering mother—that spurs her on: "I must think of my child's death in war! What is my hardship? It doesn't amount to a thing! If I don't open up the way here and now, when will my dead son and I be released from the world?"[82] Unlike the mothers of the *Therīgāthā*, then, Nakayama continues to single out her own child and work specifically on his behalf. They are *not* two strangers meeting on a road; instead, they remain mother and son. And when she finally does have an enlightenment experience that is confirmed and validated by her teacher, she speaks not of transcending or universalizing her love for her son, but of *remaining in his presence forever*—connecting this permanent union, moreover, with the doctrinal concept of "buddha mind": "Words cannot express what it is like to live and work together with my dead son. That is buddha mind. This too is buddha mind. Apart from buddha mind, there is nothing. That is joy. This too is joy. My life is full in this vast, delightful and pure world."[83] Are Nakayama's musings contradictory and confused? Or do they merely reflect the poetic nuances of a real person's life?

The material I have presented throughout the latter half of this chapter is obviously far removed from the context of premodern India. The extent to which we can extrapolate from one context to another remains highly questionable, especially in light of modern women's individualism and empowerment and their access to the Buddhist teachings themselves—all of which must result in a very different situation than existed for nuns and laywomen in traditional India. Nevertheless, I have made use of this material in order to suggest that the discourse on motherhood found in classical, male-authored Buddhist texts, with all of its ambiguities, oppositions, and contradictory images, must have lying underneath it an on-the-ground reality far more complex—and only imperfectly conceived.

Conclusion

In recent decades, feminist theory and discourse have been characterized by a fundamental tension between the imperatives of asserting women's *identity* and proclaiming their *difference*. On the one hand, feminism must assert women's *identity* with men in order to make the argument for their equal political entitlement and agency. This identity relies on the notion that both men and women possess a fully autonomous, individualist subjectivity, marked by reason, rationality, and consciousness, and distinct from the body and one's gendered embodiment. It is on the basis of this shared identity that women are entitled to the same rights, privileges, and opportunities as men. To assert this identity carries the risk, however, of failing to recognize the significance of women's unique situations and experiences—especially those surrounding female embodiment and mothering. In addition, it fails to recognize that the supposedly gender-neutral subjectivity posited for both men and women is, in fact, inherently *masculine* in nature, relying as it does on a mind/body dualism that privileges the mind as masculine and denigrates the body as feminine. For all of these reasons, feminism must, on the other hand, also assert women's *difference* from men. Asserting women's difference (particularly in terms of pregnancy, childbirth, and mothering) allows feminism to better theorize the specificity of women's lives and experiences, as well as to assert that subjectivity is always embodied—yet it also jeopardizes the very claim of identity that alone constitutes a valid argument for women's equal political entitlement and agency. Thus, asserting women's identity threatens to undermine their difference, whereas asserting their difference threatens to undermine their identity.

Patrice DiQuinzio refers to this intractable difficulty as the "dilemma of difference" and notes that this dilemma, while inevitable for feminist theory as a whole, is perhaps "most salient and most difficult to resolve at the site of mothering."[1] Mothering is the hallmark of women's difference, yet any attempt to theorize motherhood in these terms runs the risk of reinforcing the very structures of oppression that feminism intends to dismantle—by essentializing motherhood and tying it irrevocably to feminine sex and gender. The attempt to theorize mothering in a way that is liberatory, in other words, can easily slip back into what DiQuinzio calls "essential motherhood"[2]—an oppressive ideology that sees women's motherhood as natural, inevitable, and mandatory for all women, romanticizes and idealizes it, yet also describes it in terms that exclude women from individualist subjectivity. Women as mothers become associated with the body, the natural, the emotional, and the private, whereas men are associated with the mind, the social, the rational, and the public. Women are *reduced* to their maternal function and thus stripped of full agency and autonomy. Because this ideology of "essential motherhood" is never far removed from any attempt to theorize women's difference in terms of mothering, it seems that "women can be subjects of agency and entitlement only to the extent that they are not mothers," and "mothers as such cannot be subjects of individualist agency and entitlement."[3] Hence the "impossibility of motherhood" detected and analyzed by DiQuinzio within the writings of a number of feminist theorists.[4]

I mention this context only to suggest that modern feminism's struggle with the "impossibility of motherhood" is really not so different from a similar struggle among premodern Indian Buddhist monastics, who likewise can be seen to have grappled with the tension between identity and difference. We can see this tension, for example, in the Buddhist tradition's contrasting treatments of Māyā and Mahāprajāpatī (examined in chapters 3, 4, and 5): The depiction of Māyā as Mother and Birth-Giver emphasizes and celebrates women's *difference*. Yet because it comes from a male perspective and is not rooted within the experiences of actual women, this results in an essentialized, romanticized, and highly idealized picture of motherhood, paints Māyā as nothing more than an appropriate fetal container, and strips her of her autonomy, rationality, and full subjectivity—thus resulting in her depiction as a spiritually stunted (if also heavenly) creature. What is emphasized, moreover, is not only women's difference but also men's need to distinguish and separate themselves from this difference as much as possible, as manifested by Māyā's necessary, premature death as soon as her son has been born.

The depiction of Mahāprajāpatī, in contrast, disavows women's difference and instead emphasizes and celebrates women's *identity* with men—their rationality, their full subjectivity, and thus their ability to attain Buddhism's most highly valued goals. Yet this celebration is inconsistent and is accompanied by significant fear, anxiety, and repulsion on the part of its male authors, especially in connection with Mahāprajāpatī's female embodiment and mothering—her breastfeeding, her nurturance, her care—which result in her son's indebtedness and dependence and threaten to compromise his autonomy and transcendence. Women's identity with men, in other words, becomes difficult to accept and sustain once we are faced with the persisting realities of female embodiment and maternal ministrations of care—which not only assert women's difference from men in the boldest possible way, but also threaten the male's own conception of himself as an individual, autonomous being. As we saw in chapters 6 and 7, when faced with this threat, the male-dominated tradition generally responds not by theorizing pregnancy, childbirth, or breastfeeding on their own terms, but instead by co-opting the mother's reproductive abilities, recasting those abilities in a "higher" and more spiritualized form, attributing these "higher" forms of generativity to the *father*, and thus consigning the mother to the realm of animalistic instinct. In this way female embodiment and mothering come to reinforce rather than undermine male transcendence.

Māyā and Mahāprajāpatī thus form a complementary yet also contradictory pair. As I suggested before, rather than seeing either mother as "good" or "bad," we must recognize that the benefits and drawbacks (for Buddhist monasticism) of envisioning women in terms of either Māyā or Mahāprajāpatī will differ depending on the context, just as the goals of modern feminism can be pursued in some cases by asserting women's identity, and in other cases by proclaiming their difference. Thus, premodern Indian Buddhist monastics—much like modern feminists, though with very different concerns—grappled with the "impossibility of motherhood."

The same tension between women's identity and women's difference is equally discernible in the Buddhist discourse on maternal love and maternal grief (examined in chapters 1 and 2). When mother-love is elevated far above father-love, for example, there is a celebration of women's *difference*, with mothers being idealized as pure, compassionate, and self-sacrificing. Once again, however, this difference, when envisioned by male authors, also seems to render the mother somewhat mindless, irrational, and a slave to her emotions, and to contrast her with the calm reason and rationality of the father. The mother is associated with the emotional, the natural, the instinctual, and the particular, thus robbing her of her full subjectivity and leading inevitably to an *opposition* between maternal love and universal Buddhist values such as compassion, which are implicitly gendered as masculine. For such mothers to conform to universal Buddhist values—or, in other words, for women to overcome their difference and achieve an *identity* with men—they must be violently *de-mothered* (as we see in the case of the grieving mothers of the *Therīgāthā*) and, essentially, *become male*. The significance of women's mothering must be undermined to such an extent that maternal love is *banished* from the mother's heart, and her own child loses any specific identity he or she once had. Motherhood becomes untenable as soon as the mother herself is granted any agency.

As we also saw in chapter 2, however, the shadowy figures of Vaḍḍhamātā, Vāsiṭṭhī, and Hārītī—all of whom combine their mother-love with their Buddhist commitments—seem to offer us another possibility. How might this possibility be conceptualized in relation to feminist theory? The attempt to theorize women's difference in a more constructive manner, and without falling into an essentialized and romanticized motherhood, has been pursued in recent years in the literature on a feminist ethics of care. As espoused by scholars such as Carol Gilligan, Nel Noddings, Sara Ruddick, and Virginia Held, this viewpoint maintains that women's traditional (and still predominant) engagement in various forms of "caring labor" (including mothering) has given them a distinctive moral voice.[5] Caring labor, in other words, is not merely an instinctual reflex of the female sex or a necessary consequence of female biology; instead, it is a particular type of *practice* that gives rise to particular moral values, cognitive styles, metaphysical attitudes, and epistemological premises that both differ from and implicitly criticize those characteristic of men and male-dominated practices. Women thus speak with a "different voice"[6] that calls into question the universality and gender-neutrality of abstract (male) rationality. In brief, this "different voice" attributed to women is said to emphasize the value of care rather than the value of justice; relationships with and responsibilities toward other people rather than the rights, rules, and duties that govern atomized individuals; interdependence rather than individualism; moral ambiguity and open-endedness rather than clear-cut distinctions between right and wrong; a morality that is concrete and context-sensitive rather than abstract and decontextualized; a form of knowledge that is connected to rather than detached from one's body and one's emotions; and a greater attention to particular circumstances than to universal norms.

In the influential work of Sara Ruddick, this general focus on "caring labor" is further narrowed down into a specific focus on "maternal practice" and the "maternal thinking" that arises from it.[7] A "mother," in Ruddick's terms, is anyone (male or female) who is committed to meeting the three major demands implicitly and universally posed whenever children are born: the demands for *preservation, growth,* and *social acceptability.* Children demand that their lives be preserved and their growth fostered, while society demands that such children behave in socially acceptable ways. "Mothers" are those who commit themselves to meeting these three demands (whether or not they do so successfully), who regularly engage in "maternal practice" that is directed toward these ends, and who are able to engage in "disciplined reflection" on such practice, which constitutes "maternal thinking."[8] Maternal thinking has its own particular logic and rationality and can be used to criticize male modes of reasoning.

For my purposes, what is most interesting about Ruddick's enumeration of "maternal thinking"—as well as the larger feminist ethics of care from which it derives—is that several of its features seem to be strikingly harmonious with Buddhist doctrine. Children's constantly changing natures, for example, are said to demand from their mothers a metaphysical attitude of "welcoming change"[9]—which is strongly reminiscent of the Buddhist emphasis on impermanence and momentariness. Children's demand for preservation in an often dangerous world is said to foster within their mothers a distinct cognitive style Ruddick calls "scrutinizing" (a sort of watchful yet also detached alertness), as well as forcing them to engage in a constant "reflective assessment of feeling"[10]—which, together, are quite reminiscent of the Buddhist emphasis on mindfulness and attentive awareness. The obligation to respond to children's needs in particular ways at particular moments causes their mothers to develop a cognitive capacity for "concrete thinking"[11]—which is somewhat reminiscent of the bodhisattva's use of skillful means (one of the few contexts, as I noted before, in which Buddhism explicitly values attention to the particular). The general emphasis that a feminist ethics of care places on interdependence rather than individualism—or relationships *between* entities rather than the entities themselves—is strongly reminiscent of the Buddhist ideas of conditionality, dependent origination, and emptiness. And finally, the idea of "care" itself is quite similar, in many respects, to the Buddhist emphasis on benevolence and compassion.

This general sense of harmony between Buddhist doctrine, on the one hand, and a feminist ethics of care, on the other hand, suggests to me that Buddhism itself, in certain circumstances, might be hospitable to a kind of "maternal ethics," in which motherhood is seen as a legitimate basis for "higher" values and truths. In an interesting article, John Powers and

Deane Curtin have made just such a claim by asserting that the Mahāyāna Buddhist ethic of compassion and the feminist ethic of care can be directly compared to each other, since "both traditions highlight the practice of mothering as a model."[12] As a concrete illustration of this comparison, they juxtapose Ruddick's discussion of "maternal thinking" with Tsong kha pa's discussion (in the *Lam rim chen mo*) of that form of meditation (discussed in chapter 1) in which the Mahāyāna bodhisattva cultivates his compassion by first remembering his own mother and all of the many services she performed on his behalf, and then extending his resulting sense of gratitude and obligation toward all sentient beings, since all of them, at one time or another, have similarly served as his mother. Thus just as the Mahāyāna bodhisattva moves from compassion for his own mother to compassion for all sentient beings, so Ruddick's discussion moves from "maternal practice" within the home to a form of nonviolent peace politics that can be applied to the world at large. In both cases, according to Powers and Curtin, mothering becomes the "model" for a larger system of ethics.

Although interesting and often insightful, I find this comparison to be ultimately unsuccessful, for all of the reasons I enumerated in chapter 1: What Powers and Curtin fail to significantly acknowledge is that this form of meditation begins not from the perspective of the *mother* but, rather, from the perspective of the *son*, asking the son, moreover, to develop compassion *in response to*—rather than *in imitation of*—his mother's compassion toward him. Mother-love here is not an exemplary "model" for the bodhisattva; it is merely that which serves to make the mother an appealing *object* of the bodhisattva's compassion. This becomes even clearer when we recall that Tsong kha pa further fuels the bodhisattva's compassionate response by depicting this mother as *one who suffers for her various sins and wrongdoings*. The mother is painted as a pitiful object of the son's heroic endeavors, not as an active agent whose virtues he ought to imitate. To compare this form of meditation to Ruddick's treatment of "maternal thinking," then, is to miss the son-centered nature of the dominant Buddhist discourse on motherhood.

The figures of Vaḍḍhamātā, Vāsiṭṭhī, and Hārītī, on the other hand, seem to represent more promising candidates for a Buddhist variety of "maternal ethics." First, all three of them are *mothers*—not sons—who in some way reconcile their maternal love for their own particular children with their commitment to the Buddhist values of detachment and compassion. While Vaḍḍhamātā and Vāsiṭṭhī remain shadowy figures whose thinking and motivation are impossible to analyze, Hārītī receives greater treatment and comes into somewhat clearer focus. As we saw in chapter 2, Hārītī cultivates the Buddhist virtue of compassion not by *eradicating* her motherhood but, rather, by relating her own maternal love to the maternal love that is felt by others. She comes to realize—as the Buddha has told her—that "others love their children, just as you do," and they "go along the streets and lament just like you."[13] This depiction of Hārītī's realization is strikingly similar to Ruddick's discussion of the usefulness of "maternal thinking" for deployment within a wider politics of peace. Though Ruddick fully acknowledges that maternal love can be selfish and parochial in the extreme, she also claims that it need not necessarily be so: Many mothers do make the natural connection between "passionate loyalties to their particular children and a less personal imaginative grasp of what other children mean to other mothers"[14]—just as we saw Hārītī do. Mothers *can* overcome the inherent selfishness of maternal love and "widen their vision by finding in other particular mothers, children, and families passions and responsibilities akin to their own."[15] Thus does Hārītī agree to grant children to *other* mothers, once her own beloved son has been restored. The universal, in other words, *can* be seen as an imaginative union of all possible particulars, rather than as something that escapes from, transcends, and floats above all particular circumstances. Here, perhaps, it is possible to give Buddhist compassion an alternative genealogy—one that traces itself directly back to mother-love.

While the figure of Hārītī remains merely suggestive, the various modern Buddhist contexts discussed in chapter 8, in which mothering itself is seen as a form of spiritual cultivation, are even better candidates for speaking of a Buddhist "maternal ethics" and its similarities to the feminist ethics of care. The Thai Buddhist *māechī* analyzed by Sid Brown, for example, who soften the "stalwart, rule-abiding nature" of Vessantara by combining it with his wife Maddī's "nurturing, empathy, perceptiveness, and attention to particulars,"[16] can be seen as bringing together the modes of moral reasoning characteristic of men and women, respectively, as described by Carol Gilligan (in her critique of Lawrence Kohlberg).[17] The Taiwanese women of Ciji Gongdehui who strive to "make our mother love into a world love"[18] are reminiscent of Ruddick's call to transform "maternal thinking" into a nonviolent politics of peace, while their emphasis on practical, concrete actions rather than abstract virtues or ideals replicates some of the basic features of maternal practice. Dipa Ma's claim that women's greater connection to their emotions is a help, rather than a hindrance, to spiritual attainment and her careful attention to the particular kind of attentive awareness cultivated by mothers (which must move "here, there, and there, in quick succession" and be "not merely focused, but also soft and loving")[19] similarly replicate many of the basic insights into the practice of mothering and the distinctive "voice" to which it gives rise that have been proposed by feminist theorists. And finally, Nakayama Momoyo's sense that living and working together with her dead son constitutes the very definition of "buddha mind" illustrates the claim made by several feminist scholars that the "different voice" of women is one that refuses to view death in terms of separation, rupture, and transcendence, but instead emphasizes continuity, connectedness, and enduring relations between the dead and the living.[20] The growing presence of this kind of "voice" within modern Buddhist contexts suggests that Buddhism, far from being opposed to such "maternal ethics," may in fact provide for them a particularly hospitable environment.

But if the possibility of a truly Buddhist "maternal ethics" is present only within such modern Buddhist contexts—marked, as they are, by increasing female autonomy and empowerment—then what, finally, can we say about premodern Indian Buddhism and its ability to reconcile itself with motherhood? Here I would like to offer one final observation. The example of Hārītī has shown us that within the context of premodern South Asia, Buddhism's willingness to accommodate motherhood was perhaps a function of its openness toward interaction with lower-level, popular, or "folk" religious traditions, such as those surrounding the worship of local goddesses. Similarly, we saw in chapter 7 that within a localized, vernacular, Burmese ritual context—the celebration of the Tawadeintha festival—it was the mother's breastfeeding of the son that was valorized far *above* the son's salvation of the mother. Thus, as I speculated earlier, it seems that the further removed a particular context is from the level of the elite, the orthodox, and the canonical, the *more* likely it is to espouse something approaching a "maternal ethics"—perhaps simply as a result of the stronger presence and influence of actual mothers within those contexts.

In light of this generalization, it is intriguing to note the peculiar position that Buddhism holds in Susan Starr Sered's cross-cultural study of religious traditions dominated by women.[21] We should note, first of all, that these traditions have much in common with "maternal thinking" and the feminist ethics of care. For example, they treat motherhood as "a fundamental image, a key ritual focus, and a chief theological concern";[22] they "enhance, dramatize, and strengthen women's identities as mothers";[23] they "honor women less in their role as birthers than in their role as nurturers"[24] (thus emphasizing maternal practice rather than female biology); and they tend to be characterized by some of the basic features of "maternal thinking," such as an emphasis on concrete rather than abstract thought, change rather than stasis, and mutual responsibilities rather than individual rights. Buddhism, of course, is *not* one of these women-dominated religions. Nevertheless, of the twelve examples of such religions that Sered is able to identify, a full *four* of them (or one-third of the total) are found in Asian contexts in which they coexist with Buddhism.[25] Sered makes a note of this peculiar statistic and explains it by observing that "in contrast to Islam or Catholicism, Buddhism is relatively tolerant of other religions, and generally allows adherents to participate both in Buddhist and non-Buddhist religious rituals."[26]

While I would refrain from any assertion regarding Buddhism's relative "tolerance"—a generalization that I think is ill advised—I do believe that a less sweeping suggestion might be made in regard to motherhood: Perhaps Buddhism, wherever it has existed—whether in premodern South Asia, modern East or Southeast Asia, or the contemporary West—has accommodated motherhood, reconciled itself to motherhood, and, in some cases, even promoted a variety of "maternal ethics" primarily by *making a space for those who were inclined to do so.* While the dominant, male voices of the Buddhist tradition have more often essentialized, romanticized, rejected, and feared motherhood, they did, in the end, take other voices seriously and sometimes allowed those voices to filter through. I believe that the nature of our existing sources from premodern South Asia allows for only the tiniest glimpse of this process as it actually occurred.

Finally, it also seems to me that even if we restrict ourselves to the most dominant male voices of the Indian Buddhist tradition, we can see that motherhood—whatever its treatment—could never be wholly eradicated. Over and over again, the loving, affectionate, and tender emotions associated with the mother are invoked, and the son's nostalgic longing to return to his days as a baby at the mother's breast is never far away. The authors of Indian Buddhist texts were not only male renunciant monks; they were also the sons of their mothers. In their hands, the tie to the mother could be twisted, displaced, redirected, or reinterpreted—but it could never be wholly broken.

Abbreviations

Note: All Pali canonical and commentarial sources are cited from the Tipiṭaka (and commentaries) established at the Chaṭṭha Saṅgāyana or Sixth Buddhist Council held in Yangon, Myanmar, 1954–56, and available online at www.tipitaka.org. However, as is customary, the bibliographic references given are to the standard Pali Text Society editions, as noted below.

AN	*Aṅguttara Nikāya*. Ed. Morris 1885–1910.
AN-a	*Aṅguttara Nikāya Aṭṭhakathā*. Ed. Walleser and Kopp, 2nd ed., 1966–79.
Ap	*Apadāna*. Ed. Lilley 1925–27.
AP	*Aṣṭasāhasrikā Prajñāpāramitā Sūtra*. Ed. Vaidya 1960.
BC	*Buddhacarita*. Ed. Johnston, new enlarged ed., 1984.
BHS	Buddhist Hybrid Sanskrit
BHSD	*Buddhist Hybrid Sanskrit Dictionary*. See Edgerton 1953, vol. 2.
BK	[Mūlasarvāstivāda] *Bhikṣuṇī Karmavācanā*. Ed. Schmidt 1993.
BŚS	*Baudhāyana Śrauta Sūtra*. Ed. Caland, 2nd ed., 1982.
Dh	*Dhammapada*. Ed. Norman 1906–15.
Dh-a	*Dhammapada Aṭṭhakathā*. Ed. Norman 1906–15.
Divy	*Divyāvadāna*. Ed. Cowell and Neil 1886.
DN	*Dīgha Nikāya*. Ed. Rhys Davids and Stede 1890–1911.
GV	*Gaṇḍavyūha Sūtra*. Ed. Vaidya, 2nd ed., 2002.
Jā	*Jātaka* and *Jātaka Aṭṭhakathā*. Ed. Fausboll 1875–97.
LV	*Lalitavistara*. Ed. Lefmann 1902–8.
MLBV	*Mahāsāṃghika Lokottaravāda Bhikṣuṇī Vinaya*. Ed. Roth 1970.
MN	*Majjhima Nikāya*. Ed. Trenckner 1888–1925.
MN-a	*Majjhima Nikāya Aṭṭhakathā*. Ed. Woods and Kosambi 1922–38.
Mn-a	*Mahā-Niddesa Aṭṭhakathā*. Ed. Buddhadatta 1931–39.
MSL	*Mahāyānasūtrālaṃkāra*. Ed. Lévi 1907–11.

Mv	*Mahāvastu*. Ed. Senart 1882–97.
MW	*A Sanskrit-English Dictionary*. See Monier-Williams, new ed., 1979.
NRSV	Bible. New Revised Standard Version.
P.	Pali
Rgsg	*Ratnaguṇasaṃcayagāthā*. Ed. Vaidya 1961.
SbhS	*Suvarṇabhāsottama Sūtra*. Ed. Nobel 1937.
Sbv	*Saṅghabhedavastu* of the (Sanskrit) *Mūlasarvāstivāda Vinaya*. Ed. Gnoli 1977–78.
SDPS	*Saddharmapuṇḍarīka Sūtra*. Ed. Wogihara and Tsuchida 1934–35.
Skt.	Sanskrit
SN	*Saṃyutta Nikāya*. Ed. Feer 1884–1904.
Sn	*Sutta Nipāta*. Ed. Andersen and Smith 1913.
T.	*Taishō shinshū daizōkyō*
Thīg	*Therīgāthā*. Ed. Pruitt 1998a.
Thīg-a	*Therīgāthā Aṭṭhakathā*. Ed. Pruitt 1998a.
Ud	*Udāna*. Ed. Steinthal 1885.
Ud-a	*Udāna Aṭṭhakathā*. Ed. Woodward 1926.
Vin	[Theravāda] *Vinaya Piṭaka*. Ed. Oldenberg 1879–83.
Vism	*Visuddhimagga*. Ed. Rhys Davids 1920–21.

Notes

INTRODUCTION

1. *Manusmṛti* 2.145 (trans. Olivelle 2004: 34).
2. Douglas 2002: 202.
3. Throughout this book, I make use of Paul Harrison's term "Mainstream Buddhism" to refer to traditional, non-Mahāyāna Buddhism. See Harrison 1992: 77–78, n. 2.
4. Ohnuma 2007.
5. I believe this assumption is warranted, based on the North Indian homeland of Buddhism and the prevailing familial structures of Indo-Aryan culture. Nevertheless, it is also true that the occasional use of matronymics in Buddhist literature (such as the name Śāriputra, which derives from the mother rather than the father) suggests that at least some Buddhist monks grew up within matrilineal, polyandrous, or other types of familial structures.

CHAPTER 1

1. For some general considerations of the relationship between motherhood and Buddhism, see Horner 1930: 1–18; Murcott 1991: 74–91; Paul 1985: 60–73; and Gross 1993: 232–40. Two sources that deal primarily with East Asia are Faure 2003: 145–80 and Cole 1998.
2. AN i, 61; also at AN i, 131.
3. Jā v, 331 (No. 532, vv. 182–84); see also AN i, 131.
4. SN i, 228.
5. Jā v, 331 (No. 532, v. 185); see also SN i, 182.
6. Sn 22 (v. 124).
7. Jā v, 330 (No. 532, vv. 173–76).
8. AN i, 61.

9. Silk 2007: 253–54.
10. This is true, for example, of SN i, 181, and of Jā v, 312–32 (No. 532).
11. See Woodward and Hare 1932–36: i, 56, n. 5.
12. Silk 2007: 257.
13. AN-a ii, 8–9 (as cited in Silk 2007: 256). Perhaps it makes sense, then, that in the famous story of Maitrakanyaka (P. Mittavindaka) found in both Sanskrit and Pali sources, the protagonist is made to bear a blazing iron wheel on his head merely for striking his mother, much less killing her (see Brough 1957).
14. Cited in Silk 2007: 256, n. 13.
15. Trans. Cowell 1895–1913: v, 164–74.
16. Jā v, 330 (No. 532, v. 166).
17. Jā v, 331 (No. 532).
18. Ibid.
19. Jā v, 330 (No. 532, v. 169).
20. Jā v, 331 (No. 532).
21. Ibid.
22. Jā v, 330 (No. 532, v. 170).
23. Jā v, 331 (No. 532).
24. Jā v, 330 (No. 532, v. 171).
25. Jā v, 331 (No. 532).
26. Jā v, 328 (No. 532).
27. Jā v, 328 (No. 532, v. 159).
28. Cole 1998.
29. Dh-a i, 169 (on vv. 21–23).
30. P. *kucchiyaṃ vasitaputtasmiñ hi sineho balavā hoti* (Dh-a ii, 26) (on v. 62).
31. Trans. Cowell 1895–1913: iii, 107–11.
32. Jā iii, 165 (No. 354).
33. In an East Asian context, Bernard Faure (2003: 146) similarly observes that "although we often hear of mothers who have fallen into hell, and of sons who want to save them, rarely do we hear of sons saving their fathers, or daughters their mothers. This suggests the extent to which faith itself came to be gendered."
34. Sn 26 (vv. 149–50).
35. *Baudhāyana Śrauta Sūtra* 18.13 (trans. Kashikar 2003: iii, 1187).
36. BŚS ii, 358.
37. *Dhammapada Commentary*, on v. 43 (trans. Burlingame 1921: ii, 23–28).
38. Dh-a i, 331 (on v. 43).
39. Ibid.
40. Dh i, 332 (v. 43).
41. In fact, a long passage commenting on Sorreyya's sex change makes it clear that transformation from male to female is always the result of sin, whereas transformation from female to male is always the result of virtue: "For there are no

men at all who have not formerly been women, nor women who have not formerly been men. For men who commit adultery with the wives of others, upon dying, are tortured in hell for hundreds of thousands of years, and when they have attained rebirth as human beings, they are reborn as women during a hundred existences. . . . But women who perform meritorious deeds such as gift-giving and so on, who get rid of their desire to exist as women, and who form the resolution, 'May this meritorious deed of mine result in my attaining rebirth as a man,' upon dying, attain rebirth as men. And women who are devoted wives also attain rebirth as men through the power of proper behavior toward their husbands" (Dh-a i, 327) (on v. 43).

42. Trans. Tin 1923–31: iii, 788–89.
43. Vism 645.
44. Ibid.
45. Vism 646.
46. Trans. Tin 1923–31: ii, 369.
47. Trans. Jones 1949–56: ii, 199–209.
48. Mv ii, 229.
49. Ibid.
50. It is interesting to note, however, that in the parallel *Sāma Jātaka* (*Jātaka* No. 540), the mother plays a much more active role, for Sāma is restored to life by three acts of truth performed by his mother, his father, and a goddess who was his mother in a former life (trans. Cowell 1895–1913: vi, 38–52).
51. See Wayman 1991: 268–70.
52. Ibid.: 269.
53. Ibid.
54. MSL i, 88 (Ch. 13, v. 20). Although the mother is not specifically mentioned in this verse, I believe we can assume that Asaṅga has a mother in mind—especially because two verses later, the bodhisattva is further compared to "a mother pigeon who has great love for her own offspring [Skt. *kapotī svasutātivatsalā*] and constantly clasps them to her bosom" (MSL i, 88) (Ch. 13, v. 22).
55. MSL i, 123 (Ch. 17, v. 28).
56. Much the same is true, in fact, of women in general; as John G. Jones (2001: 89), speaking of the Pali *jātakas*, has noted, "Women in the Jātaka, although horrid when they are very, very bad, tend to be awesomely good when they are good."
57. Faure 2003: 147.
58. Trans. Burlingame 1921: i, 170–75.
59. Dh i, 50 (v. 5). Very similar in nature is the *Dhammapada Commentary*'s discussion of verse 291 of the *Dhammapada* (trans. Burlingame 1921: iii, 176–77), except that in this case, the rivalry is said to continue through five hundred successive rebirths. The *Dhammapada* verse recited on this occasion by the Buddha is as follows: "He who seeks for his own happiness by causing

suffering to others is tangled up in hatred. He is not free from hatred" (Dh iii, 450) (v. 291).

60. Trans. Cowell 1895–1913: iv, 304–9.
61. Jā iv, 493 (No. 510).
62. Trans. Cowell 1895–1913: v, 11–19.
63. See, for example, Wilson 1996; Falk 1974; Lang 1986; Paul 1985: 3–10. In Sutherland's words (1991: 139): "Asceticism is male and must defend itself rigorously against the seductive demands of, and attachment to, the world of the senses, which is conceived of as female." Or, in Young's words (2004: 5): "[M]en cut through to ultimate reality and women try to impede their progress; women are the opposition. Women are not participants on the same human journey, but are obstacles to it."
64. Wilson 1996: 70.
65. Faure 2003: 145.
66. Rita Gross (1993: 239) has made a similar point, observing that because of women's monopoly over early childcare, "women preside over all the incidents of frustration and limitation that initiate us into the human condition, and are subconsciously blamed for those inevitabilities. Succinctly, in Buddhist terms . . . women, more than men, introduce us to *samsara*, and are, on some level, blamed for it in a way that men are not." It is primarily men, on the other hand, who have control over the teachings that lead one out of *samsara*, again because of an unfair division of labor.
67. On this general complex of beliefs, see, for example, the following: Misra 1981: 73–80 (on child-devouring mother goddesses in Hindu, Buddhist, and Jain texts); Sutherland 1991: 137–47 (dealing specifically with *yakṣiṇīs*); Shaw 2006: 110–19 (which discusses this complex in relation to the Buddhist goddess Hārītī); Kosambi 1962 (which discusses this complex in relation to the Buddha's mother Māyā); and Brubaker 1983 and Kinsley 1986: 197–211 (both of which discuss these figures within contemporary village Hinduism).
68. See Teiser 1996; Cole 1998.
69. Trans. Tin 1923–31: ii, 107–9.
70. Vism 91.
71. P. *paridevamānā rodi* (Vism 92).
72. Vism 93.
73. The text has another monk speculate, "Surely, it's because the boy had few desires [P. *appichatā*] that he left without identifying himself" (Vism 92).
74. Trans. Tin 1923–31: ii, 348–49.
75. Trans. Cowell 1895–1913: iii, 117–20.
76. P. *puttasinehena samappitā hutvā* (Jā iii, 179) (No. 358).
77. Vism 303.
78. Ibid.
79. Trans. Tin 1923–31: ii, 340–61.

80. P. *sīmāsambhedo kātabbo* (Vism 307).
81. Mv iii, 265.
82. SN i, 110–11.
83. *Śiṣyalekha*, vv. 97–98. I rely here on the elegant translation of Michael Hahn (1998: 117), who notes that reference to the mothers' "tender love" (Skt. *vatsala*) is highly conjectural and based on the Tibetan tradition. It is interesting to note that just a few verses earlier, Candragomin draws on the idea that all sentient beings were once one's mothers in a second manner as well—one that is quite different in its sentiment: "What form and manner of existence is there that the soul has not already lived through in this world a hundred times before? . . . There is no suffering that we have not experienced many times before; there are no objects of desire that have ever satisfied us here on earth; there is no being in whose womb we have not already dwelt. How is it possible that despite all this, beings in samsara have not freed themselves from passionate attachment?" (*Śiṣyalekha*, vv. 91, 93; trans. Hahn 1998: 113–15). Here the emphasis is on the utter futility of rebirth: Over and over again, we have been conceived within the womb of one being after another—such that all beings have served as our mothers—yet we continue to pursue desires that never bring us satisfaction. Motherhood here is used as an emblem of the exhausting, utterly futile, and endless nature of samsara—an impression further reinforced by the immediately preceding verse, where Candragomin describes the bodies of women as "ugly," with "stinking secretions" (*Śiṣyalekha*, v. 90; trans. Hahn 1998: 113).
84. Trans. Lamrim Chenmo Translation Committee 2000–4: ii, 38–42.
85. Ibid.: ii, 38.
86. Gross 1993: 234.
87. Trans. Lamrim Chenmo Translation Committee 2000–4: ii, 39.
88. Ibid.: ii, 40.
89. Ibid.: ii, 41.
90. Gross 1993: 276 (emphasis in original).

CHAPTER 2

1. French trans. Lamotte 1944–80: i, 488 and n. The *Mahāprajñāpāramitā Śāstra* (*Da zhi du lun*, T. 1509) is attributed to the Indian Buddhist author Nāgārjuna but exists only in a Chinese translation made by Kumārajīva in the early fifth century CE. It is most likely a Chinese compilation, but one that is clearly based on older Indian sources.
2. French trans. La Vallée Poussin 1923–31: iii, 126.
3. French trans. Huber 1908: 205. Aside from some Sanskrit fragments, the *Kalpanāmaṇḍitikā* of Kumāralātā exists only in a Chinese translation (*Da zhuang yan lun jing*, T. 201), translated by Kumārajīva in the early fifth century CE. Though Huber misidentifies the Chinese text as the *Sūtrālaṃkāra* of

Aśvaghoṣa, it has subsequently been shown to be Kumāralātā's *Kalpanāmaṇḍitikā*.

4. *Wu mu zi jing* (T. 555), trans. by Zhi qian in the early third century CE (trans. Paul 1985: 68–70).
5. Trans. Paul 1985: 69.
6. Trans. ibid.: 70.
7. Thīg 212 (v. 302).
8. Thīg 212 (v. 303).
9. Jā i, 31.
10. Trans. Cone and Gombrich 1977: 66–73.
11. Sered 1996a. The same ideas are also treated more briefly in Sered 1996b: 89–101.
12. Sered 1996a: 6.
13. Ibid.: 6.
14. Ibid.: 20.
15. Gilligan 1982.
16. Sered 1996a: 21.
17. Ibid.: 23.
18. For Kisā Gotamī, see *Therīgāthā*, vv. 213–23 (verses and commentary trans. Pruitt 1998b: 222–32); for Vasiṭṭhī, see vv. 133–38 (ibid., 162–64); for Ubbirī, see vv. 51–53 (ibid., 73–77); for Paṭācārā, see vv. 112–16 (ibid., 143–54); for the five hundred nuns converted by Paṭācārā, see vv. 127–32 (ibid., 159–62). It should be noted that within the *Therīgāthā* itself, these verses are attributed to "Pañcasatā Paṭācārā." The commentator Dhammapāla understands this phrase to refer to five hundred (P. *pañcasata*) women converted by Paṭācārā, and provides a background story in line with this interpretation. However, K. R. Norman (1995: 88–89) believes that *pañcasatā* was originally an adjective describing a single woman named Paṭācārā (and distinguishing her from the other Paṭācārā), rather than a numeral. He speculates that *pañcasatā* originally meant "mindful of the five" and indicated that this Paṭācārā was mindful of either the five "aggregates" (P. *khandha*) or the five "obstacles" (P. *nīvaraṇa*)—both standard Buddhist doctrinal categories. Since my use of the poem does not depend on the question of whether it was uttered by one woman or five hundred women, I am following Dhammapāla's interpretation.
19. Blackstone 1998: 44. The lack of grieving fathers within the *Theragāthā* is part of a larger, gender-related pattern. In general, as Blackstone (1998: 45) notes, the monks of the *Theragāthā* pay much less attention to the social and familial relationships of their premonastic lives than do the nuns of the *Therīgāthā*: "The *Therīgāthā*'s descriptions of pre-renunciation experiences revolve around relationships. The secular world the *therī*s renounced is consistently portrayed as a social world in which they were embedded in a network of relationships, especially with family. The *Theragāthā* de-emphasizes the pre-renunciation

experiences of the *theras*, and, even in the few descriptions provided, does not dwell at length on the social interactions of the *theras*. Rather, the world the *theras* renounced is portrayed as remarkably asocial."

20. Thīg 52 (v. 51).
21. Norman 1995: 72–73.
22. Thīg 54 (v. 52).
23. P. *sallan ti laddhanāmaṃ sokaṃ taṇhañ ca* (Thīg-a 54) (on v. 52).
24. Thīg-a 55 (on v. 52).
25. Trans. Cowell 1895–1913: ii, 37–39.
26. Jā ii, 55 (No. 166).
27. P. *satiṃ paṭilabha bhaginī ti* (Thīg-a 108).
28. Thīg-a 108.
29. Dh-a ii, 265 (on v. 113).
30. Trans. Obeyesekere 2001: 129.
31. Thīg-a 114 (on v. 115).
32. Thīg-a 108.
33. See note 18 above for the uncertainties surrounding this poem.
34. Thīg 118 (vv. 127–30).
35. Thīg-a 119 (on v. 127).
36. Thīg-a 119 (on v. 128).
37. Thīg 118–19 (vv. 131–32), identical to *Therīgāthā*, vv. 52–53.
38. Thīg-a 169.
39. Ibid.
40. Ibid.
41. Thīg-a 170.
42. Thīg 171 (v. 223).
43. Dh-a ii, 274 (on v. 114).
44. Kisā Gotamī is perhaps best known for another episode in which she once again displays an overriding focus on particularistic, familial relationships: In the Buddha's life story (as related, for example, in the *Nidānakathā*), when Prince Siddhattha is riding his chariot through the city, Kisā Gotamī, in admiration of his physical beauty, utters the following words: "Satisfied, indeed, is the mother; satisfied, indeed, is the father; satisfied, indeed, is the wife, who has a lord such as him" (Jā i, 60). Because she uses the word *nibbuta* for "satisfied," however, Kisā Gotamī's statement paradoxically causes Prince Siddhattha to realize that the fires of attachment, hatred, and delusion must be completely "extinguished" (P. *nibbuta*) in order to attain liberation, and he decides to renounce the world (and his family) on that very day. The ambiguity of the term *nibbuta* is thus used to contrast the deluded woman's focus on particular, familial relationships with the enlightened man's focus on abstract spiritual truths. Incidentally, this episode is also somewhat reminiscent of a passage in the Gospel according to Luke (11:7–8), in which (as Marina Warner has noted) "a woman

cries out from the crowd: 'Blessed is the womb that bare thee, and the paps which thou hast sucked'" and "Jesus answers, again sternly deflecting his followers' thoughts from the earthly family to the spiritual community; 'Yea rather, blessed are they that hear the word of God, and keep it'" (Warner 1976: 15).

45. The *Udāna* version (Ch. 8, Sutta 8) is translated in Woodward 1935: 111–12; the *Dhammapada Commentary* version (on v. 213) is translated in Burlingame 1921: iii, 84–85.
46. Dh-a iii, 279 (on v. 213).
47. Ud 91.
48. Dh iii, 279 (v. 213).
49. Gutschow 2004: 136.
50. MacKinnon 1982: 534.
51. Faure 2003: 332.
52. *Therīgāthā*, vv. 204–12 (verses and commentary trans. Pruitt 1998b: 218–22).
53. Thīg 167 (v. 207).
54. P. *gehasitapemamatto pi vanatho . . . mayi* (Thīg-a 167) (on v. 207).
55. Thīg 168 (vv. 210–12).
56. *Therīgāthā*, vv. 133–38 (verses and commentary trans. Pruitt 1998b: 162–64).
57. *Therīgāthā*, vv. 312–37, a poem attributed to the nun Sundarī, who is the daughter of the grief-stricken man Sujāta (verses and commentary trans. in Pruitt 1998b: 288–98).
58. Durt 2001.
59. Thīg 217 (v. 316). Dhammapāla's commentary understands this phrase as referring to the words spoken to Sujāta by the nun Vāsiṭṭhī, but I am following here the Sanskrit/Chinese tradition that makes Vāsiṭṭhī/Vāsiṣṭhā equivalent to Sujāta's wife.
60. The fullest discussion of Hārītī may be found in Peri 1917. For other discussions, see Dhirasekera 1976; Misra 1981: 73–80; and Cohen 1998 (esp. 380–91).
61. *[Mūlasarvāstivāda] Vinayakṣudrakavastu* (*Gen ben shuo yi qie you bu pi na ye za shi*, T. 1451), trans. by Yi Jing in the early eighth century CE. This account has been translated into French in Peri 1917: 3–15, from which I have drawn the quotations given below.
62. French trans. ibid.: 18–19. The text in question (extant only in Chinese) is the *Guei zi mu jing* (T. 1262), translated anonymously in the late third or early fourth century CE.
63. French trans. ibid.: 31. The text in question (extant only in Chinese) is the *Mahāmāyā Sūtra* (*Mo he mo ye jing*, T. 383), trans. by Tan Jing in the late fifth century CE.
64. Only the first condition appears in the Chinese *Mūlasarvāstivāda Vinaya*; however, the second condition appears in other versions of the story, such as that found in the *Guei zi mu jing*.

65. Trans. Takakusu 1896: 37. Yi Jing's travel diary is the *Nan hai ji guei nei fa zhuan*, T. 2125.
66. Peri (1917: 32) mentions several Mahāyāna texts in which this claim occurs.
67. French trans. Peri 1917: 30. This statement is made in the *Fo ben xing jing* (T. 193), trans. by Bao Yun in the early fifth century CE.
68. Cohen 1998: 387, n. 57.
69. *Mo he mo ye jing* (T. 383), trans. by Tan Jing in the late fifth century CE. The passage concerning Hārītī has been translated into French in Peri 1917: 30–31, from which I have drawn the quotations given below.
70. For this claim in relation to Hārītī, see the several citations given in Strong 1992: 303, n. 67. See also the sources mentioned in chap. 1, note 67.
71. In relation to Hārītī, this process is most fully elucidated in Cohen 1998.
72. The text in question is the *Guei zi mu jing* (T. 1262); see n. 62 above. In this version, she has one thousand sons rather than the usual five hundred.
73. For a thorough examination of this process, as it occurred within India, see Decaroli 2004.
74. Cohen 1998: 383.
75. This short account has been translated in Decaroli 2004: 39.
76. In a somewhat similar vein, Bernard Faure has argued that "the ideology of motherhood . . . forced Buddhism to hold its fundamentalist tendencies in check and to open itself to the multiplicity of local religions" (2003: 179) and that, in this process, "Buddhist universalism was forced to yield to the process of cultural integration, and, in so doing, to open itself to female values" (2003: 362).
77. See the discussion of this shrine in Cohen 1998: 380–91, which forms the basis for my own discussion.
78. Ibid.: 389–90.
79. For a discussion of this theme and French translations of the relevant passages, see Peri 1917: 32–38.
80. French trans. ibid.: 34. (On the *Mahāprajñāpāramitā Śāstra*, see n. 1 above.)
81. French trans. ibid.: 35. (From *Za a han jing*, T. 99, trans. by Guṇabhadra in the mid-fifth century CE.)
82. French trans. ibid.: 32. (From *A pi tan pi po sha lun*, T. 1546, trans. by Buddhavarman and Dao Tai in the mid-fifth century CE.)
83. Fathers, of course, are also capable of engaging in such reasoning. In an interesting passage, Hillary Crane (2007: 124) quotes a modern Taiwanese Buddhist monk who overcame his grief at leaving behind his wife and daughter by reasoning: "But if I got ordained, and if I was very diligent in my practice, then one day I will be enlightened, and then I can go back and help them enlighten themselves. That's the way of the Buddha, we enlighten ourselves and then those around us."
84. French trans. Peri 1917: 35–36.

85. Julie Puttgen, personal communication.
86. Blum 1986: 344 (discussing Murdoch 1970).
87. MacIntyre 1981: 221.

CHAPTER 3

1. On Māyā, see, for example, Durt 1996, 2002, 2003, 2004; Obeyesekere 1973; Sasson forthcoming; Shaw 2006: 38–61; Young 2004: 23–49. On Mahāprajāpatī, see, for example, Shaw 2006: 143–52; Walters 1994, 1995; Wilson 1996: 29–32, 141–48.
2. I borrow this phrase from Sasson (forthcoming).
3. This contrast between Māyā and Mahāprajāpatī has been briefly discussed by Sasson (forthcoming).
4. Indian Buddhist traditions surrounding the birth of the bodhisattva have been extensively described and analyzed by Vanessa Sasson in two publications (Sasson 2007, esp. 90–152; Sasson 2009). My discussion here draws on many of the same sources, but with a narrower focus on Māyā as the mother.
5. See Hara 1980, which gathers together some typical passages on both *garbha-duḥkha* and *janma-duḥkha*. See also Kritzer 2009.
6. From the *Viṣṇu Purāṇa*, as cited in Hara 1980: 149.
7. Vism 500.
8. On this dilemma, see Obeyesekere 1973.
9. LV i, 60.
10. *Acchariyabbhuta Sutta, Majjhima Nikāya* No. 123 (trans. Ñāṇamoli and Bodhi 1995: 979–84); *Mahāpadāna Sutta, Dīgha Nikāya* No. 14 (trans. Walshe 1995: 199–221); *Nidānakathā* (trans. Jayawickrama 2000: 64–71); *Mahāvastu* (trans. Jones 1949–56: i, 77–78; i, 112–19; ii, 1–26); *Lalitavistara* (trans. Bays 1983: i, 29–49, 71–170); *Abhiniṣkramaṇa Sūtra* (trans. Beal 1875: 32–63).
11. P. *sato sampajāno* (MN iii, 118–24, *passim*). This phrase is used repeatedly throughout the *Acchariyabbhuta Sutta* (*Majjhima Nikāya* No. 123) in order to emphasize the conscious and deliberate manner in which the bodhisatta behaves throughout the entire birth-taking process.
12. Mv i, 143.
13. For the *Lalitavistara*, see trans. Bays 1983: i, 42; for the *Abhiniṣkramaṇa Sūtra*, see trans. Beal 1875: 32. These lists are reminiscent, of course, of the thirty-two qualities of the *mahāpuruṣa* that characterize the Buddha himself.
14. Skt. *apagatamātṛgrāmadoṣāyāḥ* (LV i, 25).
15. LV i, 28.
16. Mv i, 145.
17. P. *manussamalaharaṇatthaṃ* (Jā i, 50).
18. Skt. *yac ceha trisāhasramahāsāhasralokadhātāv ojo vā maṇḍo vā raso vā tatsarvaṃ* (LV i, 64).

19. P. *sabbaṅgapaccaṅgiṃ ahīnindriyaṃ* (DN ii, 13).
20. DN ii, 13.
21. Petchesky 1987: 268, as cited in Sasson and Law 2009: 5. For scholarship on modern fetal imaging and its effects on the politics of reproduction, see the sources cited in Sasson and Law 2009: 4, n. 1.
22. LV i, 49.
23. LV i, 29.
24. For Māyā's pregnancy cravings, see Durt 2002 (which deals with the *Saṃghabhedavastu* of the Sanskrit *Mūlasarvāstivāda Vinaya*, the Chinese *Mūlasarvāstivāda Vinaya* [T. 1450], and a Buddha biography known as the *Zhong xu mo he di jing* [T. 191]). For Māyā's supernatural powers of healing, see Durt 2003 (which deals with the Sanskrit *Lalitavistara;* its third-century Chinese translation, the *Pu yao jing* [T. 186]; its seventh-century Chinese translation, the *Fang guang da zhuang yan jing* [T. 187]; and the Chinese *Abhiniṣkramaṇa Sūtra* or *Fo ben xing ji jing* [T. 190]).
25. DN ii, 14.
26. Mv ii, 16.
27. LV i, 60.
28. Trans. Walshe 1995: 199–221.
29. Mv ii, 20.
30. As Sasson (forthcoming) has noted, "This literary tradition took great care in separating the future Buddha from his mother's body, and more particularly, from his mother's sexuality."
31. Hara 1980.
32. This passage comes from Kauṇḍinya's *Pañcārthabhāṣya*, a commentary on the *Pāśupatasūtra*, as cited in Hara 1980: 148.
33. Mv ii, 23.
34. Mv ii, 20.
35. Obeyesekere 1973: 226.
36. Skt. *māyānirmitam iva bimbaṃ* (LV i, 27); *manoramā māyakṛteva* (LV i, 28).
37. Trans. Beal 1875: 49.
38. See the translation in Cleary 1989: 259–73 (for Sutejomaṇḍalaratiśrī), 305–15 (for Māyā).
39. GV 294.
40. *māyāgatarūpavijñaptisaṃdarśanadharmatayā anāgatadharmatayā anutpādānirodhalokavijñaptisaṃdarśanadharmatayā* (GV 294).
41. *trailokyasamatikrāntena*... *sarvabhavagatyudgatena*... *pratikṣaṇadharmadhātuspharaṇena* (GV 343).
42. GV 345.
43. GV 346.
44. *sarveṣāṃ bhadrakalpikānāṃ tathāgatānām arhatāṃ samyaksaṃbuddhānām* . . . *asyāṃ trisāhasramahāsāhasrāyāṃ lokadhātau*... *asmin sarvāvati*... *lokadhātusamudre*

sarvalokadhātuvaṃśeṣu sarvalokadhātuprasareṣu sarvalokadhātuṣu sarvajambudvīpeṣv aparāntakoṭīgatān kalpān . . . (GV 348).

45. Shaw 2006: 160.
46. Ibid.: 161.
47. Ud 48.
48. Trans. Walshe 1995: 204.
49. Mv ii, 2.
50. Trans. Jayawickrama 2000: 64–66.
51. Bareau (1974: 208–9, 249–50) argues that the tradition of Māyā dying shortly after giving birth to the bodhisattva was not always an established tradition. He bases his argument, in part, on the fact that multiple accounts of the bodhisattva's later renunciation of the world mention him leaving behind both a father *and a mother*—which means that Māyā must have still been alive when Siddhārtha was a young adult. I do not quite understand this argument, however, since Māyā, as far as I can tell, is never mentioned *by name* in these accounts. Couldn't the "mother" referred to in these accounts just as easily be Mahāprajāpatī?
52. Mv ii, 3.
53. Jā i, 52. The same reason is also cited in the commentary to the *Acchariyabbhuta Sutta* (see Ñāṇamoli and Bodhi 1995: 1331, n. 1164) and the commentary to *Udāna* 5.2 (trans. Masefield 1994: ii, 734).
54. Ud-a 277.
55. Ibid.
56. Trans. Beal 1875: 63. The *Buddhacarita*, however, has a very different take. Instead of claiming that Māyā died because she was unable to regain the joy experienced during pregnancy, the *Buddhacarita* says that Māyā died because she was unable to bear the joy of seeing her magnificent son (BC i, 14, v. 2.18).
57. LV i, 98.
58. Ud-a 277.
59. LV i, 98.
60. In a somewhat similar manner, June Campbell has noted the prevalence of dead mothers within the hagiographies of many Tibetan lamas. "When the mother dies," she states, "the son is free to become enlightened, and when she is absented through the power of the lineage, his path is cleared for the monastic, spiritual life" (Campbell 2002: 93).
61. Cited in Warner 1976: xvii.
62. Luke 1:30 and 1:42 (NRSV).
63. Cited in Warner 1976: 37.
64. On the differences between Christian and Buddhist attitudes toward virginity, see Wilson 1996: 169–79.
65. Mv ii, 23.
66. Cited in Warner 1976: 45.

67. Cited in ibid.: 43.
68. Cited in ibid.: 44.
69. Ibid.: 22–24.
70. Ibid.: 236–54.
71. Ibid.: 81–102.

CHAPTER 4

1. LV i, 100.
2. Ibid.
3. BC i, 14 (v. 2.19).
4. MN iii, 253.
5. MN-a v, 69.
6. Trans. Beal 1875: 64.
7. Trans. Bays 1983: i, 174–75.
8. Trans. ibid.: i, 182.
9. Trans. ibid.: i, 207.
10. BC i, 62 (v. 6.32).
11. BC i, 64 (v. 6.45).
12. BC i, 81 (v. 8.24).
13. BC i, 86 (v. 8.51).
14. BC i, 97 (v. 9.26).
15. LV i, 201. The same thing happens in the *Abhiniṣkramaṇa Sūtra* (trans. Beal 1875: 123).
16. Wilson 1996: 70.
17. LV i, 228.
18. Mv i, 154–55.
19. Trans. Beal 1875: 126.
20. Trans. Jones 1949–56: iii, 115–16.
21. Mv iii, 116.
22. Ibid.
23. Trans. Jones 1949–56: iii, 126–33.
24. Mv iii, 130. The inflection of the phrase *uddhataśarīrāyā* ("tall body") is difficult to make sense of; I am treating it as if it were an accusative *bahuvrīhi* compound in agreement with the preceding *tāṃ* and as the object of *parimārjati snāpayati* ("bathed and wiped clean").
25. Mv iii, 131.
26. Ibid. The manuscript reading of *ekatyeṣu manuṣyeṣu caite* is emended by Senart to *ekatyeṣu manuṣyeṣu naite* (which Jones [1949–56: iii, 128] translates as "There are not many men . . ."); but I am following Edgerton (BHSD 153, s.v. *ekatya*) in keeping the manuscript reading of *caite* and thus interpreting the phrase as "there are [only] a few men. . . ."

27. Mv iii, 132.
28. Ibid.
29. It should be noted that much the same story is told of Māyā rather than Mahāprajāpatī in the *Mātiposaka Jātaka* (*Jātaka* No. 455) (trans. Cowell 1895–1913: iv, 58–61). This is one of several such instances in which stories are associated with either Māyā or Mahāprajāpatī, depending on the source. However, I would argue that the story makes better sense when told of Mahāprajāpatī. In the *Mātiposaka Jātaka*, for example, the king who sets the elephant free so that he can return to his mother is identified as a previous birth of Ānanda. The resulting relationships established between Māyā, the Buddha, and Ānanda clearly do not have the same meaning, significance, or emotional resonance as the corresponding relationships between Mahāprajāpatī, the Buddha, and Nanda. Further evidence that this story makes better sense in connection with Mahāprajāpatī than it does in connection with Māyā is offered by the *Cūlanandiya Jātaka* (*Jātaka* No. 222) (trans. Cowell 1895–1913: ii, 140–42). Here, much as we see in the *Mātiposaka Jātaka* (except with monkeys rather than elephants), the leader of a troop of eighty thousand monkeys abandons his kingship over the herd in order to devote himself full-time to the care of his old, blind mother. And here, as we would expect, the mother is a previous birth of Mahāprajāpatī, not Māyā.
30. See Ohnuma 2006, which addresses this scholarly blind spot in much greater detail, as well as repeating some of the discussion found below.
31. The episode in question appears in *Cullavagga* 10.1 and has been translated in Horner 1938–66: v, 352–56. A virtually identical account appears in the *Aṅguttara Nikāya* (trans. Woodward and Hare 1932–36: iv, 181–85).
32. Vin ii, 253.
33. Ibid.
34. Ibid.
35. Ibid.
36. Vin ii, 254–55.
37. Vin ii, 256.
38. Ibid.
39. Vin ii, 289.
40. See Heirman 2001: 275–89, which analyzes all versions of the story through exhaustive charts and lists; since I am unable to access the Chinese sources directly, I have relied on this article quite heavily. Regarding the additional sources mentioned: The *Mahīśāsaka Vinaya* is T. 1421 and exists only in Chinese. The *Mahāsāṃghika-Lokottaravāda Bhikṣuṇī-Vinaya* exists only in Buddhist Hybrid Sanskrit and is not a complete *Vinaya*, consisting of the *Bhikṣuṇī-Vinaya* portion only (ed. in Roth 1970 and trans. into French in Nolot 1991; a somewhat abbreviated English translation of the Mahāprajāpatī/ordination story itself can be found in Strong 2008: 63–68). The *Dharmaguptaka Vinaya* is T. 1428 and

exists only in Chinese. The *Mūlasarvāstivāda Vinaya* is extant in its entirety in the *Dulva* section of the Tibetan Buddhist canon; large portions are also extant in Chinese (T. 1442–1451), and significant portions in Sanskrit. The surviving Sanskrit portions do not include the Mahāprajāpatī/ordination story, and unfortunately I have been unable to consult the Tibetan version and it is not addressed by Heirman (though the summary provided by Rockhill [1884: 60–62] does not explicitly mention the motherhood argument). Two further *Vinayas* extant only in Chinese—the *Mahāsāṃghika Vinaya* (T. 1425) and the *Sarvāstivāda Vinaya* (T. 1435)—discuss only the eight "strict rules" without relating the Mahāprajāpatī/ordination story itself (the *Bhikṣuṇī Vinaya* of the former has been translated in Hirakawa 1982). The *Sūtra on Gautamī* is Sūtra No. 116 of the Sarvāstivādin *Madhyamāgama*, which exists only in Chinese (T. 26); a nearly identical version of this account also appears in T. 60, the *Fu shuo qu tan mi ji guo jing* or *Sūtra on the Story of Gautamī*. The *Da ai dao bi qiu ni jing* (T. 1478), according to Heirman, is a later *Vinaya* text possibly translated in the first half of the fifth century, though according to Hirakawa (1970: 273–74) it may be a Chinese compilation. Heirman's claim (277) that her analysis is exhaustive of "all the different versions" of this story appears to be largely correct; however, as noted before, her tables do not include any reference to the version found in the Tibetan *Mūlasarvāstivāda Vinaya*, nor do they account for the version found in a Sanskrit *Mūlasarvāstivāda Bhikṣuṇī-Karmavācanā* fragment (ed. in Ridding and La Vallée Poussin 1919, re-ed. in Schmidt 1993, and the relevant story trans. by Frances Wilson in Paul 1985: 83–94)—even though she mentions this version in a footnote (278, n. 23). This version contains neither the spiritual-capability argument nor the motherhood argument—but I will say more below about what role Mahāprajāpatī's motherhood might play in this version. According to Heirman's charts, the only extant version of this story that includes the spiritual-capability argument but not the motherhood argument is a Chinese text known as the *Pi ni mu jing* (T. 1463, *Vinayamātṛkā*?), a commentary on the *Prātimokṣa Sūtra* of an unknown school.

41. This ambivalence is addressed, for example, in Falk 1980.
42. French trans. Nolot 1991: 2–10; an abbreviated English translation can be found in Strong 2008: 63–68.
43. MLBV 12–14.
44. MLBV 14–15. Though I am unable to access the Chinese sources directly, a similar statement appears to be made in the version of the story found in the *Sūtra on Gautamī* (No. 116 of the Sarvāstivādin *Madhyamāgama*, T. 26)—at least according to the summary found in Demiéville 1929–67: i, 73–74, s.v. "Bikuni."
45. MLBV 15–16.
46. MW 664, s.v. *prati-kṛ*.
47. Buddhaghosa's commentary (AN-a ii, 122) glosses "show them this world" as follows: "If the mother and father, on the day of the child's birth, grabbed him

by the foot and threw him into the woods, into a river, or off a cliff, then he would never see the pleasant and unpleasant things in this world. But because they do not do that, because they bring him forth and nourish him, he does see the pleasant and unpleasant things in this world, thanks to his mother and father. Therefore, they are indeed those who show him this world." The bar of successful parenting that demands to be repaid, in other words, is not set very high!

48. AN i, 61.
49. Trans. Ñāṇamoli and Bodhi 1995: 1102–6.
50. Peter Harvey is one of the few scholars who has noted the parallel between these two accounts, but he refers to it merely as "a strange echo" (2000: 386, n. 15).
51. MN iii, 253.
52. Ibid.
53. The Chinese Buddhist pilgrim Xuanzang, however, seems to preserve a tradition which holds that the Buddha did accept the robes from Mahāprajāpatī, for at one point during his travels in the region of Kapilavastu, he notes: "Not far from the monastery is a stupa marking the place where the Tathāgata once sat facing the east under a big tree and accepted the gift of a robe sewn with golden thread offered by his aunt" (trans. Li 1996: 178).
54. MN-a v, 67.
55. MN iii, 253. In a collection of tales now extant only in Chinese (the *Za bao zang jing*, T. 203), it is Mahāprajāpatī herself who (rather pointedly) makes this argument: "I suckled and raised you, O World-Honored One. I have made this garment myself. And so I offer it to you, O Buddha. I hoped that you, O Tathāgata, would accept it from me. Why did you say just now to give it to your Saṅgha?" (trans. Willemen 1994: 112).
56. MN iii, 253.
57. MN iii, 254.
58. Trans. Walters 1995. For an extended discussion of this text, see Walters 1994.
59. P. *mayhaṃ aṇaṇo tvaṃ* (Ap ii, 532, v. 34).
60. Ap ii, 533, vv. 44–45.
61. Ap ii, 532, vv. 31–33.
62. Trans. in Rhys Davids 1890–94: ii, 51–56.
63. "O Ānanda, I say that in no way whatsoever does a gift given to an individual ever have greater fruit than an offering made to the Saṃgha"—even in future times, when the Saṃgha will be full of those who are "immoral and wicked." This is because such a gift is given "on account of the Saṃgha"—in other words, out of esteem for what the Saṃgha represents rather than its individual embodiments (MN iii, 256).
64. Buddhaghosa's commentary on the *Dakkhiṇāvibhaṅga Sutta* provides a completely different reason for the Buddha's refusal to accept the robes (MN-a v,

67): "But why did the Blessed One redirect what was being given to himself and cause it to be given to the community of monks? [He did so] out of compassion [P. *anukampā*] for his mother." In other words, the Buddha surmised that just as Mahāprajāpati had acquired merit from her good intention of giving him the robes, she could now double her merit by generating the same good intention toward the Saṃgha. Emphasizing the Buddha's compassion for Mahāprajāpatī here is perhaps another, more subtle way of denying his indebtedness.

65. Lamotte 1988: 699–710.
66. This manuscript was first edited in Ridding and La Vallée Poussin 1919, then re-edited in Schmidt 1993. The Mahāprajāpatī/ordination story from this manuscript has been translated by Francis Wilson in Paul 1985: 83–94.
67. BK 242.
68. BK 243.
69. See Heirman 2001: 284–89; Hirakawa 1970: 273–74 (as cited in Heirman 2001: 284, n. 48).
70. Heirman 2001: 287.
71. Ibid.: 288.
72. This is noted by Heirman herself (2001: 286), but passes without comment.
73. I am indebted to my colleague Gil Raz, whose quick perusal of the Chinese text turned up these additional references to mothers.
74. Again, this is noted by Heirman herself (2001: 286), but passes without comment.
75. Faure 2003: 161.

CHAPTER 5

1. Trans. Jones 1949–56: i, 301–2.
2. It should be noted here that the traditions surrounding Māyā and Mahāprajāpatī are multiple and often contradictory. Thus, in the *Abhiniṣkramaṇa Sūtra*, we are given the same basic story, but with the positions of the two sisters *reversed:* Mahāprajāpatī is the youngest and most desirable sister, while Māyā is the eldest (see trans. Beal 1875: 23). In the Tibetan *Mūlasarvāstivāda Vinaya*, there are only two sisters, Māyā being the younger and Mahāprajāpatī the older; this account is further confused, however, by the fact that Mahāprajāpatī is referred to as Māyā, whereas Māyā is referred to as Mahāmāyā. Because Śākyans are permitted only one wife, King Śuddhodhana, in this version, marries Mahāmāyā only, but later he is permitted to marry Māyā (i.e., Mahāprajāpatī) as well (see trans. Rockhill 1884: 14–16). Finally, in the Pali tradition, Māyā is consistently described as being older than Mahāprajāpatī (see, for example, Malalasekera 1937: ii, 522–24 [s.v. Mahāpajāpatī Gotamī] and ii, 608–10 [s.v. Māyā, Mahāmāyā]).
3. Lopez 2001: 158–60; Wilson 1996: 141–48.

4. AN i, 25.
5. Trans. in Emmerick 1970: 85–97.
6. Vin ii, 255.
7. Vin ii, 256.
8. See Skilling 2008 for a thorough discussion of this question.
9. See, for example, the version of this episode found in the *Dhammapada Commentary* (trans. Burlingame 1921: iii, 47–56). It appears, however, that the *Abhidhamma Piṭaka* preserved down on earth was believed to be a condensed version of that recited by the Buddha in heaven. In the commentary on the *Dhammasanganī*, for example, Buddhaghosa says of Ānanda that "even a disciple of such surpassing mindfulness, intelligence and fortitude would not be able to finish learning in a thousand years the sermons preached by the Teacher in three months in the way mentioned above" (trans. Tin 1920–21: i, 19).
10. Wells 1975: 104–6.
11. Trans. Burlingame 1921: iii, 47–56.
12. This occurs in the *Mahāmāyā Sūtra* or *Mo he mo ye jing* (T. 383), which, it should be noted, is most likely a Chinese composition; see the summary and translated excerpts in Peri 1917: 30–31.
13. Trans. Masefield 1994: ii, 732–36.
14. Ud-a 276.
15. Ud-a 276–77.
16. As Young (2004: 23; 49, n. 2) has noted in her discussion of Māyā and Mahāprajāpatī, the contrast between the good, dead mother and the evil, living mother is a common motif in folklore throughout the world, as evidenced, for example, by the story of Cinderella.
17. I am relying on the indexes to each volume of the Cowell translation of the Pali *Jātaka* collection (Cowell 1895–1913); I have not gone through the entire collection story by story.
18. Trans. ibid.: i, 27–29.
19. Trans. ibid.: ii, 13–17.
20. Trans. ibid.: ii, 31–34.
21. In several *jātakas* involving Māyā, the mother of the bodhisattva is simply identified as a previous birth of Māyā, but without playing any essential or distinctive role within the story. On the other hand, two *jātakas* that give Māyā a completely different role are the *Somanassa Jātaka* (No. 505, trans. Cowell 1895–1913: iv, 275–80) and the *Khaṇḍahāla Jātaka* (No. 542, trans. Cowell 1895–1913: v, 68–80). In both cases there is some sort of conflict between father and son, and the mother is aligned with the son.
22. Trans. Cowell 1895–1913: ii, 140–42.
23. Trans. ibid.: iii, 117–20.
24. Jā iii, 179 (No. 358).
25. Trans. Bays 1983: ii, 385–86.

26. LV i, 253.
27. Ibid.
28. Ibid.
29. Ibid.
30. *You xing jing*, Sūtra No. 2 of the *Chang a han jing* or *Dīrgha Āgama* of the Dharmaguptakas (T. 1), translated into Chinese in 412–13 CE.
31. Trans. in Bareau 1970–71: ii, 166–67.
32. For a nineteenth-century Chinese woodblock rendition of the scene, see Wieger 1910–13: ii, plate 185.
33. Trans. Li 1996: 189–90.
34. Durt 1996.
35. Trans. ibid.: 19.
36. Trans. ibid.: 18.
37. Trans. ibid.: 14.
38. Trans. ibid.: 17.
39. The idea that filial piety is a distinctly Chinese as opposed to Indian virtue, however, has been expertly refuted by both John Strong (1983) and Gregory Schopen (1997: 56–71).
40. Trans. Burlingame 1921: iii, 47–56.
41. Kosambi 1962.
42. Shaw 2006: 53–60.
43. Ap ii, 531, v. 20.
44. Ap ii, 535, v. 76.
45. P. *rūpena kiṃ tavānena diṭṭhe dhamme yathātathe / sabbaṃ saṅkhatam evetaṃ anassāsikam ittaraṃ //* (Ap ii, 539, v. 138).
46. P. *aho acchariyaṃ mayhaṃ nibbutāya pi mātuyā / sarīramattasesāya natthi sokapariddavo // na sociyā paresaṃ sā tiṇṇasaṃsārasāgarā / parivajjitasantāpā sītibhūtā sunibbutā // . . . atthadhammaniruttīsu paṭibhāne tatheva ca / parisuddhaṃ ahu ñāṇaṃ tasmā socaniyā na sā //* (Ap ii, 543, vv. 181–82, 186).
47. The story is translated in Burlingame 1921: i, 218; however, Mahāprajāpatī's presence at this scene and her attainment of stream-entry is only made clear at another point in the *Dhammapada Commentary* (trans. Burlingame 1921: iii, 2–4).
48. Dh iii, 164 (v. 169).
49. Trans. Pruitt 1998b: 182.
50. *Sutta Nipāta*, vv. 862–97 (trans. Norman 19966: 144–45).
51. The exhortation itself appears in the *Vinaya* (trans. Horner 1938–66: v, 359); for the claim that this exhortation resulted in Mahāprajāpatī's attainment of arhatship, see Horner 1938–66: v, 359, n. 3.
52. Ap ii, 535, v. 66.
53. P. *thīnaṃ dhammābhisamaye ye bālā vimatiṃ gatā* (Ap ii, 535, v. 79).
54. P. *appameyyaṃ bhikkhunīgaṇaṃ* (Ap ii, 536, v. 90).

55. Walters 1994.
56. Ibid.: 375, 378.
57. P. *nibbāyi dīpaccīva nirāsavā* (Ap ii, 540, v. 148).
58. Walshe 1995: 270–71.
59. P. *buddhassa parinibbānaṃ nedisaṃ āsi yādisaṃ /gotamīparinibbānaṃ atevacchariyaṃ ahu* //(Ap ii, 542, v. 173).
60. Falk 1980: 220, 222.
61. See the commentary on *Dhammapada* 53 (trans. Burlingame 1921: ii, 59–84; quotation on 76).

CHAPTER 6

1. For the *Buddhavaṃsa* account, see trans. Horner 1975: i, 9–25; for the *Nidānakathā* account, see trans. Jayawickrama 2000: 3–35.
2. Trans. Johnston 1984.
3. *Majjhima Nikāya* No. 26 (trans. Ñāṇamoli and Bodhi 1995: 253–68).
4. Strong 2001: 67–70.
5. Trans. Jones 1949–56: ii, 195–97.
6. Trans. Beal 1875: 186.
7. Mv ii, 206.
8. Trans. Jayawickrama 2000: 90–93.
9. Jā i, 70.
10. See Strong 2001: 69.
11. AN-a ii, 696.
12. For the *Mahāvastu*, see trans. Jones 1949–56: ii, 220; iii, 167. For the *Abhiniṣkramaṇa Sūtra*, see trans. Beal 1875: 346–49, 359–66. For the Sanskrit *Mūlasarvāstivāda Vinaya*, see the partial translation provided in Strong 2008: 11–24. This account also appears in the Tibetan *Mūlasarvāstivāda Vinaya* (trans. Rockhill 1884: 24, 28–29, 32–33, 56–57) and in the *Za bao zang jing* (T. 203), a collection of tales now extant only in Chinese (trans. Willemen 1994: 240–45).
13. Strong 1997.
14. Sbv i, 81.
15. Strong 1997: 115.
16. Sbv i, 106.
17. Ibid.
18. Sbv ii, 30–31.
19. Sbv i, 119.
20. Sbv i, 120; ii, 31.
21. Strong 1997: 120.
22. Trans. Willemen 1994: 240–45.
23. The title of Strong 1997 is "A Family Quest: The Buddha, Yaśodharā, and Rāhula in the Mūlasarvāstivāda Vinaya."

24. Strong 1997: 123.
25. Young 2004: 90–91. I am not sure what Young is referring to when she says that Yaśodharā's pregnancy "actively sustains [the bodhisattva] in his efforts." In my reading of the account, there is no evidence to support this.
26. Skt. *ātmīyam mātṛkāvaṃśaṃ bhagnam* (Sbv i, 82).
27. Sbv i, 82.
28. Sbv ii, 31.
29. Ibid.
30. Skt. *atyarthaṃ kāmarāgābhibhūtāyā* (Sbv ii, 37).
31. Sbv ii, 40.
32. Ibid.
33. Rgsg 365–66 (v. 10.8).
34. AP 108.
35. On this metaphor, see Macy 1977.
36. See Kajiyama 1985; Kinnard 1999: 116–30. On the "cult of the book" rhetoric of the *Prajñāpāramitā Sūtras*, see especially Schopen 2005: 25–62.
37. See, for example, the passage from the *Aṣṭasāhasrikā Prajñāpāramitā* translated in Conze 1973: 105–8.
38. Rgsg 368 (v. 12.2).
39. Rgsg 368 (v. 12.1).
40. AP 125–26.
41. Kinnard 1999: 130.
42. See the discussion in ibid.: 123–30. Conze, for example, noting a possible South Indian origin of the Mahāyāna, calls the maternal language of the *Prajñāpāramitā Sūtras* "an irruption into Buddhism of the devotion to the Mother-Goddess current in the more matriarchal Dravidian society in which it originated" (Conze 1968: 125, as cited in Kinnard 1999: 124). Elsewhere, he says that a discussion of Prajñāpāramitā contributes to "the history of the Mother-goddess who, from the Palaeolithic onwards, has occupied so great a place in human affection" (Conze 1949–50: 47, as cited in Kinnard 1999: 126). Similarly, Kinnard points to Macy's references to Prajñāpāramitā as a "pregnant zero," a "matrix of dimension," and a "clear-eyed compassionate Mama" (Macy 1977: 330, as cited in Kinnard 1999: 126).
43. Kinnard 1999: 126.
44. Ibid.: 124–25.
45. Conze 1949–50: 47, as cited in Kinnard 1999: 126.
46. Kinnard 1999: 131–43.
47. See Cabezón 1992.
48. Ibid.: 187.
49. *Lam rin chen mo* (Dharamsala: undated blockprint, folios 185b–186b), as cited in Cabezón 1992: 191.
50. Ibid.: 188.

51. Ibid.: 189.
52. The textual and philosophical issues surrounding *tathāgata-garbha* thought are exceedingly complex. Some introductory discussions include the following: Williams 1989: 96–115; Paul 1980: 47–88; Wayman and Wayman 1974: 42–55; and King 1991: 3–5, 11–21.
53. MW 349–50, s.v. *garbha*.
54. See the discussion at Paul 1980: 93–95.
55. MW 349–50, s.v. *garbha*.
56. Paul 1980: 49.
57. Grosnick 1995: 92.
58. Ibid.: 93.
59. The *Tathāgatagarbha Sūtra* (in the Chinese translation of Buddhabhadra, T. 666) has been translated in Grosnick 1995. The following quotations are drawn from both the prose and verse versions of the eighth simile (trans. Grosnick 1995: 101–2).
60. Cole 2005: 224.
61. Gross 1993: 187.
62. Ibid.: 188. Gross does admit in a footnote (188n) that "despite the contradiction involved, such symbolic valorization of birth, combined with sociological denigration of literal birth-givers, is not uncommon in world religions. In many religious contexts, the valuable birth is one's second birth, one's ritual rebirth, which may be seen as reversing the negativities of birth from a female body." Nevertheless, she seems reluctant to relate this to the concept of *tathāgata-garbha*.
63. Young 2004: 76–77.
64. Paul 1982: 96, as cited in Young 2004: 77–78.
65. Campbell 2002: 91–92.
66. Cole 2006: 301.
67. Jay 1992: 36.
68. Ibid.: xxiv.
69. Ibid.: 40.
70. Ibid.: xxiv.
71. See ibid.: chap. 8.
72. See, for one example, Heesterman 1985, esp. 26–44.
73. Many of the issues I address here are masterfully treated in Cole 1998, 2005, and 2006. Of these three works, however, only Cole 1998 (which focuses on medieval Chinese Buddhism) pays significant attention to the mother's *emotional appeal*; Cole 2005 and 2006 are more interested in the father/son discourse than in the imaginative use of the mother. In any case, my discussion remains highly indebted to Cole's body of work. Also worth mentioning here is Caroline Walker Bynum's discussion of the maternal imagery applied to male authority figures (such as abbots) in twelfth-century Cistercian writings, which

again pays ample attention to the mother's emotional appeal. According to Bynum, the mother, in these writings, is always associated with "nurturing, affectivity, and accessibility," and Cistercian writers make use of maternal imagery in order to "supplement their image of authority with that for which the maternal stood: emotion and nurture" (Bynum 1982: 154).

74. Young 2004: 70.
75. Ibid.: 78.
76. Powers 2009: 1.

CHAPTER 7

1. Trans. Hurvitz 1976: 101–9.
2. SDPS 114.
3. Ap ii, 532, vv. 31–33.
4. There is one additional context I am aware of in which the comparison between breastfeeding and the teaching of the dharma takes place—though the passage is very odd and therefore difficult to interpret. In the story of the famous laywoman Visākhā found in the *Dhammapada Commentary* (on verse 53), Visākhā convinces her father-in-law Migāra to listen to the Buddha preach, whereupon he is converted to Buddhism. What happens next (in Burlingame's translation of the episode [1921: ii, 75]) seems to involve a comparison of breastfeeding with conversion to the Buddha's teaching: "[Migāra] went forwards, and taking in his mouth the breast of his daughter-in-law [Visākhā], he adopted her as his mother, saying, 'To-day henceforth you are my mother.' And thenceforth she was called Mother of Migāra."
5. Gombrich 1972.
6. Ibid.: 67.
7. Ibid.: 69–70. The following quotations from the *Butsaraṇa* are drawn from the translations provided by Gombrich on these pages.
8. See ibid.: 71–74 for the Sinhalese text of the simile, and 74–78 for an English translation.
9. Ibid.: 75.
10. Ibid.: 76.
11. Ibid.: 77.
12. Hallisey 1988.
13. Ibid.: i, 76–77.
14. Ibid.: i, 88.
15. This is particularly appropriate, Hallisey points out, because at least one Pali commentary etymologizes the term "mother" (P. *mātā*) in relation to the concept of *mamāyana: mamāyatīti mātā*, "she is called a mother because she takes as mine" (Mn-a ii, 258; as cited in Hallisey 1988: ii, 257).
16. Andaya 2002.

17. Ibid.: 3.
18. Ibid.: 8.
19. Ibid. Similar imagery is also found in Japan and has been studied by Faure (1995: 361–64).
20. Yoe 1963: 328–33.
21. Ibid.: 328.
22. Ibid.: 330. It is perhaps worth noting that I have been unable to substantiate Scott's report of the typical subject matter of the sermon preached on this occasion by means of any more recent ethnographic reporting.
23. Whether this difference has anything to do with the fact that the former tradition pertains to Mahāprajāpatī, while the latter tradition pertains to Māyā, is unclear.
24. Teresa de Lauretis (1987: 5), for example, defines the gender system as follows: "The cultural conceptions of male and female as two complementary yet mutually exclusive categories into which all human beings are placed constitute within each culture a gender system, a symbolic system or system of meanings, that correlates sex to cultural contents according to social values and hierarchies."
25. The *Cariyāpiṭaka Commentary*, for example, states that all bodhisattvas must make five gifts throughout the course of their careers—those of wealth, children, wife, body parts, and life (see Horner 1975: part 2, 14, n. 1).
26. See Ohnuma 2007.
27. See Ohnuma 1998.
28. Although I have stated this opposition in stark terms in order to highlight the basic contrast, I realize that any such strict distinction between the "physical" and the "spiritual" is ultimately untenable in the world of Buddhist literature. The bodhisattva's "physical" gift of his body as food, for example, often leads to moral and spiritual transformation in the recipients who ingest it (see Ohnuma 1997: 226–31); likewise, the Buddha's "spiritual" gift of the dharma results in attainments that are not only spiritual or moral in nature, but also clearly reflected in one's physical form (for example, the decorous and highly controlled body of an arhat). See Ohnuma 1997: 224–26 for a further discussion of the constant interplay between physical and moral qualities in Buddhist literature.
29. *Jātaka* 313 (trans. Cowell 1895–1913: iii, 26–29); *Jātakamālā* 28 (trans. Khoroche 1989: 193–204).
30. LV i, 165–66.
31. Mv iii, 358.
32. This story exists in multiple versions—for example, *Jātakamālā* 1 (trans. Khoroche 1989: 5–9); *Suvarṇabhāsottama Sūtra* chap. 18 (trans. Emmerick 1970: 85–97); and *Avadānakalpalatā* 95. It also appears as an episode in *Divyāvadāna* 32 and *Avadānakalpalatā* 51 (trans. Das 1893).

33. SbhS 229.
34. The three Sanskrit versions I am aware of are *Divyāvadāna* 32, *Jātakamālā* [of Haribhaṭṭa] 6, and *Avadānakalpalatā* 51.
35. Ohnuma 2000.
36. Divy 471.
37. See, for example, Lang 1986; Wilson 1995, 1996; and Blackstone 1998.
38. Ed. Hahn 1992: 55, v. 34.
39. Bynum 1991; see chap. 3, "The Body of Christ in the Later Middle Ages: A Reply to Leo Steinberg."
40. Grosz 1994a: 38. Elsewhere (1994b: 14), Grosz states: "The coding of femininity with corporeality in effect leaves men free to inhabit what they (falsely) believe is a purely conceptual order."

CHAPTER 8

1. Schopen 1997: 1.
2. Ibid.: 1–22.
3. The bulk of Schopen's work has been gathered together in three collected volumes: Schopen 1997, 2004, and 2005.
4. Jā i, 90.
5. Jā i, 88.
6. Trans. Norman 1992: 4–8.
7. P. *na puttam iccheyya* (Sn 6, v. 35).
8. P. *puttañ ca dāraṃ pitarañ ca mātaraṃ . . . hitvāna* (Sn 10, v. 60).
9. P. *puttesu dāresu ca yā apekkhā* (Sn 6, v. 38).
10. P. *oropayitvā gihibyañjanāni . . . chetvāna . . . gihibandhanāni* (Sn 7–8, v. 44).
11. P. *rājā va raṭṭhaṃ vijitaṃ pahāya* (Sn 8, v. 46).
12. P. *jālaṃ va bhetvā salilambucārī* (Sn 10, v. 62).
13. P. *eko care khaggavisāṇakappo* (Sn 6–12, *passim*).
14. See p. 37 above.
15. See p. 128 above.
16. Clarke 2006: 57–72. To cite just a few examples of the former category, all taken from Sāñcī: There are donors who identify themselves as "*bhikṣu* Upasijha, brother of Phaguna"; "*bhikṣu* Bhaḍuka, son of Goti"; "*bhikṣuṇī* Isidāsī . . . mother of Sagharakhitā"; and "*bhikṣuṇī* Koṭī, mother of Ghuṇika."
17. Cited in ibid.: 67, 69.
18. Schopen 1997: 62.
19. These and the following examples (drawn from multiple sites) are cited in ibid.: 58–62.
20. Ibid.: 65 (emphasis in original).
21. These examples are cited in ibid.: 62–63.
22. Ibid.: 253.

23. Faure 2003: 162.
24. Clarke 2006.
25. Ibid.: 18.
26. I would cite, as one example of such "overstating," the following statement: "In fact, if our only source of knowledge of Buddhist monks were these documents [i.e., the Indian Buddhist *Vinayas*] . . . we might well have been forced to conclude that Buddhist monks were not celibate, but were part-time religious professionals who married and had children" (Clarke 2006: 226). Though Clarke does demonstrate many continuing ties between monks, their wives, and their children, I do not think the evidence goes quite this far.
27. Cited from the Tibetan *Mūlasarvāstivāda Vinaya*, in Clarke 2006: 99.
28. Ibid.: 106.
29. Ibid.: 110–21.
30. See ibid.: 138–240.
31. Ibid.: 169–79.
32. Schopen 2004: 170–92.
33. Clarke 2006: 235.
34. As Clarke himself states (2006: 239), "Although monks might well be monks, men were still men, and women women. No amount of monastic negotiation or legislation could change this fact."
35. Ibid.: 241–335.
36. Ibid.: 245.
37. Cited in ibid.: 263.
38. Ibid.: 282–83.
39. Cited in ibid.: 280–81. According to Clarke, however, the reading of the verb "to coo at" is very uncertain (see n. 56).
40. Cited in ibid.: 289.
41. Cited in ibid.: 291. The question of where such nuns might have come from and what kind of familial situation they were leaving behind is considerably more difficult to answer.
42. Cited in ibid.: 297.
43. Cited in ibid.: 298.
44. Ibid.: 244, 309.
45. Clarke 2008.
46. Havnevik 2000.
47. Brown 2001.
48. Kabilsingh 2000: 59.
49. Kawanami 2000: 165–66.
50. Bartholomeusz 1994: 143.
51. Ibid.: 247, n. 51.
52. To cite just a few examples, this difference between monks and nuns has been discussed in Gutschow 2000, 2004; Kawanami 2000; and Tsomo 1999.

53. Crane 2007: 123.
54. Gross 1993: 276.
55. Gutschow 2000: 114.
56. Brown 2001: 116.
57. Ibid.: 141.
58. Ibid.: 116 (quoting Nussbaum 1990: 162).
59. Ibid.: 139.
60. Ibid.: 142.
61. Huang and Weller 1998: 379.
62. Ibid.: 386.
63. Ibid.
64. Ibid.: 389.
65. On the life of Dipa Ma Barua, see Schmidt 2005.
66. Schmidt 2000: 202.
67. Ibid.: 208.
68. Ibid.: 209.
69. Ibid.: 210.
70. Wheeler 2000: 418.
71. I am indebted to Julie Gifford (personal communication) for the evocative descriptor "baby-as-zen-object."
72. Kramer 2004; Miller 2007.
73. Wheeler 2000: 419.
74. Ibid.: 420.
75. Ibid.: 419.
76. The account is translated in King 1995.
77. Ibid.: 517.
78. Ibid.: 516.
79. Ibid.: 517.
80. Ibid.: 518.
81. Ibid.: 520.
82. Ibid.: 519.
83. Ibid.: 521.

CONCLUSION

1. DiQuinzio 1999: xv.
2. Ibid.: xiii.
3. Ibid.: 13.
4. The title of DiQuinzio's book (1999) is *The Impossibility of Motherhood: Feminism, Individualism, and the Problem of Mothering.*
5. See, for example, Gilligan 1982; Ruddick 1983, 1989; Noddings 1984, 2002; Held 1983, 1987, 1993, and 2006; and the edited collection Held 1995.

6. The phrase "different voice," which is commonly used in connection with this literature, comes from the title of Gilligan 1982.
7. See Ruddick 1983, 1989.
8. Ruddick 1989.
9. Ibid.: 89–93.
10. Ibid.: 67–75.
11. Ibid.: 93–97.
12. Powers and Curtin 1994: 1.
13. French trans. Peri 1917: 18–19.
14. Ruddick 1989: 177. As a concrete, modern example of this move, Ruddick cites the mothers and grandmothers of the disappeared in Argentina and Chile. Unlike a figure such as Kisā Gotamī, these mothers, when faced with the disappearance of their children, "did not 'transcend' their particular loss and love; particularity was the emotional root and source of their protest. It is through acting on that particularity that they extended mothering to include sustaining and protecting any people whose lives are blighted by violence" (ibid.: 232).
15. Ibid.: 177.
16. Brown 2001: 139.
17. Gilligan 1982: 24–63.
18. Huang and Weller 1988: 386.
19. Wheeler 2000: 418.
20. E.g., Sered 1996a; Ruddick 1989: 215–17; Schenck 1986.
21. Sered 1996b.
22. Ibid.: 72.
23. Ibid.: 73.
24. Ibid.: 81.
25. These four traditions are (1) the indigenous religion of the Ryūkū Islands of Japan; (2) the *nat* cultic complex of Burma; (3) the indigenous shamanistic religion of Korea; and (4) the matrilineal spirit cults of Thailand.
26. Sered 1996b: 13.

Bibliography

Andaya, Barbara Watson. 2002. "Localising the Universal: Women, Motherhood and the Appeal of Early Theravāda Buddhism." *Journal of Southeast Asian Studies* 33:1, 1–30.

Andersen, Dines, and Helmer Smith, eds. 1913. *Sutta-Nipāta*. London: Pali Text Society.

Bareau, André. 1970–71. *Recherches sur la biographie du Buddha dans les Sūtrapiṭaka et les Vinayapiṭaka anciens: II. Les derniers mois, le parinirvāṇa et les funérailles*. 2 vols. Publications de l'École française d'extrême-orient, Vol. 77. Paris: École française d'extrême-orient.

Bareau, André. 1974. "La jeunesse du Buddha dans les sūtrapiṭaka et les vinayapiṭaka anciens." *Bulletin de l'École française d'Extrêmee-Orient* 61, 199–274.

Bartholomeusz, Tessa J. 1994. *Women under the Bō Tree: Buddhist Nuns in Sri Lanka*. Cambridge: Cambridge University Press.

Bays, Gwendolyn, trans. 1983. *The Voice of the Buddha: The Beauty of Compassion (The Lalitavistara Sūtra)*. 2 vols. Berkeley: Dharma Publications.

Beal, Samuel, trans. 1875. *The Romantic Legend of Sâkya Buddha: From the Chinese-Sanscrit*. London: Trübner & Co.

Blackstone, Kathryn R. 1998. *Women in the Footsteps of the Buddha: Struggle for Liberation in the Therīgāthā*. Richmond, UK: Curzon.

Blum, Lawrence A. 1986. "Iris Murdoch and the Domain of the Moral." *Philosophical Studies: An International Journal for Philosophy in the Analytic Tradition* 50:3 (Symposium on Rationality and Moral Values), 343–67.

Brough, John. 1957. "Some Notes on Maitrakanyaka: Divyāvadāna XXXVIII." *Bulletin of the School of Oriental and African Studies* 20:1/3, 111–32.

Brown, Sid. 2001. *The Journey of One Buddhist Nun: Even against the Wind*. Albany: State University of New York Press.

Brubaker, Richard L. 1983. "The Untamed Goddesses of Village India." In *The Book of the Goddess, Past and Present: An Introduction to Her Religion*, ed. Carl Olson, 145–60. New York: Crossroad.

Buddhadatta, A. P., ed. 1931–39. *Saddhamma-pajjotikā: The Commentary on the Mahā-Niddesa*. 2 vols. London: Pali Text Society.

Burlingame, Eugene Watson, trans. 1921. *Buddhist Legends, Translated from the Original Pali Text of the Dhammapada Commentary*. 3 vols. Harvard Oriental Series, Vols. 28, 29, and 30. Cambridge, MA: Harvard University Press.

Bynum, Caroline Walker. 1982. *Jesus as Mother: Studies in the Spirituality of the High Middle Ages*. Berkeley and Los Angeles: University of California Press.

Bynum, Caroline Walker. 1991. *Fragmentation and Redemption: Essays on Gender and the Human Body in Medieval Religion*. New York: Zone Books.

Cabezón, José Ignacio. 1992. "Mother Wisdom, Father Love: Gender-Based Imagery in Mahāyāna Buddhist Thought." In *Buddhism, Sexuality, and Gender*, ed. José Ignacio Cabezón, 181–99. Albany: State University of New York Press.

Caland, W., ed. 1982. *The Baudhāyana Śrauta Sūtra Belonging to the Taittirīya Samhitā*. 2nd ed. 2 vols. in one. New Delhi: Munshiram Manoharlal. Orig. pub. 1904–13.

Campbell, June. 2002. *Traveller in Space: Gender, Identity and Tibetan Buddhism*. Rev. ed. London: Continuum. Orig. pub. 1996.

Clarke, Shayne. 2008. "The Case of the Nun Mettiyā Reexamined: On the Expulsion of a Pregnant Bhikṣuṇī in the *Vinaya* of the Mahāsāṅghikas and Other Indian Buddhist Monastic Law Codes." *Indo-Iranian Journal* 51:2, 115–35.

Clarke, Shayne Neil. 2006. *Family Matters in Indian Monastic Buddhism*. PhD diss., University of California, Los Angeles.

Cleary, Thomas, trans. 1989. *Entry into the Realm of Reality. The Text. A Translation of the Gandavyuha, the Final Book of the Avatamsaka Sutra*. Boston: Shambhala.

Cohen, Richard S. 1998. "Nāga, Yakṣiṇī, Buddha: Local Deities and Local Buddhism at Ajanta." *History of Religions* 37:4, 360–400.

Cole, Alan. 1998. *Mothers and Sons in Chinese Buddhism*. Stanford, CA: Stanford University Press.

Cole, Alan. 2005. *Text as Father: Paternal Seductions in Early Mahāyāna Buddhist Literature*. Berkeley: University of California Press.

Cole, Alan. 2006. "Buddhism." In *Sex, Marriage, and Family in World Religions*, ed. Don S. Browning, M. Christian Green, and John Witte Jr., 299–366. New York: Columbia University Press.

Cone, Margaret, and Richard Gombrich, trans. 1977. *The Perfect Generosity of Prince Vessantara: A Buddhist Epic*. Oxford: Clarendon.

Conze, Edward. 1949–50. "The Iconography of the Prajñāpāramitā, Part I." *Oriental Art* 2, 46–52.

Conze, Edward. 1950–51. "The Iconography of the Prajñāpāramitā, Part II." *Oriental Art* 3, 104–9.

Conze, Edward. 1968. *Thirty Years of Buddhist Studies*. Columbia: University of South Carolina Press.

Conze, Edward, trans. 1973. *The Perfection of Wisdom in Eight Thousand Lines and Its Verse Summary*. Bolinas: Four Seasons Foundation.

Cowell, Edward B., gen. ed. 1895–1913. *The Jātaka or Stories of the Buddha's Former Births*. 6 vols. and Index. Cambridge: Cambridge University Press.

Cowell, Edward B., and Robert A. Neil, eds. 1886. *The Divyāvadāna: A Collection of Early Buddhist Legends*. Cambridge: Cambridge University Press.

Crane, Hillary. 2007. "Becoming a Nun, Becoming a Man: Taiwanese Buddhist Nuns' Gender Transformation." *Religion* 37:2, 117–32.

Das, Nobin Chandra, trans. 1893. "Rukmāvatī." *Journal of the Buddhist Text Society of India* 1:4, 1–12.

de Lauretis, Teresa. 1987. *Technologies of Gender: Essays on Theory, Film, and Fiction*. Bloomington: Indiana University Press.

Decaroli, Robert. 2004. *Haunting the Buddha: Indian Popular Religions and the Formation of Buddhism*. Oxford: Oxford University Press.

Demiéville, Paul, ed. 1929–67. *Hōbōgirin: Dictionnaire Encyclopédique du Bouddhisme d'après les sources chinoises et japonaises*. 4 vols. Paris: Librairie d'Amérique et d'Orient, Adrien Maisonneuve.

Dhirasekera, J. D. 1976. "Hārītī and Pāñcika: An Early Buddhist Legend of Many Lands." In *Malalasekera Commemoration Volume*, ed. O. H. deA. Wijesekera, 61–70. Colombo, Sri Lanka: Malalasekera Commemoration Volume Committee.

DiQuinzio, Patrice. 1999. *The Impossibility of Motherhood: Feminism, Individualism, and the Problem of Mothering*. New York: Routledge.

Douglas, Mary. 2002. *Purity and Danger: An Analysis of Concept of Pollution and Taboo*. With a new preface by the author. London: Routledge Classics. Orig. pub. 1966.

Durt, Hubert. 1996. "L'apparition du Buddha à sa mère après son nirvāṇa dans le Sūtra de Mahāmāyā et le Sūtra de la mère du Buddha." In *De Dunhuang au Japon: Études chinoises et bouddhiques offertes à Michel Soymié*, ed. Jean-Pierre Drège, 1–24. Genève: Droz.

Durt, Hubert. 2001. "The Vicissitudes of Vāsiṭṭhī/Vāsiṣṭhā Who Became Insane Due to the Loss of Her Child—From Therīgāthā to *Mahāyāna*." *Journal of the International College for Advanced Buddhist Studies* 4, 27–47.

Durt, Hubert. 2002. "The Pregnancy of Māyā: I. The Five Uncontrollable Longings (dohada)." *Journal of the International College for Advanced Buddhist Studies* 5, 43–66.

Durt, Hubert. 2003. "The Pregnancy of Māyā: II. Māyā as Healer." *Journal of the International College for Advanced Buddhist Studies* 6, 43–62.

Durt, Hubert. 2004. "On the Pregnancy of Māyā: III. Late Episodes (A Few More Words on the Textual Sources)." *Journal of the International College for Advanced Buddhist Studies* 7, 55–72.

Edgerton, Franklin. 1953. *Buddhist Hybrid Sanskrit Grammar and Dictionary*. 2 vols. New Haven, CT: Yale University Press.

Emmerick, R. E., trans. 1970. *The Sūtra of Golden Light, Being a Translation of the Suvarṇabhāsottama Sūtra*. London: Luzac.

Falk, Nancy. 1974. "An Image of Woman in Old Buddhist Literature: The Daughters of Māra." In *Women and Religion*, ed. Judith Plaskow and Joan Arnold, 105–12. Missoula: Scholars Press for the American Academy of Religion.

Falk, Nancy Auer. 1980. "The Case of the Vanishing Nuns: The Fruits of Ambivalence in Ancient Indian Buddhism." In *Unspoken Worlds: Women's Religious Lives in Non-Western Cultures*, ed. Nancy Auer Falk and Rita M. Gross, 207–24. San Francisco: Harper & Row.

Faure, Bernard. 1995. "Quand l'habit fait le moine: The Symbolism of the Kāsāya in Sōtō zen." *Cahiers d'Extrême-Asie* 8, 335–69.

Faure, Bernard. 2003. *The Power of Denial: Buddhism, Purity, and Gender*. Princeton, NJ: Princeton University Press.

Fausboll, V., ed. 1875–97. *The Jātaka Together with Its Commentary, Being Tales of the Anterior Births of Gotama Buddha*. 6 vols. and Index. London: Trübner.

Feer, Léon, ed. 1884–1904. *The Saṃyutta-nikāya of the Sutta-piṭaka*. 5 vols. and Index. London: Pali Text Society.

Gilligan, Carol. 1982. *In a Different Voice: Psychological Theory and Women's Development*. Cambridge, MA: Harvard University Press.

Gnoli, Raniero, ed. 1977–78. *The Gilgit Manuscript of the Saṅghabhedavastu: Being the 17th and Last Section of the Vinaya of the Mūlasarvāstivādin*. 2 vols. Serie orientale Roma, Vol. 49. Rome: Istituto italiano per il Medio ed Estremo Oriente.

Gombrich, Richard. 1972. "Feminine Elements in Sinhalese Buddhism." *Wiener Zeitschrift für die Kunde Südasiens* 16, 67–93.

Grosnick, William H., trans. 1995. "The Tathāgatagarbha Sūtra." In *Buddhism in Practice*, ed. Donald S. Lopez Jr., 92–106. Princeton Readings in Religion. Princeton, NJ: Princeton University Press.

Gross, Rita M. 1993. *Buddhism after Patriarchy: A Feminist History, Analysis, and Reconstruction of Buddhism*. Albany: State University of New York Press.

Grosz, Elizabeth. 1994a. *Volatile Bodies: Toward a Corporeal Feminism*. Bloomington: Indiana University Press.

Grosz, Elizabeth. 1994b. *Space, Time, and Perversion: Essays on the Politics of Bodies*. New York: Routledge.

Gutschow, Kim. 2000. "Novice Ordination for Nuns: The Rhetoric and Reality of Female Monasticism in Northwest India." In *Women's Buddhism, Buddhism's Women: Tradition, Revision, Renewal*, ed. Ellison Banks Findly, 103–18. Boston: Wisdom Publications.

Gutschow, Kim. 2004. *Being a Buddhist Nun: The Struggle for Enlightenment in the Himalayas*. Cambridge, MA: Harvard University Press.

Hahn, Michael. 1992. *Haribhaṭṭa and Gopadatta, Two Authors in the Succession of Āryaśūra: On the Rediscovery of Parts of Their Jātakamālās*. Studia Philologica Buddhica Occasional Paper Series, Vol. 1. Tokyo: International Institute for Buddhist Studies. Orig. pub. 1977.

Hahn, Michael, trans. 1998. *Invitation to Enlightenment: Letter to the Great King Kaniṣka by Mātṛceṭa. Letter to a Disciple by Candragomin.* Tibetan Translation Series. Berkeley: Dharma Publishing.

Hallisey, Charles. 1988. *Devotion in the Buddhist Literature of Medieval Sri Lanka.* 2 vols. PhD diss., University of Chicago.

Hara, Minoru. 1980. "A Note on the Buddha's Birth Story." In *Indianisme et bouddhisme: Mélanges offerts à Mgr Étienne Lamotte.* Louvain-la-Neuve, Belgium: Université Catholique de Louvain, Institut Orientaliste.

Harrison, Paul. 1992. "Is the Dharma-kāya the Real 'Phantom Body' of the Buddha?" *Journal of the International Association of Buddhist Studies* 15:1, 44–94.

Harvey, Peter. 2000. *An Introduction to Buddhist Ethics: Foundations, Values, and Issues.* Cambridge: Cambridge University Press.

Havnevik, Hanna. 2000. "The Biography of a Nun." In *The Life of Buddhism,* ed. Frank E. Reynolds and Jason A. Carbine, 109–20. Berkeley and Los Angeles: University of California Press. Orig. pub. 1989.

Heesterman, J. C. 1985. *The Inner Conflict of Tradition: Essays in Indian Ritual, Kingship, and Society.* Chicago: University of Chicago Press.

Heirman, Ann. 2001. "Chinese Nuns and Their Ordination in Fifth Century China." *Journal of the International Association of Buddhist Studies* 24:2, 275–304.

Held, Virginia. 1983. "The Obligations of Mothers and Fathers." In *Mothering: Essays in Feminist Theory,* ed. Joyce Trebilcot, 9–20. Totowa, NJ: Rowman and Allanheld.

Held, Virginia. 1987. "Feminism and Moral Theory." In *Women and Moral Theory,* ed. E. Kittay and D. Meyers, 112–27. Lanham, MD: Rowman and Littlefield.

Held, Virginia. 1993. *Feminist Morality: Transforming Culture, Society, and Politics.* Chicago: University of Chicago Press.

Held, Virginia, ed. 1995. *Justice and Care: Essential Readings in Feminist Ethics.* Boulder, CO: Westview.

Held, Virginia. 2006. *The Ethics of Care: Personal, Political, and Global.* Oxford: Oxford University Press.

Hirakawa, A. 1970. *Ritsuzō no Kenkyū.* Tokyo: Sankibō Busshorin.

Hirakawa, Akira, trans. 1982. *Monastic Discipline for the Buddhist Nuns: An English Translation of the Chinese Text of the Mahāsāṃghika-Bhikṣuṇī-Vinaya.* Patna: Kashi Prasad Jayaswal Research Institute.

Horner, I. B. 1930. *Women under Primitive Buddhism: Laywomen and Almswomen.* London: George Routledge & Sons.

Horner, I. B., trans. 1938–66. *The Book of the Discipline (Vinaya Piṭaka).* 6 vols. Sacred Books of the Buddhists, Vols. 10, 11, 13, 14, 20, and 25. London: H. Milford / Oxford University Press.

Horner, I. B., trans. 1975. *The Minor Anthologies of the Pali Canon, Part 3: Buddhavaṃsa and Cariyāpiṭaka.* Sacred Books of the Buddhists, Vol. 31. London: Pali Text Society.

Huang, Chien-Yu Julia, and Robert P. Weller. 1998. "Merit and Mothering: Women and Social Welfare in Taiwanese Buddhism." *Journal of Asian Studies* 57:2, 379–96.

Huber, Édouard, trans. 1908. *Aśvaghoṣa Sūtrālaṃkāra, traduit en Français sur la version chinoise de Kumārajīva.* Paris: Ernest Leroux.

Hurvitz, Leon, trans. 1976. *Scripture of the Lotus Blossom of the Fine Dharma (The Lotus Sūtra).* New York: Columbia University Press.

Jay, Nancy. 1992. *Throughout Your Generations Forever: Sacrifice, Religion, and Paternity.* Chicago: University of Chicago Press.

Jayawickrama, N. A., trans. 2000. *The Story of Gotama Buddha (Jātaka-nidāna).* Reprinted with corrections. Oxford: Pali Text Society. Orig. pub. 1990.

Johnston, E. H., ed. and trans. 1984. *The Buddhacarita or Acts of the Buddha,* by Aśvaghoṣa. New enlarged ed. Delhi: Motilal Banarsidass. Orig. pub. 1936.

Jones, J. J., trans. 1949–56. *The Mahāvastu.* 3 vols. Sacred Books of the Buddhists, Vols. 16, 18, and 19. London: Luzac.

Jones, John G. 2001. *Tales and Teachings of the Buddha.* 2nd ed. Christchurch, New Zealand: Cybereditions. 1st ed. orig. pub. 1979.

Kabilsingh, Chatsumarn. 2000. "Chatsumarn Kabilsingh: Advocate for a Bhikkhunī Sangha in Thailand." Compiled by Martine Batchelor. In *Women's Buddhism, Buddhism's Women: Tradition, Revision, Renewal,* ed. Ellison Banks Findly, 59–61. Boston: Wisdom Publications.

Kajiyama, Yuichi. 1985. "Stūpas, the Mother of Buddhas, and Dharma Body." In *New Paths in Buddhist Research,* ed. A. K. Warder, 9–16. Durham, NC: Acorn.

Kashikar, C. G., ed. and trans. 2003. *The Baudhāyana Śrautasūtra.* 4 vols. New Delhi: Indira Gandhi National Centre for the Arts.

Kawanami, Hiroko. 2000. "Patterns of Renunciation: The Changing World of Burmese Nuns." In *Women's Buddhism, Buddhism's Women: Tradition, Revision, Renewal,* ed. Ellison Banks Findly, 159–71. Boston: Wisdom Publications.

Khoroche, Peter, trans. 1989. *Once the Buddha Was a Monkey: Ārya Śūra's Jātakamālā.* Chicago: University of Chicago Press.

King, Sallie B. 1991. *Buddha Nature.* SUNY Series in Buddhist Studies. Albany: State University of New York Press.

King, Sallie B., trans. 1995. "Awakening Stories of Zen Buddhist Women." In *Buddhism in Practice,* ed. Donald S. Lopez Jr., 513–24. Princeton Readings in Religion. Princeton, NJ: Princeton University Press.

Kinnard, Jacob N. 1999. *Imaging Wisdom: Seeing and Knowing in the Art of Indian Buddhism.* Curzon Critical Studies in Buddhism, Vol. 8. Surrey, UK: Curzon.

Kinsley, David. 1986. *Hindu Goddesses: Visions of the Divine Feminine in the Hindu Religious Tradition.* Berkeley: University of California Press.

Kosambi, D. D. 1962. "At the Crossroads: A Study of Mother-Goddess Cult Sites." In *Myth and Reality: Studies in the Formation of Indian Culture,* 82–109. Bombay: Popular Prakashan.

Kramer, Jacqueline. 2004. *Buddha Mom: The Path of Mindful Mothering*. New York: Tarcher.

Kritzer, Robert. 2009. "Life in the Womb: Conception and Gestation in Buddhist Scripture and Classical Indian Medical Literature." In *Imagining the Fetus: The Unborn in Myth, Religion, and Culture*, ed. Vanessa R. Sasson and Jane Marie Law, 73–89. American Academy of Religion Cultural Criticism Series. Oxford: Oxford University Press.

La Vallée Poussin, Louis de, trans. 1923–31. *L'Abhidharmakośa de Vasubandhu*. 6 vols. Mélanges chinois et bouddhiques, Vol. 16. Paris: Guethner.

Lamotte, Étienne, trans. 1944–80. *Le Traité de la Grande Vertu de Sagesse de Nāgārjuna*. 5 vols. Bibliothèque du Museon, Vol. 18. Louvain, Belgium: Bureaux du Museon.

Lamotte, Étienne. 1988. *History of Indian Buddhism, from the Origins to the Śaka Era*. Trans. Sara Webb-Boin. Publications de l'Institut Orientaliste de Louvain, Vol. 36. Louvain-la-neuve, Belgium: Institut Orientaliste de l'Université Catholique de Louvain. Orig. pub. as *Histoire du Bouddhisme indien; des origines à l'ère Saka* in 1958.

Lamrim Chenmo Translation Committee, trans. 2000–2004. *The Great Treatise on the Stages of the Path to Enlightenment*. Ed. Joshua W. Cutler. 3 vols. Ithaca, NY: Snow Lion Publications.

Lang, Karen Christina. 1986. "Lord Death's Snare: Gender-Related Imagery in the Theragāthā and the Therīgāthā." *Journal of Feminist Studies in Religion* 11:2, 63–79.

Lefmann, S., ed. 1902–8. *Lalita Vistara: Leben und Lehre des Çâkya-Buddha*. 2 vols. Halle, Germany: Verlag der Buchhandlung des Waisenhauses.

Lévi, Sylvain, ed. and trans. 1907–11. *Mahāyāna-Sūtrālaṃkāra, exposé de la doctrine du Grand Véhicule selon le système Yogācāra*. Paris: H. Champion.

Li, Rongxi, trans. 1996. *The Great Tang Dynasty Record of the Western Regions, Translated by the Tripiṭaka-Master Xuanzang under Imperial Order, Composed by Śramaṇa Bianji of the Great Zongchi Monastery (Taishō, Volume 51, Number 2087)*. Berkeley: Numata Center for Buddhist Translation and Research.

Lilley, Mary E., ed. 1925–27. *The Apadāna of the Khuddaka-nikāya*. 2 vols. London: Pali Text Society.

Lopez, Donald S., Jr. 2001. *The Story of Buddhism: A Concise Guide to Its History and Teachings*. San Francisco: HarperCollins.

MacIntyre, Alasdair. 1981. *After Virtue: A Study in Moral Theory*. Notre Dame: University of Notre Dame Press.

MacKinnon, Catherine A. 1982. "Feminism, Marxism, Method, and the State: An Agenda for Theory." *Signs* 7:3, 515–44.

Macy, Joanna Rogers. 1977. "Perfection of Wisdom: Mother of All Buddhas." In *Beyond Androcentrism: New Essays on Women and Religion*, ed. Rita M. Gross, 315–33. Missoula: Scholars Press for the American Academy of Religion.

Malalasekera, G. P. 1937. *Dictionary of Pāli Proper Names*. 2 vols. London: John Murray for the Government of India.

Masefield, Peter, trans. 1994. *The Udāna Commentary (Paramatthadīpanī nāma Udānaṭṭhakathā) by Dhammapāla*. 2 vols. Sacred Books of the Buddhists, Vol. 43. Oxford: Pali Text Society.

Miller, Karen Maezen. 2007. *Momma Zen: Walking the Crooked Path of Motherhood*. Boston: Trumpeter Books.

Misra, Ram Nath. 1981. *Yaksha Cult and Iconography*. New Delhi: Munshiram Manoharlal.

Monier-Williams, Sir Monier. 1979. *A Sanskrit-English Dictionary*. New ed. Oxford: Oxford University Press. Orig. pub. 1899.

Morris, Richard, ed. 1885–1910. *The Aṅguttara-nikāya*. 5 vols. and Index. London: Pali Text Society.

Murcott, Susan. 1991. *The First Buddhist Women: Translations and Commentary on the Therīgāthā*. Berkeley: Parallax.

Murdoch, Iris. 1970. *The Sovereignty of Good*. London: Routledge and Kegan Paul.

Ñāṇamoli, Bhikkhu, and Bhikkhu Bodhi, trans. 1995. *The Middle Length Discourses of the Buddha: A New Translation of the Majjhima Nikāya*. Boston: Wisdom Publications.

Nobel, Johannes, ed. 1937. *Suvarṇabhāsottamasūtra: Das Goldglanz-sūtra, Ein Sanskrittext des Mahāyāna-Buddhismus*. Leipzig: Otto Harassowitz.

Noddings, Nel. 1984. *Caring: A Feminine Approach to Ethics and Moral Education*. Berkeley and Los Angeles: University of California Press.

Noddings, Nel. 2002. *Starting at Home: Caring and Social Policy*. Berkeley and Los Angeles: University of California Press.

Nolot, Édith, trans. 1991. *Règles de discipline des nonnes bouddhistes, le bhikṣuṇīvinaya de l'école Mahāsāṃghika-Lokottaravādin*. Paris: Collège de France.

Norman, H. C., ed. 1906–15. *The Commentary on the Dhammapada*. 5 vols. London: Pali Text Society.

Norman, K. R., trans. 1992. *The Group of Discourses (Sutta-Nipāta), Vol. 2: Revised Translation with Introduction and Notes*. Pali Text Society Translation Series, Vol. 45. Oxford: Pali Text Society.

Norman, K. R., trans. 1995. *The Elders' Verses I: The Theragāthā*. Pali Text Society Translation Series, Vol. 38. Oxford: Pali Text Society.

Norman, K. R., trans. 1996. *The Group of Discourses (Sutta-Nipāta), Volume I: The Rhinoceros Horn and Other Early Buddhist Poems*. 2nd ed. Oxford: Pali Text Society. Orig. pub. 1984.

Nussbaum, Martha C. 1990. *Love's Knowledge: Essays on Philosophy and Literature*. New York: Oxford University Press.

Obeyesekere, Gananath. 1973. "The Goddess Pattini and the Lord Buddha: Notes on the Myth of the Birth of the Deity." *Social Compass* 20:2, 217–29.

Obeyesekere, Ranjini, trans. 2001. *Portraits of Buddhist Women: Stories from the Saddharmaratnāvaliya*. Albany: State University of New York Press.

Ohnuma, Reiko. 1998. "The Gift of the Body and the Gift of Dharma." *History of Religions* 37:4, 323–59.

Ohnuma, Reiko. 2000. "The Story of Rūpāvatī: A Female Past Birth of the Buddha." *Journal of the International Association of Buddhist Studies* 23:1, 103–45.

Ohnuma, Reiko. 2006. "Debt to the Mother: A Neglected Aspect of the Founding of the Buddhist Order of Nuns." *Journal of the American Academy of Religion* 74:4, 861–901.

Ohnuma, Reiko. 2007. *Head, Eyes, Flesh, and Blood: Giving Away the Body in Indian Buddhist Literature*. New York: Columbia University Press.

Oldenberg, Hermann, ed. 1879–83. *The Vinaya Piṭakaṃ, One of the Principal Buddhist Holy Scriptures in the Pāli Language*. 5 vols. London: Williams and Norgate.

Olivelle, Patrick, trans. 2004. *The Law Code of Manu: A New Translation Based on the Critical Edition*. Oxford World's Classics. Oxford: Oxford University Press.

Paul, Diana. 1980. *The Buddhist Feminine Ideal: Queen Śrīmālā and the Tathāgatagarbha*. American Academy of Religion Dissertation Series, Vol. 30. Missoula: Scholars Press for the American Academy of Religion.

Paul, Diana. 1985. *Women in Buddhism: Images of the Feminine in the Mahāyāna Tradition*. 2nd ed. Berkeley: University of California Press. Orig. pub. 1979.

Paul, Robert A. 1982. *The Tibetan Symbolic World: Psychoanalytic Explorations*. Chicago: University of Chicago Press.

Peri, N. 1917. "Hārītī, la mère-de-démons." *Bulletin de l'École Française d'Extrême-Orient* 17, 1–102.

Petchesky, R. Polland. 1987. "Fetal Images: The Power of Visual Culture in the Politics of Reproduction." *Feminist Studies* 13:2, 263–92.

Powers, John. 2009. *A Bull of a Man: Images of Masculinity, Sex, and the Body in Indian Buddhism*. Cambridge, MA: Harvard University Press.

Powers, John, and Deane Curtin. 1994. "Mothering: Moral Cultivation in Buddhist and Feminist Ethics." *Philosophy East and West* 44:1, 1–18.

Pruitt, William, ed. 1998a. *Therīgāthā-Aṭṭhakathā (Paramatthadīpanī VI) by Achariya Dhammapāla*. Oxford: Pali Text Society.

Pruitt, William, trans. 1998b. *The Commentary on the Verses of the Therīs (Therīgāthā-Aṭṭhakathā, Paramatthadīpanī VI)*. Sacred Books of the Buddhists, Vol. 47. Oxford: Pali Text Society.

Rhys Davids, C. A. F., ed. 1920–21. *The Visuddhi-magga of Buddhaghosa*. 2 vols. London: Pali Text Society.

Rhys Davids, T. W., trans. 1890–94. *The Questions of King Milinda*. 2 vols. Oxford: Clarendon.

Rhys Davids, T. W., and William Stede, eds. 1890–1911. *The Dīgha Nikāya*. 3 vols. London: Pali Text Society.

Ridding, C. M., and Louis de La Vallée Poussin, eds. 1919. "A Fragment of the Sanskrit Vinaya: Bhikṣuṇīkarmavācanā." *Bulletin of the School of Oriental Studies* 1:3, 123–43.

Rockhill, W. Woodville, trans. 1884. *The Life of the Buddha and the Early History of His Order, Derived from Tibetan Works in the Bkah-hgyur and Bstan-hgyur*. London: Trübner & Co.

Roth, Gustav, ed. 1970. *Bhikṣuṇī-Vinaya, Including Bhikṣuṇī-Prakīrṇaka and a Summary of the Bhikṣu-Prakīrṇaka of the Ārya-Mahāsāṃghika-Lokottaravādin*. Patna: K. P. Jayaswal Research Institute.

Ruddick, Sara. 1983. "Maternal Thinking." In *Mothering: Essays in Feminist Theory*, ed. Joyce Trebilcot, 213–30. Totowa, NJ: Rowman and Allanheld.

Ruddick, Sara. 1989. *Maternal Thinking: Toward a Politics of Peace*. Boston: Beacon.

Sasson, Vanessa R. 2007. *The Birth of Moses and the Buddha: A Paradigm for the Comparative Study of Religions*. Sheffield, UK: Sheffield Phoenix.

Sasson, Vanessa R. 2009. "A Womb with a View: The Buddha's Final Fetal Experience." In *Imagining the Fetus: The Unborn in Myth, Religion, and Culture*, ed. Vanessa R. Sasson and Jane Marie Law, 55–72. American Academy of Religion Cultural Criticism Series. Oxford: Oxford University Press.

Sasson, Vanessa R. Forthcoming. "Māyā's Disappearing Act: Motherhood in Early Buddhist Literature." Unpublished ms.

Sasson, Vanessa R., and Jane Marie Law, eds. 2009. *Imagining the Fetus: The Unborn in Myth, Religion, and Culture*. American Academy of Religion Cultural Criticism Series. Oxford: Oxford University Press.

Schenck, Celeste. 1986. "Feminism and Deconstruction: Re-constructing the Elegy." *Tulsa Studies in Women's Literature* 5:1, 13–27.

Schmidt, Amy. 2000. "Transformation of a Housewife: Dipa Ma Barua and Her Teachings to Theravāda Women." In *Women's Buddhism, Buddhism's Women: Tradition, Revision, Renewal*, ed. Ellison Banks Findly, 201–16. Boston: Wisdom Publications.

Schmidt, Amy. 2005. *Dipa Ma: The Life and Legacy of a Buddhist Master*. Mamaroneck, NY: Bluebridge.

Schmidt, M., ed. 1993. "Bhikṣuṇī-Karmavācanā, Die Handschrift Sansk. c25(R) der Bodleian Library Oxford." In *Studien zur Indologie und Buddhismuskunde für Professor Dr. Heinz Bechert zum 60. Geburtstag am 26. Juni 1992*, ed. R. Grünendahl et al., 239–88. Bonn, Germany: Indica et Tibetica.

Schopen, Gregory. 1997. *Bones, Stones, and Buddhist Monks: Collected Papers on the Archaeology, Epigraphy, and Texts of Monastic Buddhism in India*. Studies in Buddhist Traditions. Honolulu: University of Hawai'i Press.

Schopen, Gregory. 2004. *Buddhist Monks and Business Matters: Still More Papers on Monastic Buddhism in India*. Studies in Buddhist Traditions. Honolulu: University of Hawai'i Press.

Schopen, Gregory. 2005. *Figments and Fragments of Mahāyāna Buddhism in India: More Collected Papers*. Studies in Buddhist Traditions. Honolulu: University of Hawai'i Press.

Senart, Émile, ed. 1882–97. *Mahāvatu avadānaṃ. Le Mahāvastu: Texte sanscrit publié pour la première fois et accompagné d'introductions et d'un commentaire*. 3 vols. Paris: Société Asiatique.

Sered, Susan Starr. 1996a. "Mother Love, Child Death and Religious Innovation." *Journal of Feminist Studies in Religion* 12, 5–23.

Sered, Susan Starr. 1996b. *Priestess, Mother, Sacred Sister: Religions Dominated by Women*. Oxford: Oxford University Press.

Shaw, Miranda. 2006. *Buddhist Goddesses of India*. Princeton, NJ: Princeton University Press.

Silk, Jonathan. 2007. "Good and Evil in Indian Buddhism: The Five Sins of Immediate Retribution." *Journal of Indian Philosophy* 35:3, 253–86.

Skilling, Peter. 2008. "Dharma, Dhāraṇī, Abhidharma, Avadāna: What Was Taught in Trayastriṃśa?" *Sōka Daigaku Kokusai Bukkyōgaku Kōto Kenkyū-jo Nenpō (Annual Report of the International Research Institute for Advanced Buddhology at Soka University)* 11, 37–60.

Steinthal, Paul, ed. 1885. *Udāna*. London: Oxford University Press.

Strong, John S. 1983. "Filial Piety and Buddhism: The Indian Antecedents to a 'Chinese' Problem." In *Traditions in Contact and Change*, ed. Peter Slater and Donald Wiebe, 171–86. Waterloo, Canada: Wilfried Laurier University Press.

Strong, John S. 1992. *The Legend and Cult of Upagupta: Sanskrit Buddhism in North India and Southeast Asia*. Princeton, NJ: Princeton University Press.

Strong, John S. 1997. "A Family Quest: The Buddha, Yaśodhara, and Rāhula in the Mūlasarvāstivāda Vinaya." In *Sacred Biography in the Buddhist Traditions of South and Southeast Asia*, ed. Juliane Schober, 113–28. Honolulu: University of Hawai'i Press.

Strong, John S. 2001. *The Buddha: A Short Biography*. Oxford: Oneworld Publications.

Strong, John S., ed. 2008. *The Experience of Buddhism: Sources and Interpretations*. 3rd ed. Belmont, CA: Thomson Wadsworth. Orig. pub. 1995.

Sutherland, Gail Hinich. 1991. *The Disguises of the Demon: The Development of the Yakṣa in Hinduism and Buddhism*. SUNY Series in Hindu Studies. Albany: State University of New York Press.

Takakusu, J., trans. 1896. *A Record of the Buddhist Religion as Practised in India and the Malaya Archipelago (*ad *671–695)*. London: Clarendon.

Teiser, Stephen F. 1996. *The Ghost Festival in Medieval China*. Princeton, NJ: Princeton University Press.

Tin, Pe Maung, trans. 1920–21. *The Expositor (Atthasālinī), Buddhaghosa's Commentary on the Dhammasaṅgaṇī, the First Book of the Abhidhamma Piṭaka*. 2 vols. Pali Text Society Translation Series, Vols. 8–9. London: Pali Text Society.

Tin, Pe Maung, trans. 1923–31. *The Path of Purity, Being a Translation of Buddhaghosa's Visuddhimagga*. 3 vols. Pali Text Society Translation Series, Vols. 11, 17, and 21. London: Pali Text Society.

Trenckner, Vilhelm, ed. 1888–1925. *The Majjhima Nikāya*. 4 vols. London: Pali Text Society.

Tsomo, Karma Lekshe. 1999. "Change in Consciousness: Women's Religious Identity in Himalayan Buddhist Cultures." In *Buddhist Women across Cultures: Realizations*, ed. Karma Lekshe Tsomo, 169–89. Albany: State University of New York Press.

Vaidya, P. L., ed. 1960. *Aṣṭasāhasrikā Prajñāpāramitā with Haribhadra's Commentary Called Āloka*. Buddhist Sanskrit Texts, Vol. 4. Darbhanga, India: Mithila Institute.

Vaidya, P. L., ed. 1961. *Mahāyāna-sūtra-saṅgrahaḥ*. 2 vols. Buddhist Sanskrit Texts, Vol. 17. Darbhanga, India: Mithila Institute.

Vaidya, P. L., ed. 2002. *Gaṇḍavyūhasūtra*. 2nd ed. Buddhist Sanskrit Texts, Vol. 5. Darbhanga, India: Mithila Institute.

Walleser, Max, and Herman Kopp, eds. 1966–79. *Manorathapūraṇī, Buddhaghosa's Commentary on the Aṅguttara-nikāya*. 2nd ed. 5 vols. Pali Text Society Publications, Vols. 97, 110, 123, 130, and 137. London: Pali Text Society. Orig. pub. 1924–57.

Walshe, Maurice, trans. 1995. *The Long Discourses of the Buddha: A Translation of the Dīgha Nikāya*. 2nd ed. Boston: Wisdom Publications. Orig. pub. 1987.

Walters, Jonathan S. 1994. "A Voice from the Silence: The Buddha's Mother's Story." *History of Religions* 33:4, 358–79.

Walters, Jonathan S., trans. 1995. "Gotamī's Story." In *Buddhism in Practice*, ed. Donald S. Lopez Jr., 113–38. Princeton Readings in Religion. Princeton, NJ: Princeton University Press.

Warner, Marina. 1976. *Alone of All Her Sex: The Myth and the Cult of the Virgin Mary*. New York: Knopf.

Wayman, Alex. 1991. "The Position of Women in Buddhism." *Studia Missionalia* 40, 259–85.

Wayman, Alex, and Hideko Wayman, trans. 1974. *The Lion's Roar of Queen Śrīmālā: A Buddhist Scripture on the Tathāgatagarbha Theory*. New York: Columbia University Press.

Wells, Kenneth E. 1975. *Thai Buddhism: Its Rites and Activities*. Bangkok: Suriyaban. Orig. pub. 1939.

Wheeler, Kate Lila. 2000. "How a Buddhist Decides Whether or Not to Have Children." In *Women's Buddhism, Buddhism's Women: Tradition, Revision, Renewal*, ed. Ellison Banks Findly, 405–24. Boston: Wisdom Publications.

Wieger, Léon. 1910–13. *Bouddhisme Chinois, Extraits du Tripiṭaka, des Commentaires, Tracts, etc*. 2 vols. Shanghai: Imprimerie de la Mission Catholique.

Willemen, Charles, trans. 1994. *The Storehouse of Sundry Valuables, Translated from the Chinese of Kikkāya and Liu Hsiao-piao (Compiled by T'an-yao) (Taishō, Volume 4, Number 203)*. BDK English Tripiṭaka, Vol. 10-I. Berkeley: Numata Center for Buddhist Translation and Research.

Williams, Paul. 1989. *Mahāyāna Buddhism: The Doctrinal Foundations*. London: Routledge.

Wilson, Elizabeth. 1995. "The Female Body as a Source of Horror and Insight in Post-Ashokan Indian Buddhism." In *Religious Reflections on the Human Body*, ed. Jane Marie Law, 76–99. Bloomington: Indiana University Press.

Wilson, Liz. 1996. *Charming Cadavers: Horrific Figurations of the Feminine in Indian Buddhist Hagiographic Literature*. Chicago: University of Chicago Press.

Wogihara, U., and C. Tsuchida, eds. 1934–35. *Saddharmapuṇḍarīka-sūtra: Romanized and Revised Text of the Bibliotheca Buddhica Publication by Consulting a Skt. Ms. and Tibetan and Chinese Translations*. 3 vols. Tokyo: Seigo-Kenkyūka.

Woods, J. H., and D. Kosambi, eds. 1922–38. *Papañcasūdanī: Majjhimanikāyaṭṭhakathā of Buddhaghosācariya*. 5 vols. Pali Text Society Text Series, Vols. 81–85. London: Pali Text Society.

Woodward, F. L., ed. 1926. *Paramattha-Dīpanī Udānaṭṭhakathā (Udāna Commentary) of Dhammapālacariya*. Pali Text Society Text Series, Vol. 143. London: Pali Text Society.

Woodward, F. L., trans. 1935. *The Minor Anthologies of the Pali Canon, Part II: Udana (Verses of Uplift) and Ittivuttaka (As It Was Said)*. Sacred Books of the Buddhists, Vol. 8. London: Pali Text Society.

Woodward, F. L., and E. M. Hare, trans. 1932–36. *The Book of the Gradual Sayings (Aṅguttara-Nikāya) or More-Numbered Suttas*. 5 vols. Pali Text Society Translation Series, Vols. 22, 24, 25, 26, and 27. London: Pali Text Society.

Yoe, Shway (Sir James George Scott). 1963. *The Burman: His Life and Notions*. New York: W. W. Norton. Orig. pub. in 2 vols., 1882.

Young, Serinity. 2004. *Courtesans and Tantric Consorts: Sexualities in Buddhist Narrative, Iconography, and Ritual*. New York: Routledge.

Index